[ABOMINATIONS]

ALSO BY LIONEL SHRIVER

[ABOMINATIONS]

SELECTED ESSAYS

FROM A CAREER OF COURTING

SELF-DESTRUCTION

LIONEL SHRIVER

HARPER

An Imprint of HarperCollins*Publishers*

HarperCollins books may be purchased for educational, business, or sales promotional use. For information, please email the Special Markets Department at SPsales@harpercollins.com.

Except where noted, the essays in this volume were previously published, or delivered, sometimes in a slightly different form in the sources cited.

FIRST EDITION

Designed by Elina Cohen

Library of Congress Cataloging-in-Publication Data has been applied for.

ISBN 978-0-06-309429-1

22 23 24 25 26 FRES 10 9 8 7 6 5 4 3 2 1

Contents

PART V: AGAINST THE GRAIN

PART VI: END PAPERS

[A B O M I N A T I O N S]

Introduction

When I first dove into this project, I was no little horrified to discover what a vast clatter of nonfiction cluttered my hard drive. I could fill out dozens of volumes this size—though don't worry, I'm not that sadistic.

The standards I've applied to the selection of these essays are loose: these pieces have stuck in my mind; they continue to pertain to the present; I can still stand to read them. Regarding three picks in particular, a fourth stipulation: after publication, they brought hell and damnation down on my head.

I came to journalism through the back door. I needed to augment meager earnings as a novelist. To that end, I recorded three-minute editorials for BBC Radio Ulster for several years in Belfast, where I also became point woman for op-eds on the Troubles for *The Wall Street Journal*. The latter comment pieces led to two three-month full-time stints on the editorial page of *The Wall Street Journal Europe*. Yet early on, it was obvious I wasn't just doing this stuff for money. I was enjoying myself. I was developing a new muscle. From the start, I especially relished supporting points of view that were underexpressed, unpopular, or downright dangerous.

Thus I was a monthly columnist for the British magazine *Standpoint* for five years, and with great pleasure I've written a fortnightly column for the London-based weekly *The Spectator* from 2017 onward. Journalism has been good discipline for me. Meeting tight deadlines has meant learning not to faff about, as the Brits would say. Filing to exact wordage—subjugating content to the geometrical demands of the rectangle—can often entail slaying favorite passages. Journalists can't afford to be precious.

I've been warned that my parallel nonfiction career has probably done my reputation as a fiction writer no favors, especially since my opinions often lie several bricks wide of the Overton window. But it's too late for regrets. The fact that Shriver supported Brexit, dislikes affirmative action, opposes lockdowns for the suppression of disease, abhors soaring national debts, defends free speech even when people use it to say something unpleasant, and resists uncontrolled mass immigration is already lodged in the public record. Readers who don't share these views could credibly enjoy my novels, which I hope don't err on the polemical side, as they might also appreciate large sections of this collection that address other matters. Still, I don't apologize for these positions, especially as the preponderance of my literary colleagues lean far to the political left, and the world of letters could sorely use counterbalance.

I'm not a natural activist. I don't go to protests or join advocacy groups. Yet in the last several years, holding the line on a range of issues has achieved a sense of urgency. In standing up to the illiberalism that has gripped so many Western institutions during the last decade, I have plenty of stalwart company in the nonfiction realm. But fellow fiction writers who've stuck their necks out to defend the freedoms on which our occupation depends have been disappointingly thin on the ground.

American by birth, I've lived the majority of my adult life in the United Kingdom, so numerous pieces here were written for British publications. I've regularized the spelling (American), but I've retained any number of British expressions and locutions ("in future"; "in hospital"), as over the years they've become my expressions and locutions. The topics these essays address should be broadly germane to readers in both countries. While most of this collection was previously published, readers would have considerable difficulty locating these thirty-five best-of essays in the morass of nearly a million Google hits on my name. I've clawed through the crammed closet of my hard drive, so you don't have to.

The Private
Sector

[PART 1]

Women of Letters
Talk for Ubud Readers
and Writers Festival

Indonesia, 2013

Dear Lionel,

I bet you're surprised to hear from me. But I'm at a literary festival in Bali—yes, *Bali*—and I've been asked to address the "time it didn't work out." In your case, it "didn't work out" for twelve solid years. "It," of course, being your career.

You're sure to find it astonishing that I look back on the murky period in which you're still mired with nostalgia. After all, you're often depressed. You've written book after book, and no one cares. Barely a soul has ever heard of you. In the rare instances that you attend social occasions, then *claim* you're a novelist, you often invite the withering inquiry, "Oh? Have you published anything?"

It's humiliating. But you suck at socializing, so you're better off staying home. Granted, it's naive to encourage anyone to ignore what other people think; everyone cares what people think. But from childhood, you've cared a smidgeon less about others' opinions of you than your peers do, and comparative obliviousness lends you an advantage. Indeed, a word of warning: in future, you will be awash in other people's opinions of you, not all of them kind, and even the fawning variety will become a curse. For now, glory in your anonymity. Being a nobody is fabulous. Other people stay out of your business. They leave you alone.

We now own a small house in London. By contrast, for most of our personal Dark Ages, you've been ensconced in the attic of a grand but disheveled Victorian manor in Northern Ireland. The Belfast flat is funky, furnished with motley castoffs from Oxfam, with slanted ceilings and lousy little gas room heaters that give off a funny smell. But though you're only renting, you have a more profound sense of *ownership* of 19 Notting Hill than we now have of the London semidetached to which we hold the deed. Your garret on Notting Hill is a weird nest in a weird city, but you have fully possessed both house and town. You give loud dinner parties for good friends, served on chipped, charity shop Victorian crockery. Mornings, you close your study door, switch on the reeking gas fire, draw the drapes, and pull up a chair to your tiny Toshiba laptop—to crawl into your own little world within your own little world. You realize that we still have dreams about Notting Hill? Because it was deeply *our house*. Now we're that much closer to death, it's now that we feel we're only renting.

OK, you're just short of broke, but you get by, even if you sometimes resort to Bulgarian wine. Your rent is derisory. Sod restaurants; you'd rather grill your own fish and not overcook it. You've no interest in clothes. You cobble together plane fare if there's somewhere you need to go. So what exactly must you do without?

I'll let you in on a secret: our income is more "comfortable" now, but nothing's changed. We still prefer to eat at home. We still buy quick-sale vegetables at the supermarket, because frugality is a state of mind—one suspicious of haughty entitlement and realistic about self-indulgence, since most pampering doesn't work. Our pleasures will remain simple, like most true pleasures: other writers' novels; three hours of tennis on affordable courts; popcorn, as close as a snack can get to free; sleep, which *is* free. With more money, you'd just be flummoxed, as we are now, by what to buy. Enjoy, then, your ingenious scrimping, the game of it. Know that in time you will be better rewarded for the fruits of your labors, and it *won't matter*.

Let's not forget, either, that during your slog in the literary trenches you have also fallen deeply in love at last. After squandering your affections on a string of cads, you finally love a man for who he is, and not some silly simulacrum you made up. (In our youth, we had a weakness for false gods—for idols of our concoction, who bore little resemblance to the disappointments next to us in bed.) This man also knows who you are and loves you anyway. On your typical evening, you watch a rented video of *The Basketball Diaries* while nestled in the arms of a smart, funny, faithful, and handsome man—so who cares if the wine is Bulgarian?

So blissful is your duo that I'm reluctant to share the news that after nine delightful years you'll part. I worry that I just broke your heart. Worse, you will break his heart, and even now I may never have forgiven us for this carelessness, which continues to cast doubt on whether we constitute a "good person." But a measure of self-mistrust has served us well. Besides, many years ago our father announced that love is the one arena in which it pays to be selfish. There, permission to be a complete jerk from your own dad. Trust that your current paramour's successor will reap the benefit of your self-reproach. You will prove a loyal wife. And falling in love twice is a lot of times.

Most of all, you have your work. That may sound pretentious, but aside from finding a hand to hold all you've really ever cared about is writing books. You can concentrate. Those rejections your agent keeps faxing may be disagreeable, but the writing of the novels themselves is still a joy. The life you signed up for is *private*.

Oh, you'll doubtless greet advance notice that your career will soon pick up as good news—and I'm glad if being wise to a little impending recognition cheers you up. But hold the champagne. We will merely swap one set of problems for another. The new problems aren't superior to the old ones, either. On the contrary, the problems that confront a so-called successful author may be grimmer than the travails you face now.

For these days we're constantly interrupted. We're ceaselessly asked to write book reviews, support charities, appear in festivals, or open libraries. To give interviews or do photo shoots. If that sounds glamorous, it's not. It's a pain in the arse. Where before we floated on a sea of solitude, now we're jostled by a crowd every morning we access our email queue. (What is email? Oh, my dear, you'll find out all too well in time.) It's official: We're incredibly lucky. We're not allowed to feel sorry for ourselves. But the right to self-pity should be enshrined in the Constitution.

As a consequence of this distraction, it now takes twice as long to write a book. Half of our time is consumed by selling it.

It really is better, if we're going to bother to write the things, for other people to read them. It's probably better not to live in such near destitution that a broken toaster plunges the household into hysteria. And it's nice to have a bit more to do with other people; we feel like part of something larger now. It's even good for our work that from time to time we talk to someone else.

But because all that comes later, you need to appreciate what you already have. You may be embarrassed at parties because no one has ever heard of you, and repeated rejection of your manuscripts is tough. Still, looking back on the years you're living now, I realize that they constituted our *prime*. Why, in a novel you haven't written yet, you will craft the following passage: "*Happiness* is almost definitionally a condition of which you are not aware at the time. To inhabit your own contentment is to be wholly present, with no orbiting satellite to take clinical readings of the state of the planet. Conventionally, you grow conscious of happiness at the very point that it begins to elude you. When not misused to talk yourself into something—when not a lie—the h-word is a classification applied in retrospect. It is a bracketing assessment, a label only decisively pasted onto an era once it is over."

In other words: you're far less miserable than you think.

Warmly,
Lionel

"Putting Away Childish Things"

Sermon in Manchester, England, 2013

[In recent times, secularism has become a standard default and no longer seems especially rebellious, much less brave. But in my childhood and adolescence of the 1960s and early '70s, pushing back against the indoctrination of organized religion still required guts—especially as I was a "PK," or Preacher's Kid. Because resistance trains the soul just as it develops muscles in athletics, being raised in a faith I came to reject probably did me a favor. This early practice in challenging received wisdom later proved a useful rehearsal for challenging some of the left-wing truisms in which I was also marinated growing up.

Thus I hesitated when approached to give a sermon, of all things. But delivering this oration, I discovered that the cadences of theological exhortation run in my blood: the rises and descents, the pauses, the elongations of vowels, the incantatory repetitions, the landings of sentences in a plaintive minor key. Although I'm usually a second-rate mimic, impersonation of my father at the pulpit turned out to be effortless, not to mention hilarious. Lo and behold, I made a cracking minister! Yet rather than go for parody, I found myself employing that liturgical lilt in all sincerity. Moving that congregation with rhetorical tools that were my birthright, I started to realize what my father got out of delivering all those sermons. Even in a deconsecrated church, uplifting that audience provided a sensation of enormous power, but a power to all appearances not derived from ego. Quite a trick, that.]

"When I was a child, I spake as a child, I understood as a child, I thought as a child: but when I became a man, I put away childish things."

Who has become a "man"? In this instance, a woman. And what "childish thing" might we put away today? The very vehicle driving the survival of this passage by the apostle Paul for two thousand years: religion. Behold, then, the antisermon sermon.

Truthfully, I put away the "childish thing" of the Presbyterian Church when still a child. As I grew more vocal in my family about not sharing my parents' religious convictions, my mother chided that on occasion it was normal—if always upsetting—to "question your faith." But I'm not sure I ever had a faith to question. I cannot recall ever swallowing without reservation the creed that I was fed from toddlerhood. I never sensed the presence of a Being looking out for me who was not one of my parents, any more than I ever believed in Santa Claus, who *was* my parents. There was always a little confusion about deity in our household anyway—where in practical and emotional terms, "God the Father" usually went by the shorter appellation "Father."

I do not understand religious faith. When it has been explained to me, I have been able to construe only that "belief" distinguishes itself from "knowledge" by being something you realize is far-fetched and unsupported by any evidence, and you profess it anyway. Mind, I won't try to sell you on the idea that I'm still profoundly "spiritual"—not a word I quite understand either, except as a lower grade of "religious" that commits you to nothing in particular while still making you unaccountably annoying at dinner parties. Ardent believers might pity me for this hole in my soul, which impoverishes my inner world, separates me from the communion of the devout, and denies me the comforts of a personal relationship with God and the promise of life everlasting. There may be none so blind as those who will not see, but so far I haven't felt deprived.

As well as a philosophical position, my alienation from religious faith is a personal matter. Both my parents have dedicated themselves professionally to Christianity. My mother was a researcher for the Presbyterian Church and later an executive in America's National Council of Churches. My father graduated from a seminary in Richmond, Virginia, and earned a doctorate from Harvard Divinity School—though it jars on my ear now that Harvard would have a school of God. He was a pastor in the small town where I was born, then an assistant minister at the church where my family worshipped. He became an academic in the religion department of North Carolina State, then in the divinity school at Emory University in Atlanta. The pinnacle of his career was becoming the president of a storied, liberally minded ecumenical institution in New York City, Union Theological Seminary, for sixteen years. I relate these achievements with a conflicted mixture of bewilderment and pride.

So you can imagine that I was raised up to the eyeballs in church. My brothers and I were compelled to attend Sunday school and worship services every week. We were roped into Bible school every summer. Joining the church in my early teens was a requirement. My parents' friends and colleagues were all ministers, church officers, biblical scholars, and theologians. Whenever my family took holidays—which nearly always involved my father's attendance at some religious conference—we spent our leisure time visiting churches. Indeed, my parents' boxes of slides include few images of my brothers and me growing up. It was a standing joke with my younger brother that whenever my father snapped a picture—of a church, of course—he'd wave at us kids to get out of the way.

To my sorrow, at a midpoint in my childhood our father abandoned his animated after-dinner readings of the storybooks we adored—C. S. Lewis's Narnia series, *The Wind in the Willows, All Hallows' Eve*—and read from the Bible instead. One of my more consternating memories is of one Sunday in junior high. I had an essay due at school the next day, composition of which I was obliged to put aside. My father had suddenly got a bee in his bonnet, and I had to read the book of Luke from start to finish that very afternoon.

Because my resistance to religious dogma began at an early age, I wiled away many a Sunday morning as a kid playing hangman or tic-tac-toe on the order of service with my younger brother, slipping the program between us while trying to avoid our mother's sharp eye. I performed tiny, unperceived acts of defiance, like keeping my eyes open during prayers. As the assumption endured that we kids would simply adopt our parents' catechism without ever being asked, my defiance grew more overt. I would refuse to recite the Apostles' Creed—though I would at least, to keep from embarrassing my parents, stand with the congregation. I often declined to sing the hymns, which in some ways was a shame, since they were the only part of a service that I enjoyed. When I was very young I was mostly bored, but by prepubescence I was furious, and spent the whole interminable hour seething in my pew. It enraged me that I wasn't allowed my own views. It enraged me that I was supposed to publicly proclaim my belief in "the Holy Ghost, the holy Catholic Church, the communion of saints, the forgiveness of sins, the resurrection of the body, and the life everlasting" when I believed in no such fictions. By the time I was twelve, my father had to drag me into the car on Sunday mornings literally by the hair.

Yet I confess that when my own father assumed the pulpit I was transfixed. I loved the often funny or touching anecdotes that illustrated his sermons. He was a fine orator, able to bend his tone into a musically ministerial minor key, using the rise and fall of a line to land with a poignancy that raised the hairs on my neck. When he lifted his hand over the congregation in benediction—*The Lord shall preserve thy going out and thy coming in from this time forth*—he made me feel protected, blessed, and safe. He's always been a handsome man, six feet tall with a square JFK jaw and the same glinting, faraway hazel eyes that he handed on to me; watching his formidable figure sweep down the aisle in a flowing black robe at the end of the service induced both an awe and a self-congratulatory sense of being well connected: my father was *the man*. Why, I have continued to find my father's public oratory moving, resonant, and trenchant throughout my adulthood, even as my ideological opposition to the institution to which he's devoted his life has grown only more entrenched.

As for why I have so little patience for religion, I don't want to pull a Richard Dawkins here, since Britain's most famous contemporary atheist can put off audiences with a caustic contempt for belief in fairy tales. I couldn't hope to match the eloquence of the late Christopher Hitchens in his debate with Tony Blair, in which Hitchens railed forcefully against the idea of any benevolent, all-powerful God who would allow the wickedness and undeserved suffering that permeates human affairs. So I will try to be succinct:

False certainty creates refuge from an ambiguity that is intrinsic to this life as I understand it. Surely that ambiguity provides one of life's great pleasures: contemplating the enigma of "what is this universe we're a part of?" and "what are we supposed to do here?" Religion is flattening and anthropocentric; it makes the world too known and so too small. The stories on which most religions are based are patently incredible—sons of God born of virgins and angels descending from the heavens—making religious belief indistinguishable from superstition. Thus religion represents to me an earlier evolutionary stage. It is a calcification of our forefathers' efforts to explain the world with magic—so maybe the "man" in First Corinthians who must put away childish things is more generally the human race. Worse, faith has divided more than united peoples historically, and for centuries has driven wars across Europe and the Middle East, while today fundamentalist Islam motivates delusional young men to enter bustling marketplaces, strapped with bombs. Faith is used to raise one group above all others, because in contrast to dehumanized "infidels" these chosen people have exclusive access to the so-called truth. Religion often imposes oppressive, joyless practical restrictions on its adherents, when life is hard enough—restrictions frequently placed most onerously on women. Religions are prone to obsess narrowly about sex, thereby casting "morality" as farcically petty.

Because I have no visceral grasp of faith, few characters in my novels profess religious beliefs—which, considering many of them are American, is demographically perverse. But for me to craft a character with strong religious convictions is to make that character unfathomable to me. An equally conspicuous omission: despite the subject matter having saturated my upbringing, I have never written fiction that wrestles with religion. To take on any larger issue in a novel, an author should give expression to rounded, often opposing views, and my views on religion are two-dimensional. I could never write a novel about faith without becoming more sympathetic with faith—more sympathetic with people who espouse faith, and with the inclination to faith.

Yet privately I have struggled with a religious conundrum for most of my life. I've great respect for my parents, for their fine characters of course, but also for their intellects. These are very smart people. They have high IQs. So how could they possibly believe that Jesus Christ is the son of God, born of the virgin Mary? Given his academic achievements, what inspired my gifted father, with a smorgasbord of challenging disciplines at his fingertips, to get a doctorate in divinity? How has this sharp, insightful couple, deeply engaged by international politics, not shared my perception that churches have riven the peoples of this earth far more than brought them together? In college, my father was a history major. I don't get it.

Just now, however, I am not in the mood for exasperation. I'm sorry to report that my father is gravely ill. At eighty-five, he may not be much longer with us. I face the prospect of losing him, and my frustration melts away. At such a somber juncture, I yearn to locate where the callings of a seminary president emeritus and his apostate daughter the novelist might intersect.

Both literature and liturgy celebrate the power of The Word— written, spoken, and sung. The cadences of the Apostles' Creed— *from thence he shall come to judge the quick and the dead*—still give me chills. Familiar hymns uplift me—"*A mighty fortress is our God, a bulwark never failing . . .*" Some hymns can make me cry—which is as much as I could hope to accomplish with any novel. Honed by generations, the incantations of religious ceremonies can transport even us disaffected folk, and I am grateful, ironically, to have been steeped in these traditions, to which I continue to respond, for if I hadn't grown up with these *sounds* in my ears I doubt I'd find them quite so moving.

Fiction and religion alike grapple with difficult moral choices. My father and I have both made a living from exploring the consequences of one's actions, and from groping to construct what constitutes a good life, a just life, a worthwhile life. Much of what my father has deployed religion to pursue I also celebrate—civil rights, the redress of political injustice but also the setting aside of historical grudges—as I have addressed in my own work the mysterious origins of evil, the iniquities of American health care, or the puzzle of how much we're obliged to personally forfeit for single members of our families. To a surprising extent, Christian values are my values, and in its own conniving, underhanded way my secular writing also elevates love, decency, charity, loyalty, responsibility, sacrifice, clemency, and the Protestant work ethic.

Both good books lowercase and the Good Book in capital letters push readers to dig below the surface, to find deeper wells of experience beneath remembering to buy butter at the supermarket and ferrying the kids to school. Clerics and fiction writers alike urge their audiences to feel more profoundly, to achieve perspective, to empathize with their neighbors, to think—although novelists may do a slightly better job at getting readerships to question received wisdom and challenge authority, if only because religion is hawking received wisdom, and ecclesiastical representatives of established churches *are* authorities.

My father and I are both preachers of a sort, and we have both been drawn to vocations that are pastoral. In the course of his duties as minister and educator, my father has comforted the bereaved, counseled the confused, and tried to pass on what wisdom he has gleaned in the form of text, private guidance, and sermons like this one. (Well. Not that much like this one.) In the best of my own work, I hope I have also helped my readership to better understand themselves and their brethren, to accept their disappointments, to inhabit their joys, to examine the darker corners of their characters where malice, envy, spite, and selfishness hide, to face death, and to relish the infernal complexity of life on this planet in the meantime.

In different manners, ministers and purveyors of less sacred texts both foster community. Humanists are often criticized for not offering the social solace of the church. Yet the readership of a particular book constitutes an ad hoc fellowship, a group of people with a common experience through which they can exchange ideas and connect with one another—although I'm leery of putting a worldwide church on a par with a book club. For that matter, I'll grant religious affiliation this advantage: the many fellow congregants who have supported my parents during my father's accelerating infirmity—by buying groceries or offering lifts to hospital—embrace a *doctrine* that defines care of the sick as an obligation, one that secular friends would be too free to regard as a choice. As a rare cleric in my 2010 novel, *So Much for That*, explains to his son, who is dismayed by the near-universal desertion of friends and family during his wife's losing battle with cancer, "Your secular friends only have their own consciences to prod them, and that's not always enough. There's no substitute for deeply held beliefs, son. They call you to your finest self. Tending the sick is hard work, and it's not always pretty. When you're relying on some flimsy notion that coming by with a casserole would be *thoughtful*, that tuna bake may not make it to the oven."

Most of all, of course, religious and secular literature are both intimately involved with *story*. I'd be the first to admit that the story of Jesus—from dangerous popularity to persecution, crucifixion, and resurrection—is a compelling narrative. In fact, I had to laugh at myself for finishing the entire first draft of my second novel, *Checker and the Derailleurs*, before I realized that I'd stolen the plot wholesale from the New Testament. So maybe my father's forcing me to read the book of Luke in a sitting at the age of thirteen wasn't wasted on me after all.

Yet fiction and religion do part ways in one crucial respect: I know, and my readers know, that *my stories are made up.* Indeed, the most destructive interpretations of sacred texts are literal. Fundamentalist readings of the Bible or the Koran insist that stories that could be illuminating as metaphors happened in exactly this way and represent the irrefutable, factual truth. Literalism leads to inflexibility and fanaticism. Certitude about the truth of stories that are scientifically impossible encourages an irrationality that spreads to everything, and that starts ominously to resemble mental illness.

Now, I've never been sure whether my intelligent father believes that Jesus of Nazareth was physically raised from the dead, or if he thinks instead that Christ's teachings live on after him and that's pretty much the same thing. I don't know if my father believes in the literal truth of Christ's feeding the five thousand with five loaves and two fishes, or if he imagines that more importantly the Redeemer fed his flock in a metaphysical sense.

But I'm not sure it matters. I will always find my father's choice of occupation curious. Yet while I may have concluded that the influence of religion on human affairs has been on balance malign, my father and I have both struggled to be good: to be good writers, good leaders, good thinkers, good citizens; to be good children and, in his case, with remarkable success, a good parent. We have both struggled to discern what it *means* to be good, which is not a simple matter, as my father would readily agree. I resemble my father, and other religious people, who are also struggling to be good, and also struggling to understand what it means to be good, far more than I differ from them.

Thus maybe the "childish thing" that we secularists need to "put away" in adulthood is our ridicule, our hostility, our incomprehension— our beloved bafflement that anyone buys this twaddle. Maybe we need to put away the atheist's belief in a superior access to the "truth," which can duplicate the very false certainty, and the very claim to membership of a privileged elect, that as religion's antagonists we would disavow. For too long, I have personally depended on rejection of faith as a substitute for faith, and as I advance into my own old age it would behoove me to shift my focus from what I don't believe to what I do. Surely it's time to release those bitter memories of being dragged to church by the hair. How much better with my father in the twilight of his life to seize not on what divides us, but on what we share.

"Terminal Friendship"

THE GUARDIAN, 2010

I met Terri Gelenian in the early 1980s at an arts camp in Connecticut. We were both in the metalsmithing workshop, and this sharply featured, appealingly surly Armenian taught me some new tricks. Her specialty was rivets and other "cold connections," an apt expression in her case. She was a willful, stubborn woman, more fiercely so than I first realized; twenty-five years later, I'd discover just how defiant my closest girlfriend could be, even in the face of the undeniable.

Terri was full of the contradictions that always captivate me in people: inclined to bear grudges but incredibly generous (often rocking up with gifts for no reason; why, I still have half a dozen pairs of her shoes). Harsh but warm. Prone to depression but with a flair for festivity. I conjure her scowling down the pavement and rolling in laughter with equal ease. She was tortured and brooding; she was terribly kind. And she was a serious artist in the best sense: not pretentious, but determined to craft interesting work well.

Back in Queens, where we both lived in our mid-twenties, we found common cause in our improbable aspirations. She wanted to become a famous artist, I a famous novelist—but Terri had then sold next to nothing, and I'd not published more than my phone number. It was a big, indifferent world out there, and an ally was crucial. We'd conspire over a six-pack in my tiny one-bedroom apartment, jovially certain that we'd still be best friends when we were "cancerous old bags." It was a running gag. We thought it was funny.

Beware the jokes of your heedless, immortal youth. Fast-forward through two and a half decades, during which Terri and I survived abusive boyfriends, marital problems, professional setbacks, my expatriation to the United Kingdom and her exile to New Jersey, Terri's painful endometriosis and four failed IVF treatments, as well as, of course, each other. During my regular summer migration to New York in 2005, Terri shared her perplexity that she'd been running a low-grade fever for weeks. I said it sounded like a tenacious virus. But shortly thereafter she rang from hospital.

She was being tested for a range of ailments, the most far-fetched of these a rare disease called mesothelioma. Thus it was quite a shock when the doctors confirmed that peritoneal mesothelioma was exactly what she had—almost certainly caused by exposure to the asbestos that laced metalsmithing materials when she was in art school. Her husband, Paul, reported grimly that the average survival rate for this ravaging cancer was a single year.

Terri was only fifty, and the timing was tragic for other reasons, too. From frustration, malaise, and exactingly high standards, through most of her career she had underproduced. Yet in recent years something had loosened up, and her output had accelerated. Better still, she was at last imbuing her creations with the feeling they'd sometimes lacked, the most touching of which was an elegy to her unavailing IVF treatments. She was finally pulling in big commissions, one of which was about to go on display at the V&A. At the same time, her brooding demeanor had brightened; she'd grown more outgoing, energetic, and relaxed. Almost . . . happy. Well, so much for that.

On the heels of her diagnosis, I was doting. I'm not tooting my own horn. I suspect being a paragon at the very start of a loved one's illness is pretty much the form. We're on the phone daily. We stop by often; we bring freshly baked scones. We follow every medical twist and turn. And we're inclined to rash promises. With a flinch, I recall declaring before Terri's surgery that I'd be willing to move into their house in New Jersey for weeks at a time! I'd be at her beck and call, running errands, preparing meals, and filling prescriptions.

Useful tip: If someone close to you falls gravely ill, at the outset, in the first flush of anguish and desperation to help? Watch the mouth.

For the timing of Terri's cancer was terrible for me as well. A month after her diagnosis, I was intending to return home to London, where a host of professional commitments could not (or so it seemed) be reneged upon. Although for most of my literary career I'd scribbled in obscurity, my prospects were suddenly looking up. My seventh novel had inexplicably hit the bestseller list in Britain and subsequently won the Orange Prize earlier that summer. (I still have the droll good-luck package Terri and Paul delivered when I made the short list: orange marmalade, orange candles, orange oil.) For the first time, I faced a smorgasbord of opportunities—festival gigs, bookstore appearances, feature assignments—and I was in the middle of a new novel.

However reluctantly, I flew back to London. After Terri's surgery, Paul phoned with the lowdown: the surgeons had discovered a patch of aggressive "sarcomatoid" cells, which meant Terri's prognosis was bleak.

I will give myself this grudging credit: I did fly back to visit Terri for Thanksgiving that November, and for a while I kept in faithful touch, ringing weekly and following every grisly detail of her punishing chemotherapy. But this is not a boast about what a wonderful friend I was in Terri's time of need. This is a mea culpa.

Little by little, I'd notice that it had been a fortnight since I'd rung New Jersey. I'd kick myself. But some book review would be due that afternoon, so I'd vow to ring tomorrow. Time and again some immediate task would seem more urgent, and I'd tell myself that I should ring

Terri when I was settled and concentrated. Watch out whenever you "tell yourself" anything; it's the red flag of self-deceit. Long hours of being "settled and concentrated" mysteriously failed to manifest themselves.

I stuck a Post-it note on the edge of my desk: RING TERRI! Over the months, the note faded, much like my resolve. On the too-rare occasions I acted on the reminder, I had to put a mental gun to my head. But why? This was one of my closest friends, and she was dying. While she was still on this earth, why was I not battling to maximize every moment? Surely the problem should have been my ringing too often, whizzing back to the States too many times, making a pest of myself.

Granted, our conversations were sometimes awkward. My own life had never gone more swimmingly, while Terri's was circling the drain. I was embarrassed. I found myself editing from our discussions anything I'd done that was exciting or fun. When I returned from an author's tour of Sweden, I portrayed the trip as a drag. This sort of cover-up reliably backfired. So I felt sorry for myself—for going to Sweden! When Terri could rarely leave the house.

I make no apologies for this, since this is what novelists do: at some midpoint in Terri's decline, I decided that my next novel would draw on this encounter with cancer. At least I had the humanity to refrain from taking notes during our phone calls, thereby relinquishing many a "telling detail" and much "great material." Consequently, I had to do an enormous amount of research on mesothelioma later, and this is what I do apologize for: not having done all those Web searches on her treatments—the surgery, the drugs, the side effects—when Terri was still suffering through them. Now I'm mortified to have Googled "mesothelioma" only when the search was for a book.

When I returned to the United States that second summer, Terri had alarmingly deteriorated. Thin to start with, she'd lost weight. She was gaunt and weak, her skin tinged a dark, unsettling orange: a chemo tan. It was obvious where this was headed. But whenever anyone acted as if she wasn't going to make it, Terri grew enraged. She resented the

"sentimental" testimonials her friends and relatives recited at her bed-
side; she thought they were delivering a death sentence. Though she
wouldn't have put it that way. I wonder if throughout her illness I ever
heard her say the word "death" aloud.

On this one count alone could I blame Terri herself for my increasingly deficient friendship. Her refusal to admit she was dying meant
that we couldn't ever talk about the macabre elephant in the room. Pretending that the treatments were working and she was going to come
through this injected an artifice in our relationship at odds with the
confidences we'd shared for twenty-five years. Days I did visit, after-
noons I did ring, we'd end up talking, lamely, about recipes. Indeed, on
a brief trip from London back to New York in November 2006, I visited
Terri in New Jersey; it was the last time I'd ever see her, and I knew
this instinctively at the time. Yet we spent an appalling proportion of
that final visit talking about mashed potatoes.

When her husband rang me in London a few days later with the
news, he was consumed with a steely rage. Obviously, Paul was angry
that he'd lost his wife. But he was also angry at other people. Oh, he
expressed his disgust in general terms, as a disillusionment with the
human race, a good riddance to our whole species. But I knew what
he meant. Paul's fury was aimed at Terri's friends and family, who had
almost universally made themselves scarce for months. His fury was
also aimed at me.

I thought I deserved it. I had visited, some. I had rung up, some. But
not nearly often enough, and in truth one of my best friends perishing
before my eyes had instilled a deep aversion, an instinctive avoidance,
a desperation to flee.

It would be a far better thing if I were a lone shithead amid an ocean
of altruists. And surely some folks really do step up to the plate when a
friend or relative falls mortally ill—wonderful people who keep popping
by with scones to the very last day. I have a new admiration for such stal-
warts, as well as a new appreciation for the Christian duty to "visit the
sick." Yet I fear this suddenly-remembering-somewhere-you-gotta-be

is a common failing of our time. In fearing and avoiding death, we fear and avoid the dying.

I'll risk sounding preachy, since I've paid for my sermon with a regret that never leaves me. Most of us will experience the afflictions of our nearest and dearest perhaps multiple times before we're faced with a deadly diagnosis of our own. So be mindful. Disease is frightening. It's unpleasant. It reminds us of everything we try not to think about on our own accounts. A biological instinct to steer clear of contagion can kick in even with diseases like cancer that we understand rationally aren't communicable. So the urge to avoid sick people runs very deep. Notice it. Then overcome it. There will always be something you'd rather do than confront the agony, anxiety, and exile of serious illness, and these alternative endeavors seem terribly pressing in the moment: replacing the printer cartridge, catching up on urgent work-related email. But nothing is more pressing than someone you love who's suffering, and whose continuing existence you can no longer take for granted. So never vow to ring "tomorrow." Pick up the bloody phone.

"My Teenage Diary"

THE GUARDIAN, 2015

[The radio appearance I mention in this essay kicked off the sole instance of my trending on Twitter because the social media crowd liked something.]

In my teens, I eyed my adulthood with trepidation, as if stalked by a stranger—one who would seize control as if by demonic possession and regard my fledgling incarnation with contempt. I was terrified of growing up to become the anti-me, maturing into a woman whom I would not recognize, and who wouldn't recognize her younger self. I doubt I was alone as a teenager in seeing adulthood as a lurking betrayal, an impending death. That may be one reason why teen suicide rates are so high: for many adolescents, growing up presents itself as a form of bereavement anyway, so it seems as if there's nothing to lose.

Asked to fill the painfully comic Radio 4 slot *My Teenage Diary*, I scrambled into my attic recently to dig up the damp, furry-cardboard covers of the journals I began keeping when I was twelve. Before re-reading them for the first time in forty-some years, I worried that I would be embarrassed. Instead, I was infuriated.

I didn't write entries with nearly the faithfulness that I remembered, and I recorded all the wrong things. I often omitted the date. I rarely described what happened: what people said, where I was, what awful incident had driven me despairingly to this notebook. No, what I mostly wrote down was *feelings*.

Sod the feelings! What was your life like? In those days, I disdained a daily "Dear diary" format, in which a girl traditionally included what happened at school, what hurtful remark from a best friend especially smarted, what punishments parents meted out for which offense, what she had for dinner. Know what? Now I would love to know what I had for dinner.

All those small, irretrievable details of the everyday would be invaluable to me now: word-for-word dialogue between classmates, the blow-by-blow of family altercations, my response to larger historical events such as the assassination of Martin Luther King Jr. These journals lack sensory information, too; I would have loved to know what my teens smelled, tasted, looked, sounded, and felt like. Even in private, I was too shy to write about sex (God forbid I should mention masturbation, at which I was already, if you will, a dab hand, but over which I suffered self-excoriating shame) or what it was like, say, to get my first period.

What I did record at length, alas, was woe-mucking about a classmate named Roger Cook. I wasn't a girl who flitted from one crush to another. I had one crush, which I sustained for five or six years, starting at age eleven. That suggests an innate constancy from which my husband now benefits. Nevertheless, I had no idea that all the textual outpouring about my unreturned affections would prove so trying decades later. Preparing for *My Teenage Diary*, I couldn't bring myself to read most of these sections, and not from embarrassment. I was bored to death.

What *was* interesting: I had forgotten quite how massive an upheaval my older brother caused in our family, and it is this saga that profitably occupies many pages—sometimes with details, with dialogue! Three years my senior, Greg dropped out of school and left home at fourteen. That was 1968, and his rebellion naturally involved drink, drugs, and sex. You gotta hand it to Greg for shacking up (as my mother would say) with not one but two fetching seventeen-year-old girls, with whom he had regular threesomes. My morally conservative parents were hysterical. While they had knock-down drag-outs with my brother, I felt sidelined—especially when he pitched up again:

Gregory's home. You can tell. He walks in and you are small. The air of importance and self-confidence enters the room; a well-traveled, experienced man. Everywhere I go, "Are you Gregory's sister?" . . . I am just a stagnant shadow. Just a small child groveling up the glory left behind by my older brother.

Their eldest out of their control, my parents fiercely pressured my younger brother and me to "not turn out like Gregory." At any sign that I, too, had wayward leanings, my mother would sob. In fact, both remaining kids were constantly subjected to my mother's moist, mucus-drizzling fits of weeping—literally on our shoulders—while we would feel trapped, hot, and secretly unmoved.

As for the writing style, of course, it's frequently lofty and affected. Take the exhortation to my older brother, in a poem written at the age of twelve: "Oh, Gregory! / Love is not gone. / It would simply flourish under / Recognition. / Yes, conversation with that which / Is three years younger may not / Be intriguing, but ought not to be ignored." *With that which is three years younger?* Please! And sure, my spelling (charade = "sherade") is atrocious. Sometimes I try out a word and I don't quite get what it means, but other times I'm impressed: I clearly understood the definition of "osmosis." I concocted my own goofy slang (a "schmerdie" was a jerk or a nerd), which turns out to have been good practice for my novel *The Mandibles*, in which I invent a new colloquial vernacular of the near future.

I suspect most of us objectify younger versions of ourselves, passing judgment, sometimes with surprising harshness, as if turning our backs on a friendship gone sour: "You idiot. How could you have squandered so much energy on that guy? He's just not that into you! They made a movie about it!" But is that impotent chastisement from the Ghost of Christmas Future really a betrayal?

As a teenager, I ached to grow up even more than I dreaded to. I craved escape from my parents' impositions on what I believed. I was determined to become a writer. I yearned to fall in love, and I constructed a fetishistic romantic ideal out of one real, perfectly nice, but probably rather ordinary boy.

Over time, I achieved all these purposes: maturity, independence, literary career, and a love of my life. I once feared that I would abandon my true self when I grew up, but the adult's pursuit of those same goals, decade after decade, has entailed a powerful loyalty to the girl. I may have tried to discard a few aspects of the 1970s Shriver: self-conscious affectation, high-flown histrionics, a weakness for unrequited infatuation. Otherwise, I wager that my younger self would recognize this wary, hazel gaze in a heartbeat. I don't think she would be too disappointed by how she turned out.

"THE BIG STORY"

FINANCIAL TIMES, 2013

The precise inspiration for a novel can be tough to pinpoint. Yet *Big Brother* derived from a single paralytic moment.

Home in London in November 2009, I wrote a column for *Standpoint* about the rise of America's "fat pride" movement. While glad to relax our literally narrow definition of attractiveness, I felt queasy about the interest group's assertion that one could be "healthy at any size." Though I'd never cited my older brother in journalism before, Greg made an irresistible example of someone whose size was anything but "healthy." Oh, I'd seen enough low-rent documentaries like *The Half-Ton Man* to recognize that, merely pushing four hundred pounds at five feet, seven inches, my fifty-five-year-old brother wasn't breaking any records in the weight department. Nevertheless, he had untreated high-blood-sugar diabetes, hypertension, and such swelling in his feet that some mornings he couldn't get his boots on. Not long before, he'd nearly died from congestive heart failure. These lines would soon haunt me: "Every time I talk to my brother, I wonder if it's for the last time. Planning to see him during an author's tour in March, I'm counting the days, actively anxious that he won't still be with us a whole three months from now." In short order, I'd stop counting those days.

For a few hours after I filed that column, my parents rang from the States. Once again, my brother was in hospital.

Because it had become too awkward for him to fly, the day before Greg had taken Amtrak from his home in North Carolina to visit our parents in Manhattan for Thanksgiving. My mother described how, shuffling thirty meters between the taxi and the elevator in their lobby, he'd had to stop and rest twice. Since my brother collected vices as some people do stamps, he was a lifelong smoker with emphysema, by then obliging him to drag an oxygen tank behind him wherever he went (which he disconnected from his nose only to light another cigarette). There was only so much paraphernalia he'd been able to drag with him on the train, so that night when he went to sleep, in the living room armchair that he preferred to a proper bed, he didn't have his sleep apnea machine.

The next morning my parents were unable to rouse their son. He was disoriented and incoherent. Consulting the laminated list of pre-scriptions and emergency numbers Greg had painstakingly printed and looped around his neck for the train trip—he had learned to prepare for medical crises—my mother rang his doctor, who urged her to get him to hospital immediately. Sleep apnea—another bane of obesity—can build up poisonous levels of carbon dioxide in the blood, and that's why he was delirious.

Yet getting Greg to hospital was easier said than done. Once the ambulance crew arrived, they were unable to lift him and had to call for a second crew to help. As both crews knelt beside that chair to hoist their unconscious, wide-load patient, my mother overheard one paramedic whisper to another, "How does this happen?"

At Saint Luke's, a few blocks away on the Upper West Side, Greg was kept sedated, because he hated to be constrained, and whenever he awoke he fought the nurses and tore the tubes out. His condition worsened when he contracted an infection, which the poor circulation and overburdened heart of a man his size made it hard for him to fight.

I was my brother's designated health proxy, meant to take medical decisions on his behalf if he was incapacitated. Eight days after Greg entered intensive care, his doctor rang me in London to say it finally seemed that Greg was out of the woods and to consult me on what came next. Saint Luke's is renowned for its treatment of obese patients, so I asked if my brother was a candidate for bariatric surgery. Yes, the doctor said, he would be well suited for a gastric bypass, and the hospital would be willing to do the operation and to undertake the protracted follow-up treatment. But there was a caveat: Greg would need someone to take care of him, and he would need somewhere to live in the New York area.

Standing in my London kitchen, I took a deep breath. I knew that my elderly parents would be unable to house and nurse Greg for many months of surgical recuperation and supervised weight loss. But my husband and I have a house in Brooklyn. It even has a "granny flat" in the basement, with a separate bathroom and kitchenette. I'm a free-lance writer, professionally mobile. Was I being called to invite him to stay with us? But my brother was very difficult! Did I love him that much? Would my husband put up with him? Could *I* put up with him? Would Greg fit through our doorways? Would our midget downstairs toilet crack under the strain? In times like these, even a committed atheist reaches for the metaphors of a Christian upbringing, and I thought: *Take this cup from me.*

That is the moment. That is where *Big Brother* comes from.

As it happened, my brother's condition abruptly plummeted again, and he died two days later. I never had to face down whether I was kind enough, loving enough, self-sacrificing enough, to take my brother on, to take my brother in. I got out of it.

BIG BROTHER IS NOT AUTOBIOGRAPHICAL. ABOUT A SISTER WHO RISKS HER marriage by setting up housekeeping with a morbidly obese older brother to help him lose weight, the novel expressly describes what *didn't* happen. Still, my brother's loss was fresh. Like the topics I'd chosen for several previous books, the issue of obesity combines the social with the profoundly private. Fat seemed like my material.

After all, I could appreciate that weight often interacts with a host of emotional and other medical problems. Greg had never been heavy until two terrible accidents in quick succession: being beaten up with a metal baseball bat and broadsided on his moped by a car. He was left in chronic pain, clinking with titanium and barely able to walk. He could hardly keep off the pounds by jogging. Disability dishearteningly curtailed his professional opportunities, further inclining him to seek what gratification lay within reach (large jars of pickled sausages).

I may have been just over a hundred pounds, but I did see how weight gain could snowball. As the brother, Edison, explains in the novel, "I used to look pretty good. Then I didn't. That's the point. Once I got sort of fat, one more baby-back didn't matter. See, when you look sharp, you got something to protect—an investment to preserve, a power to keep. But when you're already big, there's nothing to lose from getting bigger." If you're in good trim, it's easy to decline a cupcake: you're motivated; you have a social resource to preserve. But for my brother, passing on a cupcake presented itself as pure self-denial with no reward. Once you're hundreds of pounds overweight, eat it or don't eat it, what difference does it make?

Most of all, I approached this subject with sympathy. I'd often been enraged on Greg's behalf when we went somewhere together and all strangers seemed to see was some huge guy. The rebel of the family, he was a mastermind. With no formal education beyond junior high school, he taught himself to be a sound engineer from books. He started his own company while still in his teens, building sound systems and recording studios. He was Philip Glass's soundman for *Einstein on the Beach* in New York City and toured with Harry Belafonte all over Europe. He was funny, he was politically clued up, and his memorial service was crowded with devoted friends who revered him. Indeed, my primary reservation about writing *Big Brother* was that I was loath for my own exceptional big brother to be remembered solely as fat.

I HAD ANTICIPATED THAT THIS NOVEL WOULD BE DIFFICULT BECAUSE ITS origin made me sorrowful. I did not anticipate it would be hard for other reasons.

So far, only a few other fiction writers have focused on fat. Yet over-eating has been relentlessly addressed in other media, especially television and glossy magazines. I didn't want to publish dieting tips and slimming recipes, to write a thinly disguised self-help book, to rehash a clatter of conflicting scientific studies, or to go on the political warpath against fast-food companies. A literary novel needs to dig deeper. Aside from nutrition, what do we get out of eating? Is food not more "the *idea* of satisfaction, far more powerful than satisfaction itself," a promise that never quite delivers? What is so alluring about food that some of us will imperil our very survival to consume too much of it? When we meet either the grossly fat or the skeletally thin, what do we assume about their characters? Considering the tentative connection we ourselves experience between who we are in our heads and what our bodies happen to look like, why do we continue to take appearance so seriously? What does it *mean* that the populations of whole countries in the West are getting so heavy? And of course any novel about obesity has to answer the question that paramedic raised in my parents' living room: *How does this happen?*

The second section of *Big Brother*, in which Edison goes on an all-liquid diet, presented a headache if only in terms of entertainment. Weight loss is slow, and weight loss is dull—qualities no novelist courts. Lo, prose about losing weight can be every bit as tedious as the real thing. Yet I couldn't simply have you turn a page and Edison's long, grueling diet is over. I needed the reader to share the sacrifice, determination, and daily application the diet required, but ideally without boring my poor reader senseless. Furthermore, every afternoon I worked on part 2, without fail, *it made me hungry.* I'd no sooner have returned to chapter 3 in my study than I'd find myself back downstairs, staring soulfully into the refrigerator.

The other problem was structural. Any story about weight is linear—a shape no more sophisticated in literature than in geometry. I faced a range of obvious end points, none satisfying: (A.) Edison stays fat (static, not a story). (B.) Edison loses the weight and lives happily ever after (didn't sound like a Shriver novel to me). (C.) Edison loses the weight only to gain it all back again. Now, the latter structure engenders an appealing pathos. Yet as a matter of principle I could not publish a novel with the implicit message that in the long run it's impossible to lose weight and thus it's pointless even to try.

So I chose (D.).

WOULD GREG HAVE LIKED *BIG BROTHER*? I HOPE SO, THOUGH I IMAGINE HANDing him a copy with apology. Willful, brilliant, and entirely self-made, Greg Shriver was larger-than-life in a grander sense than girth. He was a bizarre hybrid of southern good-old-boy and over-aged hippie—a longhair with a hard hat. He was a magnet for other compelling characters, but also for bad luck, some of which he brought on himself, much of which simply arrived like a letter bomb. (In the mid-1990s, a small private plane freakishly crashed into Greg's rental accommodation, demolishing that one house and nothing else. Fortunately, Greg wasn't home, but he lost everything he owned. His roommate survived only because he happened to be reaching for a beer, and the open door of the refrigerator shielded him from the blast. This stuff just doesn't happen to normal people.) Edison represents a mere sliver of the complicated, formidable older brother to whom the novel is dedicated, "in the face of whose drastic, fantastic, astonishing life any fiction pales."

Greg Shriver's Memorial Tribute

Durham, North Carolina, 2009

My older brother, Greg, was a real *maverick*, so I know what a travesty it is for a conformist, cheerleader opportunist like Sarah Palin to have colonized that word. I probably looked up to Greg for the same reasons that through most of his life he was such a headache for our parents. He was an iconoclast. He was naturally disobedient, defiant, and headstrong. He did whatever he wanted to. His dropping out of school at only fourteen may have pained our well-educated parents, but at the age of eleven, when I was hardly enjoying myself at Frances Lacy Elementary School in sixth grade, I thought his cut-and-run was marvelous. He started Stage and Studio Construction as a teenager. He taught himself everything he knew—which as most of you know was a hell of a lot.

Throughout my adolescence and young adulthood, Greg was an inspiration to me, not only because he was that contemporary American rarity, the self-made man, but because he stood up to my parents. I know they didn't always find that pleasant. But like most parents, ours needed standing up to, and Greg taught me how. Greg taught me that you don't have to do what you're told. Learning to question and stand up to authority has helped to fashion not merely my family relationships, but my politics.

• • •

THE FACT IS THAT I'M TOO STUPID TO FULLY APPRECIATE JUST HOW SMART MY brother was. Obviously, he and I could connect talking about the lousy justifications for the war in Iraq, but his real brilliance was technical—scientific, electronic, mechanical—and I'm one of those people whose technical expertise runs to competently affixing a new plug onto a lamp cord and that's about it. I don't have the intellectual wherewithal to grasp everything that Greg grasped and everything that he was good at. I remember his close friend and sometime employee Paul Gabriel—another wonderful man who's sadly left us— trying to explain to me once, "Your brother, you have no idea . . ." Gabe trailed off helplessly, because Greg's sister wouldn't be able to understand the myriad situations in which Greg's intuition, improbably broad general knowledge, and innovative thinking had saved the day. So Gabe just said, "I mean, your brother Greg is *really smart*." In fact, I can't count the number of people who've told me at one time or another that Greg was "the smartest guy they'd ever met." Back when my younger brother, Timothy, and I were kids, we fiercely resented the fact that Greg had tested as having a "genius-level IQ," a treasured family factoid that our parents trotted out at every opportunity. We thought that meant that in comparison we were dumb. Well, in certain narrowly defined but still impressive respects, in comparison we probably are dumb. Or I'll speak for myself anyway. In comparison with Greg, I am dumb.

But there were other respects in which *Greg* was dumb. If he defined himself by breaking all the rules, he broke some rules that he'd have been better off adhering to. Let's not beat about the bush. Back in the day, he drank too much; bloody hell, he even drank too much *coffee*. He smoked too much, and he took too many recreational drugs. Running Stage and Studio, he slept too little, and the only exercise he ever took was climbing scaffolding and feeding plywood to his table saw. In the later years, obviously, he ate too much. Nevertheless, I treasured his appetites, which made him far better company than a militant jogger who lives on herbal tea and celery. I like people with weaknesses. Let it not go unsaid: Greg Shriver knew how to have a good time.

There were still other respects in which Greg was problematic. I wouldn't want people at my memorial service to misremember me as perfect; I think I'd find that insulting, and I'd want someone to speak up about the fact that in a lot of ways I was a pain in the ass. So, yeah, Greg could be a pain in the ass. He talked incessantly. In recent times, he often blamed his so-called logorrhea on some drug he'd been pre-scribed, and I always wanted to interrupt to object, "No, Greg, this isn't some new pharmaceutical side effect; you've always been this way; you've *never* been able to shut up"—but of course he wouldn't let me get that word in edgewise. Greg wasn't a good listener, and that's an understatement. If for no other reason than that, he may have been a nightmare as a husband, and it's hard to blame two wives for not going the distance. Still, I do wish he hadn't ended up by himself. It's the very people who have such a hard time connecting who most desperately need companionship.

I think it's worth talking a little about Greg's last few years. I found his circumstances incredibly painful, and that's the main reason that I didn't see him or ring him as often as I wish I had and should have. Especially when I saw him in person, his woeful physical condition moved me to tears. As you all probably know, owing to two nasty ac-cidents a couple of years apart, Greg had a hard time getting around even with a cane; he was in constant pain, and respiratory problems required him to drag that portable oxygen tank behind him wherever he went, like a faithful dog. And again, let's not beat about the bush, he got fat. Because my brother never did anything by halves his whole life, when Greg got fat, he got fat with a vengeance.

What pained me most about his weight was that lots of people couldn't see him anymore. All they saw was some big geez who they hoped didn't squeeze in next to them on the bus. I hated Greg's having become at once so big but also, to strangers, invisible. The home stretch of his life was agonizing, and there's a way in which he died by degrees. That's the sole thing that's good about his passing: getting it over with. I will miss him fiercely, but for the last few years Greg was in such a state of constant physical suffering that he seemed to be sticking around in large part as a favor to his friends and family. As I told my mother after he died, that car that broadsided him on his moped, and very nearly killed him? Well, in the end it did kill him. Took a decade, but that car did kill him.

Still, it's worth remembering that behind all that bloat and disability was an extraordinary person—a brother, a son, a father, a friend, and, yes, a genius—if only to remember that other distended and damaged bodies disguise unusual people whom families and friends desperately love. That's one thing I learned from Greg during his latter life; I think he increased my compassion. That's a compassion that we can all continue to spread around to folks who are still with us.

So I think it's fitting to take this opportunity to thank two people who showed so much compassion toward Greg Shriver when his health became compromised, which also made it hard for him to keep making a living. That's my parents. I probably know better than anyone that Greg was a difficult son. There were whole years during which he didn't communicate with his family at all, and we had no idea where he was living. But that didn't stop our parents from coming to his aid when he needed their help. Greg's determination to visit our parents in New York for Thanksgiving last month was a testimony to his love for them; he was willing to risk a journey that he really wasn't well enough to undertake. I'm sorry that trip plunged him into a last medical crisis from which he never recovered, but I'm glad for his and their sakes that he was in New York, where our parents could visit every day and hold his hand. I'm hopeful that Greg knew, however dimly, that they were there. I'd also like to thank his close friends Scott and Markie, who really stuck by Greg, and who were always there when he needed them. Greg talked to me about you both all the time.

I don't plan on remembering my brother at four hundred pounds and hardly able to walk. I'll always picture him instead in that cavernous basement workshop on Franklin Street in Raleigh, where I used to visit him in my teens and twenties. You know, with his army truck parked in the drive. The shop was always hazy with sawdust, littered with encrusted coffee cups, and cluttered with salvaged machine parts that Greg just might find a use for someday. It was always dark, not only because it had no windows to speak of, but because Greg, with typical I'll-do-it-my-way perversity, slept all day and worked all night. That basement was clamorous with shrieks from the table saw and Greg's shouted directions to his employees above the din. In those days, Greg always wore black jeans shiny with machine oil, and he trooped that concrete floor in lace-up black boots with inch-thick corrugated soles, his long, dark hair swinging—more perversity—in not two but three tight braids. His rimless glasses were tinted yellow, like the tobacco-stained fingers of his right hand. I'll always remember his signature smirk, with that wisp of a mustache that took years to grow in. I'll remember my brother as thin. And I'll remember my brother as vigorous, galumphing across that basement slightly bent forward as if fighting an oncoming gale, lunging from side to side, always clutching another cup of coffee, already cold.

Greg, if you're out there? I'll always regret not having been able to talk to you one more time—since there's a kind of talk you have only when you both know it's your last conversation. If I were given that chance, I'd tell you how much I've always looked up to you, and how much I still do. How grateful I was when things finally started to go a little my way professionally, but in tragically perfect concert with things going to hell for you. You didn't fly into a fit of sibling rivalry. Instead I got, "You go, girl." There's a way in which you and I were always allies, in collusion, in the end not so much against our parents as against the whole bossy, petty, normative world that told us what we could and could not do. You've always given me courage to swim against the tide. I love you, and for your many failings I forgive you, since your failings had a splendor all their own. There will never be anyone else like you. Your life was epic, baroque, outrageous, built on a grand scale, even if you paid for your eccentricities on the same grand scale. Our family is smaller, more ordinary, and more boring without you. Anything I accomplish in future will be a measure less gratifying because I can't share it with my older brother. I wish that you'd come around for even a few minutes at Saint Luke's hospital, just so you'd have known that I was ringing every day, and worrying every day. I can't tell you how much I hate having flown to North Carolina all the way from London this week on your account, and you don't even know it. Because if you'd only woken up, I'd have so much more gladly flown to New York last month, to whisper in your ear that you were always the renegade, the outlaw, the real revolutionary in our family who had not only talent and brains but guts, and I was proud to be your sister.

"What Did You Do in the War, Mommy?"

[PART II]

"Fiction and Identity Politics"

BRISBANE WRITERS FESTIVAL OPENING ADDRESS, 2016

I hate to disappoint you folks, but unless we stretch the topic to the breaking point this address will not be, as advertised, about "community and belonging." In fact, you have to hand it to this festival's organizers: inviting a renowned iconoclast to speak about "community and belonging" is like expecting a shark to balance a beach ball on its nose.

The topic I submitted instead—for which I was given the official go-ahead months ago—was "Fiction and Identity Politics," which may sound on its face equally dreary. But I'm afraid the thorny issues that cluster around "identity politics" have got all too interesting, particularly for people pursuing the occupation I share with many gathered in this hall: fiction writing. Taken to their logical conclusion, ideologies recently come into vogue challenge our right to write fiction at all. Meanwhile, the kind of fiction we are "allowed" to write is in danger of becoming so hedged, so circumscribed, so tippy-toe, that we'd indeed be better off not writing the anodyne drivel to begin with.

Let's start with a tempest in a teacup at Bowdoin College in

Brunswick, Maine. Earlier this year, two students, both members of student government, threw a tequila-themed birthday party for a friend. The hosts provided attendees with miniature sombreros, which—the horror—numerous partygoers wore.

When photos of the party circulated on social media, campus-wide outrage ensued. Administrators sent multiple emails to the "culprits," threatening an investigation into an "act of ethnic stereotyping." Partygoers were placed on "social probation," while the two hosts were ejected from their dorm and later impeached. Bowdoin's student newspaper decried the attendees' lack of "basic empathy." The student government issued a "statement of solidarity" with "all the students who were injured and affected by the incident," and demanded that administrators "create a safe space for those students who have been or feel specifically targeted." The tequila party, the statement specified, was just the sort of occasion that "creates an environment where students of color, particularly Latino, and especially Mexican, feel unsafe." In sum, the party favor hats constituted—wait for it—"cultural appropriation."

Curiously, across my country Mexican restaurants, often owned and run by Mexicans, are festooned with sombreros—if perhaps not for long. At Britain's University of East Anglia, the student union has banned a Mexican restaurant from giving out sombreros, deemed once more an act of "cultural appropriation" that was also racist.

Now, I am a little at a loss to explain what's so insulting about a sombrero, a practical piece of headgear for a hot climate that keeps out the sun with a wide brim. When I was small, my parents brought a sombrero back from their trip to Mexico, the better for my brothers and I to unashamedly *appropriate* the souvenir to play dress-up. For my part, as a German American on both sides, I'm more than happy for all those who don't share my genetic pedigree to don Tyrolean hats, pull on some lederhosen, pour themselves a *weissbier*, and belt out the Hofbräuhaus song.

But what does this have to do with writing fiction? The moral of the sombrero scandals is clear: *you're not supposed to try on other people's hats.* Yet that's what we're paid to do, isn't it? Step into other people's shoes and try on their hats.

In the latest ethos, which has spun well beyond college campuses in short order, any tradition, any experience, any costume, any way of doing or saying things that is associated with a minority or disadvantaged group is ring-fenced: look but don't touch. Those who embrace a vast range of "identities"—ethnicities, nationalities, races, sexual and gender categories, classes of economic underprivilege and disability—are now encouraged to be possessive of their experience and to regard other peoples' attempts to participate in their lives and traditions, either actively or imaginatively, as a form of theft.

Yet were their authors honoring the new rules against helping yourself to what doesn't belong to you, we would not have Malcolm Lowry's *Under the Volcano.* We wouldn't have most of Graham Greene's novels, many of which are set in what for the author were foreign countries, and which therefore have Real Foreigners in them, who speak and act like foreigners, too. In his masterwork *English Passengers,* Matthew Kneale would have restrained himself from including chapters written in an aboriginal's voice—though these are some of the richest, most compelling passages in that novel. If Dalton Trumbo had been scared off of describing being trapped in a body with no arms, legs, or face because he was not personally disabled—because he had not been through a World War I maiming himself and therefore had no right to "appropriate" the isolation of a paraplegic—we wouldn't have the haunting 1938 classic *Johnny Got His Gun.* We wouldn't have Maria McCann's erotic masterpiece, *As Meat Loves Salt*—in which a straight woman writes about gay men in the English Civil War. Though the book is nonfiction, it's worth noting that we also wouldn't have 1961's *Black Like Me,* for which John Howard Griffin committed the now unpardonable sin of "blackface." Having his skin darkened—Michael Jackson in reverse—Griffin found out what it was like to live as a black man in the segregated American

South. He'd be excoriated today, yet that book made a powerful social impact at the time.

The author of *Who Owns Culture? Appropriation and Authenticity in American Law*, Susan Scafidi, a law professor at Fordham University who for the record is white, defines "cultural appropriation" as "taking intellectual property, traditional knowledge, cultural expressions, or artifacts from someone else's culture without permission. This can include unauthorized use of another culture's dance, dress, music, language, folklore, cuisine, traditional medicine, religious symbols, etc." What strikes me about that definition is that "without permission" bit. How ever are we fiction writers to seek "permission" to use a character from another race or culture, or to employ the vernacular of a group to which we don't belong? Do we set up a stand on the corner and approach passersby with a clipboard, getting signatures that grant limited rights to employ an Indonesian character in chapter 12, the way political volunteers get a candidate on the ballot?

I am hopeful that the concept of "cultural appropriation" is a passing fad (albeit one not passing fast enough). People with different backgrounds rubbing up against one another and exchanging ideas and practices is self-evidently one of the most productive, fascinating aspects of modern urban life. But this latest and no little absurd no-no is part of a larger climate of supersensitivity, giving rise to proliferating prohibitions supposedly in the interest of social justice that constrain fiction writers and prospectively make our work impossible.

So far, the majority of these farcical cases of "appropriation" have concentrated on fashion, dance, and music: At the American Music Awards 2013, Katy Perry was castigated for dressing like a geisha. According to the Arab American writer Randa Jarrar, for someone like me to practice belly dancing is "white appropriation of Eastern dance," while the *Daily Beast* claimed that Iggy Azalea committed "cultural crimes" by imitating African rap and speaking in a "blaccent." The felony of cultural sticky fingers even extends to exercise: at the University of Ottawa in Canada, a yoga teacher was shamed into suspending her class, "because yoga originally comes from India." She offered to retitle the course "Mindful Stretching." And get this: the purism has even reached the world of food. Supported by no less than Lena Dunham, students at Oberlin College in Ohio have protested "culturally appropriated food" like sushi in their dining hall (lucky cusses—in my day, we never had sushi in *our* dining hall), whose inauthenticity is "insensitive" to the Japanese. Seriously, we have people questioning whether it's *appropriate* for white people to eat pad Thai. Turnabout, then: I guess that means that as a native of North Carolina, I can ban the Thais from eating hush puppies.

This same sensibility is coming to a bookstore near you. Because who is the appropriator par excellence, really? Who assumes other people's voices, accents, patois, and distinctive idioms? Who literally puts words into the mouths of people different from themselves? Who dares to get inside the very heads of strangers, who has the chutzpah to project thoughts and feelings into the minds of others, who steals their very souls? Who is a professional kidnapper? Who swipes every sight, smell, sensation, or overheard conversation like a kid in a candy store, and sometimes *takes notes*, the better to purloin whole worlds? Who is the premier pickpocket of the arts? The fiction writer, that's who.

This is a disrespectful vocation by its nature—prying, voyeuristic, kleptomaniacal, and presumptuous. And that is fiction writing at its best. When Truman Capote wrote from the perspective of condemned murderers from a lower economic class than his own, he had some gall. But writing fiction takes gall.

As for the culture police's obsession with "authenticity," fiction is inherently inauthentic. It's fake. It's self-confessedly fake; that is the nature of the form, which is about people who don't exist and events that didn't happen. The name of the game is not whether your novel honors reality; it's all about what you can get away with.

In his 2008 novel *The Other Hand*, Chris Cleave, who as it happens is participating in this festival, dared to write from the point of view of a fourteen-year-old Nigerian girl—though he is male, white, and British. I'll remain neutral on whether he "got away with it" in literary terms, because I haven't read the book. But in principle, I admire his courage—if only because he invited this kind of ethical forensics in a review out of San Francisco: "When a white male author writes as a young Nigerian girl, is it an act of empathy, or identity theft?" the reviewer asked. "When an author pretends to be someone he is not, he does it to tell a story outside of his own experiential range. But he has to in turn be careful that he is representing his characters, not using them for his plot."

Hold it. OK, he's necessarily "representing" his characters, by portraying them on the page. But of course he's using them for his plot! How could he not? They are his characters, to be manipulated at his whim, to fulfill whatever purpose he cares to put them to.

This same reviewer recapitulated Cleave's obligation "to show that he's representing [the girl], rather than exploiting her." Again, a false dichotomy. Of course he's exploiting her. It's his book, and he made her up. The character is his creature, to be exploited up a storm. Yet the reviewer chides that "special care should be taken with a story that's not implicitly yours to tell" and worries that "Cleave pushes his own boundaries maybe further than they were meant to go."

What stories are "implicitly ours to tell," and what boundaries around our own lives are we mandated to remain within? I would argue that any story you can *make* yours is yours to tell, and that trying to push the boundaries of the author's personal experience is part of a fiction writer's job. I'm hoping that crime writers, for example, don't all have personal experience of committing murder. Me, I've depicted a high school killing spree, and I hate to break it to you: I've never shot fatal arrows through seven kids, a teacher, and a cafeteria worker, either. We make things up, we chance our arms, sometimes we do a little research, but in the end it's still about what we can get away with— what we can put over on our readers. Because the ultimate end point of keeping our mitts off experience *that doesn't belong to us* is that there is no fiction. Someone like me permits herself to write only from the perspective of a straight white female born in North Carolina, closing on sixty, able-bodied but with bad knees, skint for years but finally able to buy the odd new shirt. All that's left is memoir.

And here's the bugbear; here's where we really can't win. At the same time that we're to write about only the few toys that landed in our playpen, we're also upbraided for failing to portray in our fiction a population that is sufficiently various. My most recent novel *The Mandibles* was taken to task by one reviewer for addressing an America that is "straight and white." It happens that this is a multigenerational family saga—about a white family. I wasn't instinctively inclined to insert a crossdresser or bisexual, with issues that might distract from my central subject matter of apocalyptic economics. Yet the implication of this criticism is that we novelists need to plug in representatives of a variety of groups in our cast of characters, as if filling out the entering class of freshmen at a university with strict diversity requirements.

You do indeed see just this brand of tokenism in television. There was a point in the latter 1990s at which suddenly every sitcom and drama in sight had to have a gay or lesbian character or couple. That was good news as a voucher of the success of the gay rights movement, but it still grew a bit tiresome: "Look at us, our show is so hip, one of the characters is homosexual!" We're now going through the same fashionable exercise in relation to the transgender character in series such as *Orange Is the New Black*.

Fine. But I still would like to reserve the right as a novelist to use only the characters who pertain to my story.

Besides: Which is it to be? We have to tend our own gardens, and write only about ourselves or people just like us because we mustn't pilfer others' experience, *or* we have to people our cast like an "I'd like to teach the world to sing" Coca-Cola advert?

For it can be dangerous these days to go the diversity route. Especially since there seems to be a consensus regarding the notion that

San Francisco reviewer put forward that "special care should be taken with a story that's not implicitly yours to tell."

In *The Mandibles*, I have one secondary character, Luella, who's black. She's married to a more central character, Douglas, the Mandible family's ninety-seven-year-old patriarch. I reasoned that Douglas, a liberal New Yorker, would credibly have left his wife for a beautiful, stately African American because arm candy of color would reflect well on him in his circle, and keep his progressive kids' objections to his betrayal of their mother to a minimum. But in the end the joke is on Douglas, because Luella suffers from early-onset dementia, while his ex-wife, staunchly of sound mind, ends up running a charity for dementia research. As the novel reaches its climax and the family is reduced to the street, they're obliged to put the addled, disoriented, often violent Luella on a leash, to keep her from wandering off. The family is desperate, with no money or transport; how else would you control her?

Behold, the reviewer in *The Washington Post*, who groundlessly accused this book of being "racist" because it doesn't toe a strict Democratic Party line in its political outlook, described the scene thus: "The Mandibles are white. Luella, the single African American in the family, arrives in Brooklyn incontinent and demented. She needs to be physically restrained. As their fortunes become ever more dire and the family assembles for a perilous trek through the streets of lawless New York, she's held at the end of a leash. If 'The Mandibles' is ever made into a film, my suggestion is that this image not be employed for the movie poster." Your author, by implication, yearns to bring back slavery.

Thus in the world of identity politics, fiction writers better be careful. If we do choose to import representatives of protected groups, special rules apply. If characters happen to be black, they have to be treated with kid gloves, and never be placed in scenes that, taken completely out of context, might seem disrespectful. But that's no way to write. The burden is too great, the self-examination too paralyzing.

The logical result of that kind of criticism in the *Post* is that next time I don't use *any* black characters, lest they do or say anything that is short of perfectly admirable and lovely or anything disagreeable is ever allowed to happen to them.

In fact, I'm reminded of a letter I received in relation to my seventh novel from an Armenian American—who objected, Why did I have to make the narrator of *We Need to Talk About Kevin* Armenian? Because he didn't like my narrator, he felt that her ethnicity disparaged his community. In my reply, I took pains to explain that I knew something about Armenian heritage, because my best friend in the States was Armenian, and I also thought there was something dark and aggrieved in the culture of the Armenian diaspora that was atmospherically germane to that book. Besides, I despaired, everyone in the United States has an ethnic background of some sort, and she had to be something!

Especially for writers from traditionally prosperous demographics, the message seems to be that it's a whole lot safer just to make all your characters from that same demographic, so you can be as hard on them as you care to be, and do with them what you like. Availing yourself of a diverse cast, you are not free; you have inadvertently invited a host of regulations upon your head, as if just having joined the European Union. Use different races, ethnicities, and minority gender identities, and you are being watched.

I confess that this climate of scrutiny has got under my skin. When I was first starting out as a novelist, I didn't hesitate to write black characters, for example, or to avail myself of black dialects, for which, having grown up in the American South, I had a pretty good ear. I am now much more anxious about depicting characters of different races, and accents make me nervous. In describing a second-generation Mexican American who's married to one of my main characters in *The Mandibles*, I took care to write his dialogue in standard American English, to specify that he spoke without an accent, and to explain that he dropped Spanish expressions only tongue in cheek. I would certainly think twice—more than twice—about ever writing a whole novel, or even a goodly chunk of one, from the perspective of a character whose race is different from my own—because I may sell myself as an iconoclast, but I'm as anxious as the next person about attracting vitriol. But I think that's a loss. I think that indicates a contraction of my fictional universe that is not good for the books and not good for my soul.

Writing under the pseudonym Edward Schlosser on *Vox*, the author of the essay "I'm a Liberal Professor, and My Liberal Students Terrify Me" describes higher education's "current climate of fear" and its "heavily policed discourse of semantic sensitivity"—and I am concerned that this touchy gestalt, in which offendedness is used as a weapon, has spread far beyond academia, in part thanks to social media. Why, it's largely in order to keep from losing my fictional mojo that I stay off Facebook and Twitter, which could surely install an instinctive self-censorship out of fear of attack. Ten years ago, I gave the opening address of this same festival, in which I maintained that fiction writers have a vested interest in protecting everyone's *right* to offend others—because if hurting someone else's feelings even accidentally is sufficient justification for muzzling, there will always be someone out there who is miffed by what you say, and freedom of speech is dead. With the rise of identity politics, which privileges a subjective sense of injury as actionable basis for prosecution, that is a battle that in the decade since I last spoke in Brisbane we've been losing.

Worse: the Left's embrace of *gotcha* hypersensitivity inevitably invites backlash. Donald Trump appeals to people who have had it up to their eyeballs with being told what they can and cannot say. Pushing back against a mainstream culture of speak-no-evil suppression, they lash out in defiance, and then what they say can be pretty appalling.

Regarding identity politics, what's especially saddened me in my recent career is a trend toward rejecting the advocacy of anyone who does not belong to the group. In 2013, I published *Big Brother*, a novel that grew out of my loss of my own older brother, who in 2009 died from the complications of morbid obesity. I was moved to write the book not only from grief, but also from sympathy: in the years before his death, as my brother grew heavier, I saw how dreadfully other people treated him. He'd be seated off in a dark corner of a restaurant, and the staff would roll their eyes at one another after he'd ordered, though he hadn't requested more food than anyone else. I was wildly impatient with the way we assess people's characters these days in accordance with their weight. I tried to get on the page my dismay over how much energy people waste on this matter, sometimes anguishing for years over a few excess pounds. Both author and book were on the side of the angels, or so you would think.

But in my events to promote *Big Brother*, I started to notice a pattern. Most of the people in the signing queues were thin. Especially in the United States, fat is now one of those issues where you either have to be "one of us," or you're the enemy. I verified this when I had a long email correspondence with a "Healthy at Any Size" activist, who was incensed by the novel, which she hadn't even read. Which she refused to read. No amount of explaining that the novel was on her side, that it was a book that was terribly pained by the way heavy people are treated and how unfairly they are judged, could overcome the scrawny author's photo on the flap. She and her colleagues in the fat rights movement did not want my advocacy. I could not *weigh in* on this material because I did not belong to the club. I found this an artistic, political, and even commercial disappointment—because in the United States and the United Kingdom, if only skinny-minnies will buy your book, you've evaporated the pool of prospective consumers to a puddle.

I worry that the clamorous world of identity politics is also undermining the very causes its activists claim to back. As a fiction writer, yeah, I do sometimes make my narrator an Armenian. But that's only by way of a start. Merely being Armenian is not to have a character as I understand the word. Membership of a larger group is not an identity. Being Asian is not an identity. Being gay is not an identity. Being deaf, blind, or wheelchair-bound is not an identity, nor is being poor. I reviewed a novel recently that I had regretfully to give a thumbs-down, though it was terribly well intended; its heart was in the right place. But in relating the Chinese immigrant experience in America, the author put forward characters that were mostly—Chinese. That is, that's sort of all they were: Chinese. Which isn't enough.

Not only as writers but as people, surely we should seek to push beyond the constraining categories into which we have been arbitrarily dropped by birth. If we embrace narrow group-based identities too fiercely, we cling to the very cages in which others often try to trap us. We pigeonhole ourselves. We limit our own notion of who we are, and in presenting ourselves as one of a membership, a representative of our *type*, an ambassador of an amalgam, we ask not to be seen.

The reading and writing of fiction is obviously driven in part by a desire to look inward, to be self-examining, reflective. But the form is also born of a desperation to break free of the claustrophobia of our own experience. The spirit of good fiction is one of exploration, generosity, curiosity, audacity, and compassion. Writing during the day and reading when I go to bed at night, I find it an enormous relief to escape the confines of my own head. Even if novels and short stories do so only by creating an illusion, fiction helps fell the exasperating barriers between us, and for a short while allows us to behold the astonishing reality of other people. The last thing we fiction writers need is restrictions on what belongs to us. In a recent interview, our colleague Chris Cleave conceded, "Do I as an Englishman have any right to write a story of a Nigerian woman? . . . I completely sympathize with the people who say I have no right to do this. My only excuse is that I do it well."

Which brings us to my final point. We do not all do it well. So it's more than possible that we write from the perspective of a one-legged lesbian from Afghanistan and fall flat on our arses. We don't get the dialogue right, and for insertions of expressions in Pashto we depend on Google Translate. Halfway through the novel, suddenly the protagonist has lost the right leg instead of the left one. Our idea of lesbian sex is drawn from wooden internet porn. Efforts to persuasively enter the lives of others very different from us may fail: that's a given. But maybe rather than having our heads chopped off, we should get a few points for trying. After all, most fiction sucks. Most writing sucks. Most things that people make of any sort suck. But that doesn't mean we shouldn't make anything. The answer is that modern cliché: to keep trying to fail better. Anything but be obliged to designate my every character an aging five-foot-two smart-ass, and have to set every novel in North Carolina. We fiction writers have to preserve the right to wear many hats [*put on hat*]—including sombreros.

"Liberals Now Defy the Etymology of the Word"

THE NEW YORK TIMES, 2016

[Mind, this is a slight expansion of what I originally filed, not the crimped, eviscerated piece The New York Times *published.]*

Happily, most of the folks listening to my opening address for the Brisbane Writers Festival earlier this month laughed and clapped in all the right places. Yet I learned subsequently that, midway through, Yassmin Abdel-Magied, a twenty-four-year-old engineer of Sudanese extraction and the author of a single memoir, had walked out—at length followed by her concerned mother. In the press, these two departures later morphed into a stampede for the exit by most of the audience.

The young woman's indignant blog post the next day might have sunk into obscurity along with my speech, had it not been picked up by *The Guardian*—which initially requested a transcript of the address in order to "fact-check" the blog, then couldn't be bothered to corroborate a screed that did indeed misquote my speech, and published Ms. Abdel-Magied's counterargument without the argument: "We were 20 minutes into the speech when I turned to my mother, sitting next to me in the front row. 'Mama, I can't sit here,' I said, the corners of my mouth dragging downwards. 'I cannot legitimize this . . .'" In what *Breitbart* headlined "The Worst Article Written by Anyone Ever" (look, you can't choose your friends online, and a renowned Trump-supporting website jumping on my bandwagon pertains to my larger point), Ms. Abdel-Magied went on, "As I stood up, my heart began to race. I could feel the eyes of the hundreds of audience members on my back: questioning, querying, judging. . . . The faces around me blurred. As my heels thudded against the grey plastic of the flooring, harmonizing with the beat of the adrenaline pumping through my veins, my mind was blank save for one question. 'How is this happening?'"

I'm asking the same thing.

Briefly, what so horrified this audience member was a speech (the majority of which she did not hear) in which I urged that fiction writers be allowed to write fiction. Ultimately, the contrived taboo of so-called cultural appropriation means we can safely write only autobiography. And if fiction writers are criticized for both stealing other people's stories *and* failing to portray a diverse cast, we can't win. Honestly, my thesis seemed so obvious, even anodyne, that I'd initially worried I was taking on a paper tiger, and the speech would seem bland.

Nope—not in the topsy-turvy universe of identity politics. The festival immediately disavowed the embarrassing address as representing my views alone, not those of the administrators, who claimed to the press that I did not speak "to my brief"—whereas in fact the festival's organizers had approved an extensive lowdown of the talk's content months in advance. The public accusation that I'd gone rogue at the podium impugned my professionalism. A more litigious speaker might sue.

Right before my main solo appearance to discuss my new novel, I was mugged in the greenroom by two "fellow" writers, who physically braced me on the way out the door. The larger, more intimidating of the pair asserted she had not attended my address and so "wouldn't attack me," and then proceeded to attack me: I had come ungraciously to another country to criticize its minorities! (The address hadn't mentioned Australian minorities even once.) The festival hastily organized a rowdy "Right of Reply" protest directly across the hall from my event, which was *surprisingly* underattended. Rioting indignation from a few feet away sometimes drowned out my remarks about the destabilizing effects of high sovereign debt. On Bookmaker.com.au, I'd wager a fair whack of change that none of the protesters had heard the speech, of which I still possessed the sole copy.

Days later, at the request of my publicist, *The Guardian* finally ran the speech itself. Social media (which I ignore) apparently went ballistic, followed by a torrent of mainstream articles, both with me and against me, all over the world. Journalists universally misreported that I had insolently worn a sombrero for the entire address, whereas in truth I donned it as an emphatic flourish for the lecture's last two words. Leaving aside the fact that there's nothing pejorative about wearing a sombrero, portraying me as having heavy-handedly made the point that "fiction writers wear many hats" for forty-five solid minutes insulted my dramatic judgment.

Since not everyone is treated to such a personalized headline, I plan on printing out *The New Republic*'s "Lionel Shriver Should Not Write About Minority Characters" and taping it as a chiding little re-minder above my desk. I'll also preserve the magazine's subsequent headline "Lionel Shriver Thinks a Sombrero Is Just a Hat" as an unusually accurate capitulation of my viewpoint—although if I also plaster my wall with Izzy Lyon's comment piece on spiked-online.com, "Lionel Shriver Is Right," my marriage is bound to suffer.

First off, that account of Ms. Abdel-Magied's now-legendary sense of injury looks dodgy. This is a performance of injury, an opportunistic and even triumphant display of injury, affront molded into a cudgel. It's hard to imagine that the poor purported victim ended the evening alone in her room in a puddle of tears. For the no-platforming identity-politics movement originating in American liberal arts colleges, be-havior such as huffing out of an address, assaulting an older, more established speaker in a literary festival greenroom, and stirring up a lynch mob on social media on the basis of hearsay is par for the course. Broadly, these ructions are an assertion of generational power. Among millennials and especially those coming of age behind them, the race is on to see who can appear more righteous and more aggrieved—thus who can displace the boring old civil rights generation with a flashier brand.

When I was growing up, conservatives were the voice of oppression, conformity, and orthodoxy. It was the Right that imposed restrictions on liberty: we were all supposed to espouse Christian beliefs, remain virgins before marriage, say no to drugs, eschew profanity, and comply with the draft. It was the Right that was suspicious, sniffing out a Communist under every bush, and the Right that subjected public figures to scrutiny, especially of their patriotism.

Now the role of oppressor has passed to the Left. In Australia, where I gave that speech, Section 18C of the Racial Discrimination Act makes it unlawful to do or say anything likely to "offend, insult, humiliate or intimidate," providing alarming latitude in the restriction of free speech. It is Australia's right wing arguing for the amendment of this law, which the Left defends.

Raised in a liberal household and a lifelong Democrat, I am dismayed by the ever-growing list of what one can and cannot do or say coming out of left-wing activists—by their impulse to control, to instill self-censorship as well as to promote real censorship, and to deploy sensitivity to be brutally insensitive. Counterproductively, progressives who repress others with whatever inane version of virtue they've cooked up this week give rise to potent pushback—from people tired of being bossed around for whom these frenzies about cultural appropriation, trigger warnings, and safe spaces are self-evidently crazy. In a word, the tyranny of the shrill, goofball Left helps give rise to *Trump*.

Ironically, the primary focus of attacks from the identity-politics crowd is older fellow travelers. Only other liberals will be shamed into silence by terror of being labeled a racist (a slur generously lobbed at me in recent days, and one that, however unfounded, tends to stick). But there's still such a thing as a real bigot and a real misogynist. In obsessing over "microaggressions," like the sin of uttering the commonplace

Americanism "you guys" to mean "you all," activists persecute the very folks who already care about decency and equal rights, while providing fodder for proper retrogrades, who can dismiss concerns about still-pervasive discrimination as so much twaddle.

Moreover, people who would hamper free speech always make the mistake of assuming that they are designing a world in which only their enemies will be forced to shut up. But the clamorous college campus crowd is just as dependent on the right to speak their minds in a tolerant public square as their detractors.

Yet in an era of weaponized sensitivity, participation in public discourse is growing so perilous—so fraught with the danger of being caught out for using the wrong word or failing to toe the line of the latest dogma in relation to disability, sexual orientation, economic class, race, or ethnicity—that many of us are apt to bow out. Perhaps bullying their elders into silence is the intention of the identity-politics cabal, too—and there may be something to be said for throwing them all in the gladiatorial ring and letting them tear one another apart over who seemed to imply that Asians are good at math. Meanwhile the rest of us will withdraw, abandoning all hope of discussing heavily land-mined subjects with any but our most intimate companions, safely behind closed doors with a bottle of wine, and only if the company has been carefully vetted beforehand.

Is that the kind of life we want? Is that the kind of public dialogue we wish to foster—anxious, evasive, scrupulously cleansed of any whiff of controversy, lest we destroy our careers? Is that the kind of social life we want—whereby we are so horrified by the prospect of inadvertently giving offense that we don't ever speak to members of racial or sexual minorities, period? Is that the kind of fiction we want—whereby for a novelist of European heritage to create a character from Pakistan presents a prospect so booby-trapped with potentially fatal pitfalls that the universes inside the novels of white writers all look like John Cheever's homogeneous Connecticut suburbs of the 1950s, in befuddling contrast to the world outside their covers?

Ms. Abdel-Magied at least got the question right: *How is this happening?* How did the Left in the West—not only in the United States, but also in Europe, Down Under—come to embrace control, restriction, censorship, and the imposition of a credo at least as tyrannical as the anti-Communist, pro-Christian conformism I grew up with? "Liberals" have ominously relabeled themselves "progressives," forsaking a noun that at least had its roots in *liberalis* (*Webster*: "suitable for a freeman, generous," from *liber*, free). "Progress" merely means go forward, and you can go forward into a pit.

"Writers Blocked"

PROSPECT, 2018

In the 1980s, pop psychology promoted the shibboleth that "you can't argue with what people feel." Since then, that line has brought many a contentious conversation to an impasse. The consequences of anointing emotion as beyond interrogation are vividly illustrated in Mark Lawson's biting novel *The Allegations*: when an aggrieved party *feels* bullied, it means, ipso facto, that he or she *has* been bullied, and employment tribunals are mere formalities. Sacked by the BBC for the same offense, but never allowed to confront his anonymous accusers, Lawson should know.

But you *can* argue with what people feel. Emotions range from the justifiable—grief that a brother just died—to the irrational, unreasonable, and disproportionate: spitting fury that you're not allowed a chocolate cream, but only a caramel. That was me, throwing a tantrum aged ten. Pity I wasn't born twenty years later. I might have screamed at my mother when she sent me to my room: "But you can't argue with what people feel!"

Worse, in English "I feel" and "I think" are roughly synonymous. If we enshrine as a truism that "you can't argue with what people think," we can throw in the towel on intellection in perpetuity. Which, the way things are going, maybe we should do.

One emotion has grown so sacrosanct that an astonishingly large segment of Europeans now think that provoking it should be illegal: umbrage. According to a 2015 Pew Research Center poll, only the barest majority of Britons—54 percent—and a scant 27 percent of Germans believe that government should allow people to make statements offensive to minorities. (Why only minorities? Wouldn't equality under the law argue for banning speech offensive to anyone?)

Thus in January 2018, in an interview with the Canadian free-speech advocate Jordan Peterson that went viral, *Channel 4 News* presenter Cathy Newman referred casually to the "right not to be offended," as if the entitlement were a familiar point of common law. Though Peterson got the better of her in that instance—we don't often see Newman flustered—defenders of the "right not to be offended" are starting to prevail in European public opinion.

It doesn't take much parsing to conclude that protecting all and sundry from the terrible experience of having your feelings hurt is the end of free speech. Since nowadays "you can't argue with what people feel," umbrage is freed from rational justification. Given that the better part of the human race is crazy, stupid, or both, there's nary a thought in the world whose airing won't offend somebody. Doesn't Darwin offend creationists? Furthermore, in granting so much power to woundedness, we incentivize hypersensitivity. If we reward umbrage, we will get more of it. We do reward umbrage, and we're buried in it by the truckload.

Time was that children were taught to turn aside tormentors with the cry, "Sticks and stones may break my bones, but words will never hurt me!" While you can indeed feel injured because Bobby called you fat, the law has traditionally maintained a sharp distinction between bodily and emotional harm. Even libel law requires a demonstration of palpable damage to reputation, which might affect your livelihood, rather than mere testimony that a passage in a book made you cry.

That words-will-never-hurt me rejoinder is out of fashion. The "safe spaces" cropping up on university campuses aren't shelters to protect students from hailstorms, or havens for young women whose boyfriends beat them up, but bubbles in which to hide from ideas—to hide from words. When in a recent tweet the journalist Matt Baume decried Ryan Anderson's controversial book on transgenderism, *When Harry Became Sally*, as "violent," he didn't mean it was full of gory shoot-outs. Baume meant it was full of opinions that he didn't like.

Emotion cannot be disputed, especially umbrage. Words and sticks-and-stones are on a par. If words that cause umbrage are acts of violence, the state has every excuse to impound your dictionary.

THE END OF FICTION

Up against the wall in a dark alley, I'd personally say the sword is mightier than the pen. But all this power to break bones imputed to mere language may seem a boon for folks whose medium is wordsmith-ing. Aren't we writers menacing? Unfortunately, authors now contend with a torrent of dos and don'ts that bind our imaginations and make the process of writing and publishing fearful. Being a novelist in the era of "call outs" for supposedly offensive content is far less fun than it once was.

When I drafted my famous—or infamous—speech for a 2016 appearance at the Brisbane Writers Festival, I'd barely heard of "cultural appropriation." Fast-forward a mere eighteen months, and this ostensible taboo has grown firmly established in literary circles. (Social fads can color not only the present but also the past. It now seems as if we've been battling over "cultural appropriation" for years and years.) The notion often crops up in creative writing programs, leaving upcoming writers confused about what material they're "allowed" to use in their work and racking their brains over how in heaven's name they're supposed to seek permission to borrow a cup of sugar from "marginalized peoples." Earlier this year, having enrolled in one such MFA program in the Midwest, my own poor niece, Julia, endured a three-hour-long class entirely devoted to deploring the views on this issue promoted by this ghastly woman Lionel Shriver. Only near the end of the session did Julia allow that her surname was no coincidence, and the ogre under discussion was her aunt. The relationship didn't make her popular. Unsurprisingly, Julia is quitting the program.

These days, straight white fiction writers whose characters' ethnicity, race, disability, sexual identity, religion, or class differs from their own can expect their work to be subjected to forensic examination—and not only on social media. Publishers of young adult fiction and children's literature hire "sensitivity readers" to comb through manuscripts for perceived slights to any group with the protected status once reserved for distinguished architecture.

The publishing magazine *Kirkus Reviews* assigns "own voices" reviewers with a matching "marginalized" pedigree to assess young adult books that contain a diverse cast. Last autumn, the magazine yanked both a positive review and its coveted "star" after online activists accused Laura Moriarty's dystopian novel *American Heart*, which imagines a future in which Muslims in the United States are sent to internment camps, of using a "white savior narrative." Yes, whole plotlines are becoming unacceptable. This year's film *Three Billboards Outside Ebbing, Missouri* has attracted heavy flak because its racist cop rounds into a half-decent human being. Writers can refurbish murderers into good guys, but must never redeem a racist.

As for adult literature, it's impossible to gauge the degree of politically correct censorship going on behind the scenes at publishing companies and literary agencies. Editors and agents are unlikely to assert directly that a submission's content is too hot to handle. Having tackled divisive subjects or deployed characters who don't hew to the rules of identity politics—rules that are often opaque, or at least until you break them—authors are left with uneasy suspicions about why their manuscripts are attracting no takers, but with no hard evidence.

Equally impossible to gauge is the extent of writers' collective self-censorship. The tetchiness and public shaming of "call out" culture has to be influencing which subjects writers feel free to address and which they shy from, as well as making many writers reluctant to include a diverse cast. Does the edict to eschew stereotypes mean a black character can never be a drug dealer? (So much for *The Wire*, then. Or *Clockers*.) Rather than tiptoe through this minefield, plenty of writers must be playing it safe with characters, topics, and plots that won't get them into trouble. But this caution is invisible. Literary roads not taken are mapped privately in a writer's head, behind a screen, with the drapes drawn. We have no record of what a host of individual authors have decided to avoid.

IMAGINARY FRIENDS

Writing my first novel in the 1980s, I didn't hesitate to include black characters—not only Americans, but a whole invented African tribe. I freely included occasional dialogue in black English. Despite a continued conviction that I have as much right to create black characters as black writers have to create white ones, I've grown more self-conscious. Accents and dialects, now decried as "othering," make me nervous. I'm more hesitant to fold a range of ethnicities, races, gender variants, and classes into my work. Unless I push back against my own prudence, my literary palate will pale.

Overcoming my anxiety, in late 2016 I permitted myself to create another black character in a short story called "Domestic Terrorism." Jocanda is the alluring girlfriend of a young white layabout. Her willingness to cross the racial divide for this waster helps push the reader to puzzle, "What on earth does she see in the guy?" Counter to cliché, Jocanda's background is upper middle class, so to the degree that she speaks as if she's from the 'hood—"He don't need to become nothing"—it's an affectation. I constrained the black English to light touches. Jocanda is lively, smart, savvy, and appealing.

Yet despite the positive portrayal, the cutting across class stereotype, and the restrained rendition of her speech, my agent warned me about the story's poor prospects at a magazine that had published me in the past. In the touchy climate following my speech in Brisbane that September, she said "We'll never know" whether it would be rejected because I had the gall to craft a black character. She invited me to revise the story using a white girlfriend. I held my ground. The story was indeed declined. Why? Maybe the editor just thought it was crummy. *We'll never know.*

I've plenty of recent experience of using nonwhite characters in my novels, only to have them singled out and scrutinized for thought crime. It's funny how consistently folks looking for affront tend to find it. (I envy a series like Charlie Brooker's *Black Mirror*, whose futuristic settings enable characters to merely *happen to be* nonwhite.) I have an obstreperous streak a mile wide. I hate being bullied, especially at the keyboard. If even writers like me are starting to wonder if including other ethnicities and races in our fiction is worth the potential blowback, then fiction is in trouble.

One crucial but now imperiled fictional device is that of imbuing characters with thoughts and emotions that the author may or may not share. When characters speak and think, the writer has plausible deniability. The contractual understanding with the reader—that the content of dialogue and internal reflection does not necessarily represent the author's own perspective—facilitates putting contradictory feelings and ideas in the same work, providing it balance and depth. Freedom from a reader's assumption that every character is necessarily a mouthpiece for the author's opinions allows for the exploration of characters who don't embrace progressive orthodoxies—who are bigots, opponents of gay marriage, advocates of more restrictive immigration, or (the ultimate stretch of the imagination) Tory supporters.

Yet the "it wasn't me, it was my imaginary friend" defense has been challenged ever since Bangladeshis successfully protested against the filming of Monica Ali's *Brick Lane* in their area not because of what her novel said, but because of what her *characters* said. At the 2016 Sewanee Writers' Conference in Tennessee, fellow authors accused Allen Wier of a "microaggression" because three old men in a baseball park ogled a young woman *in his short story*.

Is "hate speech" in dialogue prosecutable? Not long ago, I'd have said of course not. Now I'm not so sure. Minnesota has just withdrawn from its school syllabus two great American classics, both scathing examinations of southern racism—Mark Twain's *The Adventures of Huckleberry Finn* and Harper Lee's *To Kill a Mockingbird*—because the novels' bigoted dialogue might make students feel "humiliated and marginalized." Readers motivated to find fault often embrace deliberately unsophisticated interpretations of literary texts, for it's easy to make passages sound atrocious just by taking characters' assertions and word choice out of context. Indeed, searching for hidden offenses has become social media's updated version of the Easter egg hunt.

Impositions from the Left also extend to language. Any fiction writer who wants to strain the reader's patience with gender-neutral pronouns is welcome to them, but I dread the day that artificial contrivances like *ze* and *zir* become ideologically mandatory. Though preferring plural constructions, I resist female pronouns in the general instance. Using "she" in reference to both sexes is merely reverse discrimination, and these intrusions of authorial righteousness are distracting. I'm a throwback, so I'm not fussed about "mankind," "unmanned," or "man up!" (an exhortation to embrace resilience that we can heartily fling at women). Elaborate avoidance of words whose etymology has nothing to do with race, like "blackball" or "blacklist," serve no purpose beyond preening. The notion that "nitty-gritty" must be retired because it once referred to the detritus at the bottom of emptied slave ships is an activist invention; the noun came into use only in the 1930s. And don't get me started on atrocities like "chestfeeding."

Rather than scramble to keep up with all the new rules about what words a writer can and cannot use, we might better question who is-sues these rules, by what authority, and why on earth we're obliged to obey them.

THE PERILS OF PRIVILEGE

In the wake of #MeToo, hasty, due-process-free sackings in response to sexual-misconduct allegations and the consequent popular conflation of art and artist potentially makes the publishability of authors' work dependent on how we comport ourselves at parties. As with actors, directors, and painters, writers, too, can now be silenced—and have their previous work withdrawn from sale, if not have the fruits of entire careers effectively erased—by the exposure of some impropriety off the page.

Writing about #MeToo can itself trigger the reflex to gag. When *Harper's Magazine* was about to run an article by Katie Roiphe out-ing the anonymous creator of a widely circulated blacklist of men in the media accused of sexual misconduct, there was a concerted online campaign to stop the magazine from publishing, including jamming its switchboard and instructing other writers slated for the same issue to withdraw their work.

Writers are already stifled by expressing the wrong opinions outside their fiction. In 2014, Black Lawrence Press (BLP) dropped a novella from an anthology because the author, Elizabeth Ellen, had published on an unrelated website a controversial essay with which the BLP ed-itors disagreed. Do publishers now need to endorse everything you've ever written in order to print your work? In today's polarized political climate, it's perilous for writers to speak out about controversial sub-jects, lest they alienate a portion of their readership and be banished from progressive literary mags and presses. Professionally speaking, my voicing public support for Brexit was shooting myself in the foot.

We now have a whole new category of writer—and person, for that matter—who isn't permitted to say anything about anything. Sticking up for the rights of straight white males is less fashionable than sticking up for smokers. More broadly, enjoying any kind of "privilege" means you sacrifice your right to free speech. Sorry to go all American on you, but our Constitution's First Amendment protecting freedom of expression doesn't come with an asterisk: "*Unless you've hitherto had it too good." I've heard from multiple male colleagues that they'd like to champion free speech, but sitting at the very bottom of the victimhood totem pole they "can't say anything." To quote an ex-president whom I quite miss: "Yes, you can."

Not all repression, however, is coming from the Left. In the United States, libraries and school boards are so ban-happy that the American Library Association holds a "Banned Books Week" every September to highlight its annual "Top Ten Most Challenged Books." With a single exception—Bill Cosby's Little Bill series, which was singled out for the author's alleged sexual assaults—last year's most proscribed books were exclusively targeted for content that affronts prudish, Christian conservatives: gay or transgender characters, sexually explicit scenes that might lead to "sexual experimentation," drugs, atheism, cursing, and profanity. Chuck Palahniuk's Make Something Up: Stories You Can't Unread was censured not only for sexual licentiousness, but also for being "disgusting and all round offensive"—a badge of honor that makes me jealous.

VIRTUE BY IRON FIAT

What is the purpose of literature? To shape young people into God-fearing adults who say no to drugs? To accurately mirror reality? To act as a tool for social engineering? To make the world a better place? Certainly fiction is capable of influencing social attitudes, or trying to. But the novel is magnificently elastic. Fiction is under no obligation to reflect any particular reality, pursue social justice, or push a laudable political agenda. The purpose of any narrative form is up to the author. Yet contemporary university students are commonly encouraged to view literature exclusively through the prism of unequal power dynamics—to scrounge for evidence of racism, colonialism, imperialism, and sexism. What a pity. What a grim, joyless spirit in which to read.

How did we get so obsessed with *virtue*? A narrow version of virtue at that—one solely preoccupied with social hierarchy, when morality concerns far more than who's being shafted and who's on top. If all modern literature comes to toe the same goody-goody line, fiction is bound to grow timid, homogeneous, and dreary.

I don't want to read solely about nice people, and I don't turn to novels to be morally improved. I was drawn to writing fiction in the first place because on paper I completely control my world—where I can be mischievous, subversive, and perverse. Where I follow no one else's rules but my own. Where I can make my characters do and say abominations. I have never confused sitting down at my desk with attending Sunday school. And I frankly do not understand readers who go at novels making prissy judgments of the characters and author both and can't just sit down to a good story.

We live in denunciatory times. Cynical times, too; we assume decency will descend only through legislation or an iron-fisted cultural fiat. Raise the issue of free speech at any gathering, and first thing everyone piles on with all the ways in which this awful freedom must be constrained.

Perhaps because the cause of free speech has been—catastrophically, in my view—allowed to become the preserve of the Right, too many left-leaning writers (i.e., most writers) in the West have been discouragingly tepid in their defense of a liberty on which their art and livelihood depend. When PEN America gave *Charlie Hebdo* a freedom of expression award (under heavily armed guard) after Islamists murdered twelve of the magazine's staff for its irreverent content, more than two hundred huffy authors protested. For the dissidents, sticking up for Muslims' "right not to be offended" was more important than free speech.

Following the Brisbane foofaraw, the *Guardian Review* ran a two-page spread in which eleven authors addressed whether fiction writers should feel free to "appropriate" others' experience. The equivocation was astonishing. Even writers who tentatively defended imaginative "theft" did so only after hedging the point to death. A commonplace thread ran that it was all right to write about characters different from yourself, but only after exhaustive homework, and only if you were really good at it, which they were, of course, but most people weren't. The writers willing to defend their liberty without a snowstorm of qualification numbered exactly one. Good on you, Philip Hensher.

The presses with their sensitivity readers. *Kirkus* with its "own voices" reviewers. The academy, now content to assess the canon in the reductive terms of "intersectionality." The whole apparatus of delivering literature to its audience is signaling an intention to subject fiction to rigid ideological purity tests, unrelated to artistry, excellence, and even entertainment, that miss the point of what our books are for. Let's see a little more courage, people—in the work and in the world.

"Cruel and Unusual Punishment"

HARPER'S MAGAZINE, 2019

I have a new fear. And this one's a doozy.

I write a fortnightly column for the British barely right-of-center magazine (that's left of center, in the United States) *The Spectator*. Having weathered more than one social-media shitstorm, I'm one column away from the round of mob opprobrium that sinks my career for good. As Roseanne Barr and Megyn Kelly can testify, it doesn't take a thousand words, either. A single unacceptable sentiment, a word usage misconstrued, or a sentence taken out of context suffices these days to implode a reputation decades in the making and to trigger McCarthyite blacklisting. When I've floated this anxiety past the odd friend or colleague, the universal response has been a sorrowful shake of the head. Repeatedly I hear, "You're exactly the sort of person this happens to."

But that isn't the fear in its entirety. Suppose a perceived violation of progressive orthodoxy translates into the kind of institutional cowardice on display in the forced resignation of Ian Buruma from the *New York Review of Books*. Amazon, Barnes & Noble, Waterstones in the

United Kingdom, my literary agent, my publishers in translation, and HarperCollins worldwide could all decide they can no longer afford association with a pariah. My current manuscript wouldn't see print, nor would any future projects I'm foolish enough to bother to bash out. Journalistic opportunities would dry up. Yet what I most dread about this bleak scenario is my thirteen published titles suddenly becoming unavailable—both online (gosh, would piracy sites be morally fastidious, too?) and in shops.

Because that's the direction we're traveling in. For reasons that escape me, artists' misbehavior now contaminates the fruits of their labors, like the sins of the father being visited upon the sons. So it's not enough to punish transgressors merely by cutting off the source of their livelihoods, turning them into social outcasts, and truncating their professional futures. You have to destroy their pasts. Having discovered the worst about your fallen idols, you're duty bound to demolish the best about them, too.

After Roseanne Barr's notorious tweet last May slagging off the former Obama adviser Valerie Jarrett in racial terms (Barr claims, charmingly, that she "thought the bitch was white"), ABC canceled her new revival sitcom, *Roseanne*. Viacom pulled reruns of the revival across all its channels, as well as reruns of her original series. Roseanne the person may continue to mouth off, but, however iconic, *Roseanne* the series has been disappeared from television listings (though it is still available online). Last fall's eleven-episode spin-off, *The Conners*, used the same cast minus a certain someone, burying the character six feet under with an opioid overdose. Now that's what I call overkill.

After being exposed, if you will, for masturbating before multiple underwhelmed women, the comedian Louis CK had his film *I Love You, Daddy* withdrawn a week before its American release and subsequently shelved. HBO dropped his series *Lucky Louie* and several stand-up specials from its on-demand platform. Once Bill Cosby was convicted of sexual assault, he was sentenced not only to three to ten years but also to cultural near-oblivion. Amazon has held out, and

DVDs are kicking around stores, but otherwise no trace remains of
The Cosby Show on any other channel or platform. Although Garrison
Keillor initially claimed that he merely touched a woman's bare back
to console her, and later confessed to a "mutual email flirtation with a
freelance writer," Minnesota Public Radio booted its elderly stalwart
out the door, ended distribution and broadcasts of *The Writer's Al-
manac* and rebroadcasts of *A Prairie Home Companion*, and blocked
public access to Keillor's radio archive. When the author Junot Díaz
was accused of sexual impropriety last spring—of which investigations
by MIT and the Pulitzer Prize board have since exonerated him—
bookstores began removing his books from their shelves. Indicted by
multiple women for salacious behavior in his studio, the photo-realist
painter Chuck Close had a major solo retrospective "indefinitely
postponed"—a synonym for "canceled"—at the National Gallery in
DC, which also "postponed" a Thomas Roma photography show after similar accusations were made against him. It's this bad: in last
summer's *New York Times* article "Food Writing in the #MeToo Era,"
Kim Severson asked, with no apparent drollery, "Should home cooks
throw out the cookbooks from chefs exposed for regularly grabbing
and propositioning women?"

Back in the day when your mother spotting your name in the
newspaper was mortifying, sheer social embarrassment was punishment enough. But in the rush to judgment of the modern shaming
mill, disgrace is no longer sufficient. In numerous instances during
the #MeToo scandals, accusation has stood in for due process, and
criminal offenses like rape (Cosby and Weinstein) and unwelcome
advances (Keillor) have been thrown indiscriminately into the same
basket. Thus the career consequences of violating the law and violating
subjective norms of "appropriateness" have too often been identical.
Culprits are sentenced to cultural erasure.

In some instances, that erasure has been unnervingly literal. Having learned that Steven Wilder Striegel is a sex offender, Twentieth
Century Fox completely eliminated a scene from *The Predator* in which

the actor appeared. Since some might regard "the predator" as his handle, Kevin Spacey was removed from Ridley Scott's completed *All the Money in the World*, at considerable expense. Disney deleted Louis CK's voice from the animated TV show *Gravity Falls* and redubbed the part. In late 2017, when the actor Ed Westwick was accused—but not convicted—of sexual assault, the BBC took out all the scenes in which he'd performed in an Agatha Christie adaptation (titled, ironically, *Ordeal by Innocence*) and reshot them with a replacement actor—a great show of purism on the public's dime, in the service of a dreary miniseries I couldn't bring myself to finish watching.

Most judicial systems distinguish between high crimes and misdemeanors. Trials in the court of public opinion appear to do no such thing. It's not fashionable to defend Roseanne Barr, but I've studied that tweet of hers, which was clumsy, insensitive, and self-destructively idiotic (at this point, who doesn't realize that putting the word "ape" anywhere near an African American is social suicide?). Still, I can't help but wonder if the price Barr paid for that careless one-liner (supposedly a joke, but not a funny one, and it's the unfunny jokes that will do you in) wasn't a bit high. She lost her show, relinquished her rights to the franchise, and is now, as far as I can tell, roundly unemployable. On top of all that, ABC and Viacom have attempted to quarantine the better part of her life's work—as if the purported racism of its leading actor were radioactive.

WHAT ARTISTS OF EVERY STRIPE CARE ABOUT MOST IS WHAT THEY HAVE made. The contemporary impulse to rebuke disgraced creators by vanishing their work from the cultural marketplace exhibits a meanspiritedness, a vengefulness even, as well as an illogic. Why, if you catch someone doing something bad, would you necessarily rub out what they've done that's good? If you're convicted of breaking and entering, the judge won't send bailiffs around to tear down the tree house you built for your daughter and to pour bleach on your home-made pie.

For artists, the erasure of their work may be a harsher penalty than incarceration or fines. Eliminating whole series from streaming platforms, withdrawing novels from bookstores, and canceling major gallery retrospectives constitute, for those in the creative professions, cruel and unusual punishment.

Though I've never been especially interested in making connections between the biographical details of artists' lives and what they make, I accept that art and artist are not unrelated. But with Roseanne Barr having been officially christened a racist, it seems to me that to pull her original series you would still have to separately prove that *Roseanne* the program was racist. To remove any of Louis CK's series from streaming platforms, you should have to demonstrate that *Louie* the program is abusive of women. Instead, the content of these banished products is clearly immaterial. The films, series, books, and paintings are tainted by association.

This erasure impulse hails primarily from terror: that the roving black cloud of calumny will move on to any individual or institution complicit in distributing a vilified artist's work. If you join in denouncing whoever's persona non grata this week, presumably they won't come for you. Severing ties even to an artist's output also provides cultural middlemen a precious opportunity for public moral posturing, to the benefit of the brand. Erasure is also a form of rewriting history—a popular impulse of late. In this touched-up version of events, we were never taken in by these disgusting specimens. In the historical rewrite, there was always something fishy about Bill Cosby; he was never America's dad.

Only a restricted range of misbehaviors qualifies one for being disappeared: any perceived intolerance of minorities and any delinquency to do with sex. Other misdeeds are less likely to be career ending: fraud, tax evasion, or drug possession, say. Winona Ryder recovered from being caught shoplifting. Domestic violence will get you into trouble, but other outbursts of violence are survivable. Yet there's no sensible reason that only bigotry and sexual misconduct should doom artists to cultural purdah. The question is whether we condition our consumption of what artists produce on their moral purity.

Do we really require the people who make our movies, fiction, and artworks to be above reproach in their personal lives? If so, how are they to understand their own material—in the main, the lewd, scheming, cheating, thieving, covetous, malign, murderous, hateful, and rapacious human race? I worry that requiring artists to be perfect means either no art or bad art.

We seem to have established a protocol of imposing total social and professional exile for having said something deemed distasteful or for small lapses of judgment wildly shy of illegality. Even during the post-trial communal shunning of O. J. Simpson—when what was at issue was double murder—there was no campaign to take reruns of *Roots*, *The Naked Gun*, and *The Towering Inferno* off the airways. Nowadays, those who violate progressive pieties risk ejection from the tribe and the wholesale effacement of their handiwork. Mirroring the Scientology custom whereby anyone who bad-mouths the church is ostracized as a nonperson, the practice smacks of a cult.

And is one's exile for life? It's still up for grabs which targets of juggernauts like #MeToo will ever be considered to have paid their dues and be allowed to rejoin the faithful. Last September's ouster of Ian Buruma suggests not. Weak-but-still-interesting essays by perpetrators of sexual misconduct in the *New York Review of Books* and *Harper's Magazine* triggered social-media outrage. The *NYRB*'s publisher capitulated by forcing his editor's resignation.

On the other hand, Minnesota Public Radio restored access to the archives of Keillor's shows after only six months of punitive unavailability. Performing at multiple comedy clubs less than a year after his #MeToo downfall, Louis CK has tested the waters on how long one of these exclusion orders may last. Though he has sometimes received standing ovations at these appearances, a few patrons have walked out, and the gall of resuming stand-up so soon kicked off a range of huffy op-eds. Nevertheless, his audiences' broad openness to a comeback suggests that, at least for the more beguiling artists, the careers of the fallen aren't necessarily scotched forever. But I'm even more concerned about the blacklisted work: Is the unavailability permanent? Or, having sat mutely on its metaphorical dunce chair at the back of the class, can *The Cosby Show* ever be rerun on network television once its serial-rapist star has also served his time?

If the price exacted for short-of-criminal offenses has sometimes seemed disproportionate (Garrison Keillor's sacking was dubious; Al Franken should never have had to resign his Senate seat), most art involves multiple creators, many of whom may be blameless. Even books require a host of ancillary staff to publish. Shelving TV shows and films penalizes all the other actors, directors, writers, crew, and cameramen. Their work is also erased. Remedying this injustice (and capitalizing on a successful series), Amazon is going ahead with a fifth season of *Transparent* absent the wandering hands of Jeffrey Tambor. Good luck with that. Tambor played the only faintly bearable character in the drama, and without him the show abandons its premise.

WHICH BRINGS US TO THE PARTY WHO REALLY PAYS FOR THE NEW PURITANISM: the arts consumer.

Assume you actually buy into Dylan Farrow's fishy recollections of having been sexually assaulted by her father at seven, despite those allegations having been exhaustively investigated. Assume as well that you endorse the notion that exposure to the work of the less than pure of heart gives you cooties. Then you're well within your rights to refuse to watch Woody Allen movies. You may withhold your tiny financial contribution to the director's livelihood, just as we're all free to decide not to buy Israeli goods to protest settlements in the West Bank (just see how much difference it makes). Product boycotts for political, so-cial, or environmental reasons have a long history.

But in the instances we're examining here, the distributor decides for us. As if we need to be protected. (Or the distributor needs to pro-tect itself—from association with sin. Clearly the real motivation here is to appear immaculate.) In truth, we're being punished, too, along with the alleged perpetrators. We've been robbed of a halfway watch-able season of *Transparent* that includes Jeffrey Tambor. I wanted to see the new Louis CK movie. But presumptuously, patronizingly, I'm not *allowed*. Who's really deprived when we can't access *A Prairie Home Companion*? What does that accomplish? In ditching the revival of *Roseanne*, we've lost the one program that exhibited the kind of di-versity of which this country is starved: it sponsored a real live Trump supporter. And after much soul-searching, I can't see who benefits if I throw away Mario Batali's recipe for lemon tart.

I'm faintly open to the idea that Kevin Spacey may present a work-place safety issue, but he's still not been convicted of sexual assault. Please, couldn't he have been allowed on set under guard? Because the party that's really been roundly punished for his purported trans-gressions is the audience for *House of Cards*. I had the disagreeable experience of watching the first few episodes of season 6 on a long flight recently. Since Spacey's character of Frank Underwood has been erased, the show is even more dreadful than I feared. Now, I've long been of the view that the American version lost its mojo as soon as Frank-cum-Iago stopped scheming behind the scenes and actually be-came president. Yet thereafter Spacey could still carry the show with his over-the-top camp. Whether from weak acting, the gaping hole in the cast, or her constrictingly icy character—whose further develop-ment comes down to watching her go for another bleeding run—Robin Wright can't carry it. I want my protagonist back. I feel personally pe-nalized for Kevin Spacey's peripatetic prick.

I'm one of those throwbacks perfectly content to watch *Rose-mary's Baby* for a fourth time, even if Roman Polanski has admitted to statutory rape. It's a good film. That's what I care about. I'm a cultural materialist. I want the stuff, and in truth I wouldn't be all that bothered if the director were an ax murderer. I can see differing with me on this point, but I want us all to be able to act according to our own rubrics.

More broadly, I can't be the only one to find this contemporary convention of levying total banishment for often relatively small, non-criminal offenses against progressive mores a little creepy. I wish I would read more often about some actor vilified for making an unwelcome pass on set, and the agent, for example, says, "Know what? I'm sticking by my client. We'll weather the storm." Instead, I read repeatedly that "all ties have been severed," all doors slammed in the scoundrel's face. Herd behavior is by nature mindless. Parties to modern excommunication never seem to make measured decisions on the merits for themselves and in consideration of the depth of the relationship, but race blindly to join the stampede. Ian Buruma and the *NYRB*'s publisher, Rea Hederman, had been friends for thirty years. That didn't count for beans.

"Lefty Lingo"

The only letter I've ever sent to *The New York Times* was in the 1980s, objecting to the paper's suddenly pestilent use of "draconian." During Iran-Contra the complaint must have seemed trivial; the letter never saw print. Yet that seminal annoyance in my twenties marked an awakening to word-as-contagion.

Every era has its fashionable argot. Take the turn of this century, when we were eternally "on the same page" and getting "wake-up calls" while confessing "My bad!" or pronouncing ourselves "good to go." Meanwhile, the British were christening everything in sight "brilliant" and prefacing their every sentence with "to be honest." Alas, the Brits' grating compulsion to denounce initiatives and bodies as "not fit for purpose" has yet to burn out. Maybe it's time to write another letter.

Propelled by digital technology that spreads rhetorical fads like herpes, this decade's lengthy left-wing lexicon has impressively penetrated both mainstream media and everyday speech, while carrying ideological baggage so overstuffed that it wouldn't fit in an airplane's

overhead compartment. The idiom is persistently negative. Many of
the cringe-inducers I grew up with in the 1960s conveyed enthusiasm: "Way to be!" "Outta sight!" "Far out!" and "Dig that!" Subsequent
generations have also latched on to effusive expressions, such as "Awesome!" and "That's sick!" But the glossary particular to today's Left is
joylessly accusatory: "fat-shaming," "victim blaming," or "rape culture"
(which indicts not only men but pretty much everything). As we said
in 1970, what a drag.

Front and center in overused progressive vocabulary is, of course,
"privilege." From Lyndon Johnson onward, we've expressed concern for
the "underprivileged." Shining a spotlight instead on the "privileged"
fosters resentment in people who feel shafted and an impotent guilt in
people at whom the label is hurled. The word functions something like
a rotten tomato without the mess. I myself have been decried in the
Independent as "dripping with privilege," while the writer Ariel Levy
was portrayed in *The New Republic* as "swaddled in privilege." This is
a shape-shifting substance in which one can bathe or nestle.

Whereas *a* privilege can be acquired through merit—for example,
students with good grades got to go bowling with our teacher in sixth
grade—privilege, sans the article, is implicitly unearned and undeserved. The designation neatly dispossesses those so stigmatized of any
credit for their achievements, while discounting as immaterial those
hurdles an individual with a perceived leg up may still have had to
overcome (an alcoholic parent, a stutter, even poverty). For privilege is
a static state into which you are born, stained by original sin. Just as
you can't earn yourself into privilege, you can't earn yourself out of it,
either.

Even taken on its face, the concept is elusive. "Privilege is an unbelievably hard thing to define," the British journalist Douglas Murray
observes in *The Madness of Crowds*:

> It is also very nearly impossible to quantify. . . . Is a person with inherited
> wealth but who has a natural disability more privileged or less privileged

than a person without any inherited wealth who is able-bodied? Who can work this out?

Not I, although I confess I'm undermotivated.

Yet in practice, while "privileged" may also mean "straight and male," it almost always means "white." In *The Tyranny of Virtue*, the academic Robert Boyers observes that these days the label is deployed in a way that "makes it acceptable to target groups or persons not because of what they have done but because of what they are." That sounds awfully like a workable definition of racism. Thus it's intriguing that the P-bomb is most frequently dropped by folks of European heritage, either to convey a posturing humility ("I acknowledge my privilege") or to demonize the Bad White People, the better to distinguish themselves as the Good White People.

Boyers himself has been shut down in his classroom at Skidmore College by a student accusation that he exercised "privilege," which he describes as "a noise word intended to distract all of us from the substance of our discussion." Its invocation is meant to punish its object "by making him into a representative of something he could not possibly defend himself against." He writes, "Nothing is easier than to wield the charge of privilege and thereby to win instant approval." In other words, it's a cheap shot.

Sometimes the cheap shot backfires. A September *Guardian* editorial scorned David Cameron's experience of having his disabled six-year-old son die in his arms as "privileged pain." The attempt to deny the former British prime minister the integrity of his suffering went down so poorly even with the paper's loyal readership that the editors were forced to admit the editorial "fell far short of our standards" and to provide an amendment. Yet for the sneering dismissal ever to have seen the light of day speaks volumes. The privileged are denied even the right to anguish.

Meanwhile, it isn't clear what an admission of privilege calls you to do, aside from cower. That tired injunction "Check your privilege" translates simply to "STFU"—and it's telling of our era that "shut the fuck up" is now a sufficiently commonplace imperative to have lodged in text-speak.

BECAUSE THE LEFT'S COLLECTIVE VOCABULARY FUNCTIONS AS A T-SHIRT, the better for the like-minded to recognize one another like campers on a field trip, members of this in-group have naturally adopted a hip descriptor for themselves. In *The Problem with Everything*, Meghan Daum identifies "woke" as borrowed from the civil rights movement, when the term "signaled one's allegiance to a more general ethos of progressive righteousness." Sadly, the resurrected buzzword has already backfired, having rapidly proved an inadvertent gift to conservative commentators, who'd wearied of their shopworn swipes at "social justice warriors."

In more and more commentary, the term "woke" and attendant mischievous improvisations are delivered with a smirk. The monosyllabic tag has turned out to be wonderfully adaptable for the purposes of derision. Snide variations abound: "the wokery" (mine), the "wokerati" (Lisa Simeone), "the woke-ing class" (Julie Bindel), or Daum's shorthand for "NPR-listening, *New Yorker*–reading, *Slate* podcast–downloading elites": the "wokescenti."

The wokescenti's biggest terminological success is surely "people of color," whose nearly universal installation in public discourse shouldn't reprieve the term from scrutiny. (After all, what does that make everyone else, "people of whiteness"?) While this curiously archaic construction is commendably inclusive, erstwhile "minorities" also encompassed a range of skin tones. Savor the historical irony that the expression "people of color" referred to black Americans in post–Civil War Jim Crow legislation. And there's no avoiding the absurdity that "colored people," which the more modish phrase strains to avoid, is a dated 1950s term that came to be construed as disrespectful.

"Linguistically," Murray notes, the distinction is "without a meaningful difference." Yet when poor Benedict Cumberbatch appeared on *Tavis Smiley* in 2015 and carelessly alluded to "colored actors," all hell broke loose: outcry, public apology ("I make no excuse for my being an idiot and know the damage is done"), the works. "Throughout this episode," Murray reminds us, "nobody seriously claimed that Cumberbatch was a racist." He had merely committed, Murray observes, a "crime of language."

The same demented theatrical deference has abruptly made the noun "slave" almost unprintable. Therefore in a long *New York Times* article in September about Virginia Theological Seminary's historical complicity in slavery, we find reference to "enslaved people," "slave labor," "the enslaved," victims of "involuntary servitude," "people who were sold," people who were "once owned," "enslaved laborers," "enslaved men and women," and previous faculty who had "owned black people"—but, scrupulously, never one use, outside of direct quotations, of "slave" as a noun.

These circumlocutions are meant to emphasize the fact that Africans traded like chattel were not, in their essence, slaves but human beings. With similar deference to a referent's humanity, "the obese" has given way to the prolix "people living with obesity," as if all that excess weight is merely renting a spare bedroom down the hall. Yet the logic of this prohibition taints any noun that refers to a person. If I'm a "Londoner" or a "libertarian," is that all I am? Aren't these words, by identifying me via a mere location or creed, reductive? Given that butchers and bakers and candlestick makers cannot, in their essence, be distilled to their professions, perhaps we should say instead "butchering people" and "baking people" and "people of candlestick making."

Another popular substitute for the neutrally proportionate word "minorities," "marginalized communities" conveniently assumes the conclusion: that all minorities are exiled to the social edges. Cultural "appropriation" likewise assumes the conclusion that cultural cross-fertilization equates with theft. To force an antagonist of the concept to employ the term is therefore to win while skipping the argument. Underhanded, but effective.

The premier example of this linguistic skullduggery—that is, winning an argument without the bother of actually conducting one—is the Left's increasingly successful imposition of the disagreeable-sounding term "cisgender." The logic of the 1990s contrivance—*cis* being Latin for "on this side of," as opposed to *trans*, meaning "on the other side of"—feels forced and inorganic. More crucially, to employ the adjective is to endorse the view that sex is "assigned" at birth rather than recognized as a biological fact. The word no sooner raises thorny debates regarding sex and gender than shuts them down.

Denoting, say, a woman born a woman who thinks she's a woman, this freighted neologism deliberately peculiarizes being born a sex and placidly accepting your fate, and even suggests that there's something a bit passive and conformist about complying with the arbitrary caprices of your mother's doctor. Moreover, unless a discussion specifically regards transgenderism, in which case we may need to distinguish the rest of the population ("nontrans" would do nicely), we don't really need this word, except as a banner for how gendercool we are. It's no more necessary than words for "a dog that is not a cat," "a lamppost that is not a fire hydrant," or "a table that is actually a table." Presumably, in order to mark entities that are what they appear to be, we could append "cis-" to anything and everything. "Cisblue" would mean blue and not yellow. "Cisboring" would mean genuinely dull, and not secretly entertaining after all.

"Microaggression" is a perverse concoction, implying that the offense in question is so minuscule as to be invisible to the naked eye, yet also that it's terribly important. The word cultivates hypersensitivity. The ubiquitous "transphobic," "Islamophobic," and "homophobic" are also eccentric, in that the reprobates so branded are not really being accused of fearfulness but hatred. (Sorry—*hate*. "Hatred" has gone the way of the floppy disk.) "Lived experience" is interchangeable with "experience," save that the redundant double-barrel is pompous. The alphabet soup of "LGBTQ" continues to add letters: LGBTQIAGNC, LGBTQQIP2SAA, or even LGBTIQCAPGNGFNBA. A three-year-old bashing the keyboard would produce a more functional shorthand.

Rare instances of left-wing understatement, "problematic" and "troubling" are coyly nonspecific red flags for political transgression that obviate spelling out exactly what sin has been committed (thereby eliding the argument). Similarly, the all-purpose adjectival workhorse "inappropriate" presumes a shared set of social norms that in the throes of the culture wars we conspicuously lack. This euphemistic tsk-tsk projects the prim censure of a mother alarmed that her daughter's low-cut blouse is too revealing for church. "Inappropriate" is laced with disgust, while once again skipping the argument. By conceit, the appalling nature of the misbehavior at issue is glaringly obvious to everyone, so what's wrong with it goes without saying.

EVERY LINGUISTIC SUBSET CONSTITUTES A CODE. BUT THIS VERNACULAR isn't as innocently contagious as "groovy." In left-wing circles, neglecting to ape what has been tacitly declared as What We Say Now marks you as suspect. Conversely, weaving the ordained jargon into conversation signals ingratiatingly to your political clan, "I'm one of you." (Hence when mainstream media outlets embrace these terms, they brand themselves as partisan.) In today's political climate, deployment of progressives' conformist vocabulary is also defensive. It broadcasts benevolence and an elaborate, gesturing respect for others meant to keep the wolves from the door.

The whole lexicon is of a piece. Its usage advertises that one has bought into a set menu of opinions—about race, gender, climate change, abortion, tax policy, #MeToo, Trump, Brexit, Brett Kavanaugh, probably Israel, and a great deal else. Reflexive resort to this argot therefore implies not that you think the same way as others of your political disposition but that you don't think. You have ordered the prix fixe; you're not in the kitchen cooking dinner for yourself. "The seductions of this shorthand," writes Daum, are that there is "no need to sort out facts or wrestle with contradictions when just using certain buzzwords" grants "automatic entry into a group of ostensibly like-minded peers." This vocabulary is lazy.

Assumption of the Left's prescriptive patois may indicate solidarity with fellow travelers, but it also betokens the insularity and closed-mindedness of any indiscriminate embrace of fundamentalist dogma. It instantly alienates people who don't sign up for the same set menu of views—which may sometimes be the intention. Referencing the "cis-heteronormative patriarchy" in discussions with strangers suggests either that you presume these people already agree with you on virtually everything, or that you're interested in talking to them only if they do. Even when speaking to moderates, much less conservatives (who have their own coded lingo, such as "snowflakes," "virtue signaling," and "grievance culture"), you have shut down conversation.

Standardized lefty catchphrases are now routinely employed to test allegiance and to exclude people who fail the test. Boyers notes that cherished left-wing concepts like identity and inequality are now used "to label and separate the saved and the damned, the 'woke' and the benighted, the victim and the oppressor," thereby "yielding not significant redress but a new wave of puritanism and a culture of suspicion." This moral division of wheat from chaff sows confusion about the difference between "sponsoring injustice and simply living more or less modestly in an imperfect world."

Like all new slang, the current crop has the attraction of seeming ultracontemporary. But as quickly as these ideologically loaded expressions proliferate, they also become hackneyed—a problem beyond politics. When students at Cardiff University petitioned in a buzzword-strewn diatribe to disinvite the feminist Germaine Greer, who does not see trans women as women, because "hosting a speaker with such problematic and hateful views towards marginalized and vulnerable groups is dangerous," they displayed not only that they could not think for themselves, but that they could not write.

CONFESSIONS

OF AN EXPAT

PART III

"Bye-Bye Belfast"

1997

[Let an essay age long enough, and it can mature from dated to historical. The lessons of this small, personal tale—if not small at the time for me— also pertain to the fierce us-and-them polarization of the present. While you might maintain a semblance of neutrality by being phlegmatically apathetic, you can't engage with national politics riven by the likes of Trump or Brexit without taking sides. There is no safe harbor. Worse, larger social divisions running hot are likely to incur collateral damage of the most intimate sort. In the last several years, many a Christmas dinner on both sides of the Atlantic has been ruined by hoarse-voiced disputes, and rarely over the consistency of the cranberry sauce. Furthermore, at ground level the personal and political inseparably intertwine. Did a friend-turned-antagonist disavow you because of a disagreement over current events, or did he or she never really like you to begin with?

I might note that Sinn Féin, the political wing of the IRA, and more broadly Northern Irish nationalists—who all seemed back in the day to treasure their grievances far more than their aspirations to a united Ireland—basically invented identity politics. The obsession with language, the supersensitivity, the preening sanctimony, the attachment to victimhood: Northern nationalists got there way before American college students. Immediate recognition of that whole huffy gestalt may help explain the extremity of my aversion to the illiberal faction in the culture wars.

This essay was originally commissioned by Granta and then rejected. The temptation being irresistible, I'm taking this opportunity to right what I like to think was a tiny injustice.]

I moved to Belfast in 1987 to set a novel, a mission I learned on arrival was clichéd. A better question than why I came is why I stayed. Ten years later, I remain.

My routine answer to taxi drivers runs that Belfast is, ironically, a quiet town, a good place to write, both friendly and cheap. This is rubbish. In truth, I'm hooked on the Troubles soap opera and its pleasant confusion of politics and gossip. I cherish Belfast's dark cachet. I enjoy violence sufficiently nearby to be titillating, yet rare enough to put me at little personal risk—rather like having your violence and not having it eat you, too. I relish the opportunity—amply available on both sides—to act self-righteous.

Yet what I like about Northern Ireland has become what I dislike. That is, I dislike myself for liking it. I may have acquired a perverse taste for Ulster infighting, but you can acquire a taste for plenty of things that are not very good for you. So the best question is why, after a decade in Northern Ireland, this American woman needs to leave.

I first met the young man I will call Cory in Lavery's, a gungy cross-sectarian pub near Queen's University that has singularly resisted a makeover of retro-chic milk churns or Mickey Mantle Americana. Lavery's is an unabashed shithole.

In those days I still went to pubs, though after enough conversations like the one Cory rescued me from—about some punter's exciting holiday at Disney World—I would forswear them. For a visiting American, the only alternative to this standard ach-I've-a-cousin-in-Fort-Lee fare was an earnest explanation of what the Troubles are *really* about. In time I'd prefer Disney World, but that evening I was frantic; I'd not come all the way from New York to talk about the Seven Dwarfs Mine Train, and I was grateful for Cory's reprieve.

This was early 1988, what would prove a fun-packed year in the Northern Irish calendar. Still to come: the Gibraltar and Michael Stone shootings, the Andytown lynching, the summer's Ballygawley bus bomb. I'm sometimes nostalgic for 1988. 1997's sporadic check-point booby traps, stalled political talks at Stormont Castle, and shakily restored IRA cease-fire cannot compare. The Troubles are a spectator sport. During off-seasons, syncopated only by yammer about "parity of esteem" and "cross-border bodies with executive powers," voyeurs feel cheated; locals grow torpid.

Cory was refreshingly candid. To assertions like the above he would mischievously accede. Then in his midthirties, Cory was short, bearded, and impish, with a wicked grin and gorsey eyebrows that invited the cringe-making allusion to a leprechaun. He dressed shabbily, which I have always found winning, though by this standard most of Northern Ireland's men are very winning indeed. A modest paunch gave his figure an unpretentious solidity, though he had slim, vegetarian wrists and bookish wire-rims. A diffident manner belied an immediate intent to pick me up, though his gaze had a spark. Sadly, I have since watched those eyes hood and harden. When we met he glittered through them, and these days Cory simply peers out suspiciously from behind his walled pupils like everyone else.

My first novel had just been released in the United Kingdom. Cory recognized my name, and informed me, with a note of reluctance, of my first British review in that weekend's *Observer*. He asked me round for coffee to obtain a copy at his flat.

That novel had been decently received in America, so when Cory pulled out the crumpled newspaper in his tumbledown bedsit I wasn't prepared. Now six books on I've toughened up, but my more honest instinct when confronted with a pan as a neophyte was to cry.

Poor Cory must have been embarrassed, but he handled the situation with grace and invited me to collapse on his shoulder. He didn't take advantage of my blubbering to cozy me onto his bed, but made me that cup of coffee. Whatever else has happened since, I will always remember his kindness that evening. Given my endurance in Belfast, that night was properly the beginning of a lifelong friendship. As matters turned out, the friendship was simply long.

In Northern Irish terms, I have thus far failed to describe Cory at all. Never mind the eyes. All right: Cory is Catholic. A then-fledgling freelance journalist, he was born in working-class Andersonstown, a republican stronghold. But to Cory, IRA volunteers weren't courageous freedom fighters sacrificing their young lives that their people might throw off the yoke of British oppression, but dull-witted, fascistic thugs who tyrannized their own "community"—a word Cory framed, astutely, with quotation marks.

As for the Border, which in the North draws character more starkly than boundaries, Cory was an infidel. Regarding the God of Catholicism he was merely agnostic; regarding West Belfast's earthly deity—Gerry Adams—he was defiantly atheistic. The counterpart of the Green Prod (decoratively guilty, ostentatiously liberal, self-consciously "Irish"), Cory was an Orange Taig. Alternatively, devout nationalists would denounce him as the corollary of an Uncle Tom: a "Castle Catholic," in reference to the former seat of Protestant power, Stormont Castle. But Cory wouldn't see himself as a suck-up to the unionist establishment, or what was left of it by 1988, of which he was also critical. Instead, he argued for the pragmatic economic advantages of British citizenship. Though he tepidly accepted the "consent principle" that Irish unification should come about only with the assent of the Northern majority, his politics were driven not by such democratic niceties but by gut antagonism. He detested the IRA.

In Northern Irish terms, I've also failed to describe myself. I won't be coy. I'm one of the only American unionists on the island of Ireland. Without a drop of Gaelic blood in my veins as far as I know, I arrived in Belfast at the age of thirty with no local political predisposition whatsoever. Sheer pig-ignorance as well as an absence of ancestral sentimentality may have protected me from the republican propaganda to which many Irish Americans are notoriously susceptible. Yet from the outset I distrusted republicans' wolfish right-wing behavior dressed up in lacy left-wing rhetoric, the way you might instinctively look twice at a grandma with big teeth.

Distrust blossomed into hostility. Like my new friend Cory's, my thinking was soon fueled by loathing. To this day, IRA apologists can still color my cheeks an apoplectic purple and constrict my throat until my diatribes grow unattractively nasal. Another writer charged recently that, in my vitriolic bias, I've become "part of the problem." I've lost my objectivity and thereby my understanding. I concur, to a point. But if you are not part of the problem—if you do not appreciate the depth of antipathy that Northern factions feel toward one another, which you can truly plumb only by feeling it yourself—you cannot possibly understand Northern Ireland. Should it be true that an outsider can contribute solely through nonpartisanship, then I have traded my utility for grasp.

Politically, of course, loathing backfires. One man's poison is another man's meat. Self-styled as beyond the pale, Provisional IRA republicans eat Protestant firebrand Ian Paisley's condemnatory adjectives for breakfast: "depraved," "satanic," "fiendish," "unspeakable" . . . It would be cannier to ignore than to denounce these attention-seekers, but this judicious policy is almost impossible to follow, if only because vilifying the Provisionals is so much fun. Vampirically, Provos gorge on revulsion, but unionists and even constitutional nationalists also need to feel revolted, as some people have to jump-start the morning with caffeine.

There ensued my Northern Irish heyday. I evolved a jocular social circle, in which Cory was pivotal. In retrospect, our crew was cliquish and off-puttingly insular—like cliques everywhere. Even transient members of our tongue-in-cheek salon were also novelists, journalists, or academics: passive observers who hoped that sufficiently vociferous observation would reprieve us from our passivity (it didn't). We were often smug and glib, but at least in the early years we had a good time. A benevolent glow augmented the niggardly gas fire when the usual suspects assembled in my offbeat living room, its cream upholstery grayed from resting *Belfast Telegraph*s against the arms of the chairs. None of us had much money, and we ate a lot of pasta and popcorn. We made up for the quality of our Bulgarian wine with quantity.

Our idea of fun in those days was to career up the Antrim coast to the Young Unionists Conference, where we'd shake our heads at the great unhip and their heartbreaking answer to the leather-clad republican wiseguy look: geeky gray suits, polka-dot ties, spotty complexions, brutally short hair. We'd secure admission to conferences of the Social Democratic and Labour Party (SDLP) the way London coteries might book seats at the West End. We'd insinuate ourselves, fox-in-the-henhouse, into republican events at the Felons Club and ask Gerry Adams embarrassing questions, or we'd gather intelligence at the Sinn Féin Ard Fheis and pointedly refuse to join the crowd's refrain of "Up the Ra!" Whether or not the Troubles function as entertainment for the larger Northern population, they were certainly entertainment for us, and after these forays we would regularly repair to my sprawling, drafty flat to be droll.

I inhabit the attic of a ramshackle Victorian manor that looms at the end of a potholed cul-de-sac. Slanted ceilings shaft every side of my top floor, cutting the rooms where we gathered into odd shapes whose lopsided skew seemed apt. By tacit conceit, none of us fit in the neat square boxes that Northern Ireland fashioned for its "two communities." I was that unheard-of creature, an American unionist; Patrick, just as incongruously, was unionist and gay; Cory and his BBC sidekick Francis were both Orange Taigs; Virginia was a liberal Prod who'd crossed the holy Border to attend university in Dublin and, though quietly unionist, rose above by finding it all so depressing that she was constantly threatening to move to France. (A local pastime: self-indulgent despair, masturbatory disgust, and impotent threats that after this last pointless murder you're *really* going to quit this Brigadoon once and for all . . . These resolutions sickly o'er like a smoker's vows that he is definitely going to quit—next week.)

We had other conceits. When we met, Cory had recently returned from four years in India; Francis, fluent in Spanish, had lived in Spain and Turkey; Patrick had a hand in another world, Belfast's underground gay scene; Virginia flirted dangerously with the forbidden Irish Republic; a later addition, a visiting lecturer at Queen's, Alan hailed from a genuinely foreign country, mainland Britain; I was a well-traveled Yank. Ostensibly, we all knew there was life outside Northern Ireland, and once in a while another country would actually arise in conversation. We liked to think that we kept Ulster's squabble in perspective, and that we had a sense of humor about its foibles. Well, we *must* have had a sense of humor, to have so abundantly lost it this last year.

But as for our exception from Northern boxes, we were kidding ourselves. We were all "unionists with a small 'u'"—the pat phrase for our kind, meaning that union*ism* was palatable by democratic default, and union*ists* (accidentally in the right, but stodgy, straitlaced, po-faced dullards you would never ask over for a drink) were painful. Like everyone else in Ulster, we had comfortably fortified ourselves with others who concurred on the Border, a social vetting system I'll be glad to see the back of. In Belfast, the Border not only dominates local politics and the press, but dictates personal ties as well. Countless friendships with nationalists have died on my vine. I never systematically picked greenies off one by one, but they withered of their own accord. We'd ring one another with decreasing frequency after too many fearful evenings of tiptoeing across a minefield of explosive subject matter, to end up talking about the food. Yet I was alerted to my cronies' factional homogeneity only when Cory introduced into this circle of unionists-with-a-small-"u" a Nationalist with a capital "N."

At first, all our number were single and unattached, intensifying our sensation of being free thinkers—though our lack of romantic encumbrance grew burdensome once we dispersed. Alone, I'd glare morosely at the black mold blooming on my slanted ceiling, stereo static crackling through my empty flat because I was too bereft to flip the Sinéad O'Connor tape to the B side. Cory and I grew especially close by putting off this confrontation with solitude into the wee-smalls, sharing our misbegotten adventures with the opposite sex. A flirtatious undercurrent to our relationship remained only that. Not, blessedly, quite each other's type, we settled instead on the relationship that so often outlives romance, that of Best Friends.

Any tightly knit singles crowd is traumatized by the pairing off of its members. Although we were no exception, I thought we managed the transition to coupledom with relative grace, at least at first.

The woman I will call Muriel is a pleasant, earnest, hospitable Catholic then in her early thirties, and the unabashed frankness with which Cory's new girlfriend shared that she had one glass eye was appealing. In her formative social outings with Cory, Muriel was eager to be accepted by his politically loudmouthed cohorts. We didn't make it easy for her. Oh, we inquired politely about her teaching job on the Falls Road; we left her some popcorn. But we were accustomed to letting fly on the issues of the day, and in Belfast there was only one issue. So we'd rail against the IRA bombing of Frizzell's fish shop on the Shankill, which killed nine civilian Protestants in October of '93; Muriel would be far more exercised about the retaliatory pub strafing at Greysteel by loyalist gunmen on Halloween (the shooters shouted gleefully as they opened fire, "Trick or treat!"). Once you have chosen sides, you inevitably get a wee bit more emotional about some atrocities than others. Accordingly, I've never heard Muriel voice outrage about a single IRA operation. If a soldier was shot, it was "a shame," or as Adams would say, "regrettable"; the truck bombing of Canary Wharf in 1996 that killed two and caused £150 million in commercial damage wasn't treacherous but "disheartening."

Muriel is a sentimental nationalist. She's enchanted by the idea of Irishness, and the whole Yeats-Joyce-Heaney cultural package. Though I'm fairly sure that she votes for the nonviolent SDLP, Muriel (who reveres the republican rabble-rouser Bernadette Devlin McAliskey— the cow) is a closet Provo. After all, if you're a soft touch for nationalist romance, natty Gerry Adams makes for a swoonier pinup than the sweaty, disheveled SDLP leader John Hume. Muriel has an eagle eye for sectarianism toward Catholics but unselfconsciously writes off

Protestants as troglodyte clods. After all, deeply held prejudice always presents itself to its custodian as plain fact. So naturally I'd assert that Muriel's defense of Irish nationalism was devoid of rational argument and wholly reliant on hysterical outburst as *plain fact.*

I hasten to add that Muriel was generous as both hostess and guest, often arriving with flowers and an extra bottle of wine. She was inquisitive about my affairs, and even, good lord, read one of my books. I may have found her feminism a little ornamental, but at least she was not, like most Northern Irish women, afraid of the word. We had some stylistic differences. Muriel wore dresses with color-coordinated accessories and pumps, while I was given to 1950s night-shirts and slouch socks. Muriel served sit-down starters with cilantro sprigs, while I threw cut vegetables into the middle of a company in piles. So what? I found her perfectly convivial company so long as we avoided politics.

We never avoided politics. I now think it probable that Muriel's kindness and social solicitation were an act, scripted by the decorum of the middle class with matching place mats to which she aspired, successfully disguising a simple, blanket dislike. In that instance I'm embarrassed, for I was certainly taken in. But even in the early, careful days of our acquaintance, I was never in any doubt that when the Border arose in conversation it drew a line not only between the north and south of Ireland but also between Muriel and me.

At which times she unquestionably despised me. As far as Muriel was concerned, I was an impertinent interloper who could never hope to understand the tortuous ins and outs of her native land. She never got beyond the ad hominem argument that, as I was American, ipso facto I didn't know what I was talking about. (Were she to live in my own city of New York for several years she'd have had not only a right to but a duty to form views on, say, welfare reform, but the Northern Irish concede no such comparisons.) The Troubles might be squalid, but they were *Muriel's* Troubles, which she would clutch to her breast like an orphan with one grubby doll that she refused to share. Northerners seem to fear—and so do themselves an injustice—that they are exclusively distinguished by intractable bickering, and so are determined to corner the market on belligerence if on nothing else. They appear to regard this pugnacity as in short supply, though in my experience there is plenty to go round. Buttinskies with a penchant for writing things down are perceived as thieves, who will bundle away precious sectarian subject matter and so leave less for everyone else. Visiting scribblers' paragraphs are swag bags bulging with Ulster's glittering complexities, destined to be fenced to foreign publishers for a fraction of their true value. Consequently, the Troubles must be hoarded, protected from the pilfering of strangers, like crown jewels made of paste. The Troubles are a national treasure.

Muriel's resentment of my presumption peaked around their dinner table in East Belfast, when she objected to the glossary in my third novel, the only book I've set in the North, *Ordinary Decent Criminals*. The Northern Irish shouldn't require "special explanations." My definitions of "republican" and "Anglo-Irish Agreement" denoted a population that was "other." "Otherness" had generated a preponderance of the world's historical woes, she said, as it connoted aliens who were short of fully human, and besides which, novels did not have glossaries.

"That novel was written for Americans," I said measuredly, with more patience than this barking conversation deserved. "So according to you, even if my readers haven't a clue what a 'unionist' is, I'm supposed to leave them stymied and risk their putting my book down just to avoid any suggestion of 'otherness'?"

Muriel burbled something about how the Northern Irish "have families and go shopping like everyone else."

"Yes," I granted, "but it is not the fact that the Northern Irish go shopping that interests the rest of the world, is it?"

Well, it *should* be.

I needn't have proceeded to defend the elastic novel form as readily incorporating an appendix, because Muriel was not really incensed by my glossary but by my whole book. By its existence. I had no right. I hadn't paid the price by being spanked to life by the brutal red hand of Ulster, yet I had profited shamelessly from the tragic suffering of Muriel's riven people. Waving the hardback, a gift to her boyfriend whose chummy inscription must have rankled, Muriel grew beet-faced, consternated by the *otherness* of these lovely people who go shopping.

"Have you read that novel?" I interrupted squarely.

"Well, no, but I've flipped—"

"I refuse to have an argument over a book that you haven't read." Closure that an English teacher might have deployed herself.

But then, I'd run into Muriel's brand of get-your-hands-off-my-Troubles before. Cory's rising territoriality perturbed me more. He'd once flattered me as "understanding Northern Ireland better than any foreigner he knew." Rare graciousness for Ulster; in turn, I gave him credit for giving me credit. But Cory's compliments had grown sparse. The New Cory was a Troubles guru, whom Dutch news crews sought out to liaise with West Belfast joyriders, whose IRA kneecappings then attracted international fascination. Admiring anyone else's observations would involve listening to them first. Why would he do that? And so leave, as Patrick remarked ruefully in private, that much less time to be "wise"?

For Cory had evolved into an archetypal Catholic success story. He'd bought a house, a Zip drive. When we met, he was freelancing for the skinflint Catholic *Irish News* and teaching at a business college. Years on, he wrote a column for the better-paying Protestant *Telegraph*, recorded packages for BBC Radio Ulster, published in the *New Statesman*, and had secured a book contract with Blackstaff Press. The ultimate arrival anywhere: Cory was on TV. Though as a presenter of local documentaries Cory had already acquired mainstream credentials, he'd also enrolled in Queen's University to earn a PhD in politics that he didn't need. On the other hand, for a bootstrapped Andytown Taig, perhaps the yearning to be called "Doctor" was forgivable.

In short, my best friend had gone from irreverent outsider wag to establishment pundit. I offer his case as cautionary, because in the self-important confines of Northern Ireland Cory's metamorphosis seems not only common but inevitable. Perhaps the North is simply bad for character. Cory's mastery of the quarrel he grew up with provided him an artificial sense of worldliness, when in actuality he was becoming more provincial. Once you pick your team, a neatly polarized moral universe throws up Truths on a weekly basis, so it's a doddle to be *wise*. More, too much sanctimony makes for an excessively rich intellectual diet. Indignation clogs the arteries and makes your mind slow and fat.

Accommodating my metaphor, Cory's wee paunch had ballooned, as if he were literally full of hot air. He'd pat this tummy with self-satisfaction after making a trenchant point. His anti–Sinn Féin stance had begun to suffer contradictions: he was obliged to impute ever more sophisticated strategy to the IRA in order to reap the prestige for discerning the movement's sly intent.

The biggest casualty of Cory's expertise was his sense of perspective. Once I could quote a British professor's characterization of the Troubles as "a conflict between two groups of losers arguing over yesterday's problems," and Cory would laugh. By the early 1990s, he couldn't afford even to grin. Throw enough energy into this black hole, and to diminish the Troubles is to diminish yourself. A sense of proportion rapidly becomes an admission against interest. Since neither Cory nor I can assert in print that the North doesn't deserve the very scrutiny we ourselves subject it to, the emperor soon acquires a very fine suit of clothes indeed.

I can't speak for Cory, but this constraint actively corrupts my journalism. Were I to portray the Troubles as an infantile feud inflated by violence, or dare to intimate that some incremental turn of the wheel is of minor consequence, I'd effectively be advising my readers to move on to another op-ed. Yet the alternative is to continually service the statelet's vanity, and implicitly my own vanity as well, over being so knowledgeable about this big, boggling conundrum. At the BBC radio program for which I record weekly political commentary, the prime taboo is ridicule, lest victims' relatives perceive their suffering as mocked. That you are deriding the reason for which people died but not diminishing the tragedy of their deaths is a distinction too subtle by half for talk radio, and itself cold comfort. Maybe the only loss more unbearable than sacrificing loved ones for a cause is sacrificing them for nothing.

Frankly, I found Cory's transformation disturbing because it mirrored my own. We'd both become sonorous, complacent. I, too, had stopped listening—since somehow you never make the connection that, in a culture where no one listens to anybody, no one is listening to you, either. I, too, was giddy with sanctimony, and my own sense of perspective had ebbed. That is, the conflict dominated my conversation even during my summers back in New York, making Lionel the Dinner Guest a crashing bore. So it's astonishing that amid all my posturing and sounding off some unsuspecting American fell in love with me.

Enter our last character. The man I'll call Jack to protect his privacy was a caustic, wiseacre journalist I met in Manhattan in the summer of 1993, and his "visit" to my garret in Belfast that autumn has now lasted four years. I'm sometimes nostalgic for his initial skepticism of the Troubles, his instinctive reluctance to participate. Jack made an effort with my friends all right, but he was staggered by the tightly circumscribed boundaries of their concerns. Fresh from Nairobi and East Africa's monumental problems—real problems, such as runaway population growth and obscene poverty—and still digesting the lessons for humanitarian aid in the UN debacle he covered in Somalia, Jack understandably found five-hour dissections of "Protestant identity" inane. Nevertheless, this newest import to our salon was jaunty, brash, and self-assured. He disliked having to ask so many questions. Understandably, he hated feeling left out. Whip smart, he's by nature a quick study; besides, as I've tried to indicate, Northern Ireland-as-puzzler is closer to a five-letter anagram than a Rubik's Cube. So in short order, Jack could hold his own with the best of them. Yet his original vow not to pander to Northern Irish navel-gazing had an integrity that, alas, circumstance demanded that he relinquish.

Because Jack had to support himself. I had dragged him to this bog. To live with me, he had to write about the bog, and thereby become complicit at least nominally with its self-regard. Given that some un-measurable proportion of Northern violence constitutes performance for a global audience—an audience that rewards only extremism, ex-aggeration, and butchery with its attentions—both Jack and I have in-deed become "part of the problem."

If Jack was skeptical of the Troubles, Cory was skeptical of Jack. Ostensibly worried about my safety, my best friend took me aside early on to observe that Jack radiated the "capacity for violence." An ironic warning. The capacity for violence, in an emotional sense, simmered not in my new boyfriend but in Cory.

Their relations were cordial but wary. Although Cory and I had never been involved, that didn't seem to preclude an element of posses-siveness on his part, and even of jealousy. (When I had a run-in with British immigration, Cory offered to marry me—for only the purpose of legal convenience, of course.) And while we're at it, need I spell it out? Muriel was palpably jealous of me and my suspiciously inti-mate friendship with the man who became her husband. At the risk of sounding catty, I'd characterize her looks as, well—nondescript? Which must have intensified her insecurity. As a double whammy, she harbored her own literary ambitions and resented my occupation as a novelist. In that capacity, I have to say it's disappointing when the dynamics between a story's characters are this stock and that obvious.

It was also predictable that Cory would not appreciate another blow-in journalist pissing around his patch. (I'm sympathetic. I've been unattractively cool to visiting American writers myself.) This subtle turf war heated up when Jack not only published Troubles articles in *The New Republic* but snagged a contract with the Free Press in the United States to write a book on Northern Irish paramilitaries.

Between 1993 and 1996, my crew still gathered, superficially civilized—perhaps too. We no longer dropped in on one another unannounced. We served dinners with cloth napkins; we issued invitations tit for tat. Our most animated conversation now took place behind one another's backs; face-to-face, we asked about the latest less from curiosity than courtesy. Though no doubt a routine development as cliques pair off, age, and enter the middle class, this necrotization of social discourse was no less a loss for being ordinary. As compensation, our increasingly stilted mealtimes provided front-row seats for regular after-dinner theater: Cory and Muriel would fight.

We all know couples who row in public, but these were Northern Irish rows. That is, they were about—what else?—the Border. Muriel was a closet Provie; Cory was still an Orange Taig. The odd evening the rest of us would leave them to it and gawk. More often, unfortunately for Muriel, we leapt into the fray. Lord knows it wasn't fair. Not only was the overwrought Muriel not rhetorically equipped for these battles, but she was grotesquely outnumbered. Jack had been an early convert to unionism-with-a-small-"u," and as a former practicing lawyer with a photographic memory for atrocities (he's the only man I know who has sat and read *An Index of Deaths from the Conflict in Ireland, 1969–1993* cover to cover), he made a devastating addition to Our Side. Besieged Muriel had to fight her corner all by herself. Hell, I give her credit for fighting it, if not always well. We never made the slightest inroad into her nationalism, nor did we expect to. So what were we doing, besides pushing her around? If anything, we only confirmed as a group that unionists were bullies.

For a long time I thought that Cory and Muriel going at it like that (Muriel acceleratingly shrill, Cory condescendingly reasonable) was a sign of a healthy, vital relationship. Even after the two got married, they preserved their own views and apparently sustained an energetic dialogue about the constitutional question. I was impressed that such a marriage was possible, and that Muriel could hold her own amid all these unionists without punching us each in the gob. But now I take that back. Such a marriage is not possible, not in Ulster. You simply don't meet couples who disagree about the Border, not couples that stay couples. Furthermore, I think Muriel did, in the end, punch me metaphorically in the gob.

Last chapter: Jack's book on paramilitaries came out in November of '96. Days before he flew to the United States for its publication, he received a phone call from the US Immigration and Naturalization Service, whose lawyers had noticed his book. The INS was attempting to deport an ex-IRA man, Brian Pearson, who had lied on immigration forms about his criminal record and overstayed his tourist visa by eight years. Had he been Nigerian, Pearson would have been waving bye-bye to New York State from a plane. But Pearson was Northern Irish and had claimed political asylum. The notorious Martin Galvin, publicity director for NORAID (an American fund-raiser for the IRA), was Pearson's attorney. Galvin would argue that IRA volunteers are not terrorists but legitimate civil insurgents, and that Pearson's blowing up an RUC police station was not a crime. Though Pearson could have been deported to the Republic of Ireland, where he would be safe as houses, Galvin asserted absurdly that his client's life would still be endangered by roving bands of loyalist paramilitaries and the North's bigoted, Tonton Macoute–esque Protestant police force in the South, where the RUC enjoyed no jurisdiction. Knowing bugger all about Northern Ireland, the INS asked my boyfriend to act as a consultant in the case.

I was envious. After so much text and tirade, I'd not swayed the tide of history an inch. *Ordinary Decent Criminals* had, at best, entertained. Holding forth in my living room had served only to annoy Muriel. All my radio editorials had never changed the minds of my heedless listeners, most of whom still assumed I supported the IRA because I had an American accent. And here my partner could be potentially instrumental in defeating what was to become a republican cause célèbre. Still, the INS was not going to solicit the advice of a novelist. Jack was a trained lawyer and would do a much better job. I kissed him goodbye and wished him luck.

I had only one role in the Pearson case: to keep my trap shut. Prior to the hearing, INS lawyers preferred to keep their sources under wraps. I'm an inveterate gossip, and not blabbing down the phone about Jack's consultancy was a tall order. More, only one Belfast resident rivaled me in the gossip department, and that was Cory. Jack abjured me that I was to keep particularly mum with the man I'd once considered my best friend. This was easier than it should have been. Cory rarely rang anymore. For reasons I was reluctant to identify, we'd grown apart.

In only one instance was Cory briefly drawn in. Jack suggested from the United States that I "ask around" about who such-and-such was. Easy enough. In passing, I asked Cory over the phone if he recognized the name. He didn't, and then he bridled. Why did Jack want to know? I said I wasn't sure (I wasn't), assured him that the information didn't seem very important, never mind. A casual inquiry I would regret.

Around Christmas, the usual suspects gathered in my flat for what was to prove a last time. As usual, Cory and Muriel fought. As usual, the scrap concerned the Border. I stayed out for once. When they left, the couple still looked out of sorts—Cory tight-lipped, Muriel flushed.

In January, I joined Jack in New York for a fortnight, my arrival coinciding with the initial days of the Pearson hearing. I got an unexpected cross-Atlantic phone call from Francis, who exclaimed breathlessly that Jack's role in the Pearson case was on the front page of the *Irish News*. Huh, I said. What of it?

According to Francis, Cory was livid. No longer sure "who Jack really was," Cory was spreading the rumor that my partner worked for the CIA. Or the UK's domestic equivalent, MI5. Or both.

I laughed. Francis didn't.

When Jack and I returned to Belfast, Francis made an appointment. He arrived with the air of an adjutant who'd been dispatched with a message to the enemy and was authorized to bear back a reply. These were my friends, yet the imagery that came to mind was military.

Francis laid out Cory's position: the *Irish News*—a broadsheet that maintains the journalistic standards of a shopping flier—had published snippily that this Jack person "wasn't even a lawyer." Hence Cory now realized that Jack's claim to have practiced law in New York before turning to journalism was a cover story. Clearly my boyfriend had been a government agent all along, deviously deploying the great Troubles pundit himself as a tool of security interests. (This construction made *me* either a dupe as well—living with a man who was merely using me to infiltrate Belfast pasta suppers—or another Machiavellian fiend. Hell, maybe I was working for the CIA myself. In which case, I thought, it was about time they sent a check.)

I had trouble taking Cory's theories seriously, because they were so trite. Underneath Belfast's how's-about-ye conviviality festers a tout-under-every-bush paranoia. If locals want to smear you, the first thing they reach for is capital letters: SAS, MI5, CIA, RUC. Conspiracy-mongering follows from grandiosity. I think it plausible, for example, that the CIA has no case officer whatsoever stationed in Northern Ireland. The place just isn't that vital to American interests, but try telling this to a Northerner, nationalist *or* unionist. Why would the CIA not send operatives to the center of the universe? With his recent loss of perspective, Cory, too, might picture the whole world's intelligence services as angling to penetrate the Irish Continuity Army. But his belief that a real CIA agent would spend an abundance of his time eating popcorn with a *Belfast Telegraph* columnist and a few BBC associate producers displayed a pretty low opinion of my country's spies.

Jack saw Francis off at the door downstairs and said, "Thanks for coming by"—a line that usually elicits "No problem" or "It was great to see you." Instead, Francis replied soberly, "You're welcome."

I rarely dread phoning friends, but I put off ringing Cory for three days. Cory picked up, and within thirty seconds my cheeks flamed; my few intrusions were stuttering and hoarse. Choking incoherence on my end allowed Cory to recite his monologue intact. Each assertion sounded rehearsed, his delivery one-two-three, as if he'd been practicing on other people for days. I will try to do his grievances justice, since this was the last time I spoke to Cory.

One: As for the Pearson case, Jack was on the wrong side. Pearson was a nice man with a lovely family who had proved a model American citizen, and it would be a terrible shame to uproot such a harmless fellow. (In this sweetly sentimental reasoning, heedless of legal precedent, I could hear: *Muriel*.)

Two: Cory played down the CIA business—perhaps the theory simply sounded too preposterous when advanced to me—substituting the broader charge that Jack was Working For The Government. (Never mind which government; Cory's working-class roots may have surfaced, since for proles Government is singular, malign, and monolithic.) Hence Jack had violated "journalistic ethics." A freelancer so compromised had sacrificed his objectivity and independence of thought.

Three: Association with Jack had ruined Cory's reputation with his "republican sources." Since the story had broken, all of Cory's Sinn Féin contacts were carping, "You told us to trust him, and now look."

Four: I had kept the case a secret. I was duty bound to have told Cory all.

Five: Cory remembered that who-is-such-and-such phone call. Such-and-such turned out to be a witness for Pearson's defense. *What if* Cory had gone around West Belfast asking who this person was, and *what if* someone in Sinn Féin heard him asking around, and *what if* they discovered the inquiry was for Jack, who was Working For The Government . . . Why, in that instance, I'd have endangered his life and the life of his family!

The upshot: Cory could no longer "afford" to mix with "us."

At this point I went into shock. I knew we were having a fight, and I knew it had grown acrimonious. But Cory had been a good friend of mine for over nine years, and I'd had no idea until that moment that what was on the table was our entire relationship. Which, it seemed, was over. There was a silence. If my face was red, Cory's was certainly white. We hung up. We didn't say goodbye.

Forgive me if I take a moment and sigh. Several months have now passed, and recounting this shabby tale depletes me. In fiction, I'd have contrived a grander climax to sever such a long friendship—I don't know, a bomb? But real stories throw up piquancies that the made-up kind, in their coarse high drama, would miss.

You know how, after a phone call like that, you repeatedly mutter all you might have said and didn't? Indulge me.

If Pearson was a nice man who liked the United States, more was at stake than his contentment. As it happens, the original decision, now being appealed, did find for Pearson. The black judge, who may have fallen for the brothers-in-oppression ploy, agreed that IRA members were not necessarily terrorists and (incredibly) that Pearson's bombing of a police station was an act of legitimate political protest. Should the ruling stand, any IRA member, retired *or active*, could successfully claim asylum in the United States—a state of affairs that small-"u" Cory should decry. But he's married to a staunch nationalist. And he wants to stay married. So little by little Cory's politics have had to bend.

As for the short course on "journalistic ethics": journalists are frequently employed at American trials, and commentators like Jack and Cory don't pretend to objectivity, but espouse viewpoints. Jack believed in what he was doing for the INS, and that, to me, was the end of it. So I was less intrigued by this mysterious rule that journalists must never hire out to "Government" than by Cory's resort to high-flown principle, never mind that grotty business of his having never much cared for my boyfriend as a person. For a place that has sponsored so much depravity, Ulster is bizarrely agallop with principles. Even Northern Ireland's lowlifes are mounted on high horses, all jousting for the moral high ground, all portly from that steady diet of indignations, which get to be a habit, like donuts.

Cory's "republican sources" were offended? His one regular "republican source" whom I know of is Anthony McIntyre, known matily as "Mackers"—an ex-lifer convicted of shooting a Protestant in the 1970s. Mackers is still a hard-line Chucky, who condemned the 1994 IRA cease-fire as a sellout; he's the type who, on learning that an English shopping center just blew up, smiles slyly over an extra beer. I invited Mackers to our flat a couple of times. Though I found him intelligent and amiable, alien politics precluded his ever becoming more than a specimen. I remember treating him with funny scientific deference, as if handling a Moon rock through rubber gloves. Not many Real Live Republicans had lounged on that sofa.

Now Mackers was mad. He felt he'd been had. The single interview subject whom Cory had shuttled Jack's way, and who had featured unbecomingly in Jack's book, Mackers had given Cory an earful, aggrieved by both the book and Jack's role in the Pearson case. The poor retired assassin had only himself to blame. He had presumed that any Yank would be in thrall to the IRA, and the lines that hang him in the book are direct quotes.

Though personally dismaying to me, it was illuminating of Northern Irish journalism that Cory treasured the goodwill of an unrepentant convicted murderer more highly than our nine-year friendship. A Belfast hack closely guards his "republican contacts," for anything to do with the IRA is always the hot story. In fact, Sinn Féin manipulates freelancers by withdrawing interview access when their coverage of republicanism is too negative. Gerry Adams is treated like the pope even by journalists who ostensibly revile him. (For that matter, these days Adams's audience is as difficult as the pope's to gain.) Ironically, an honest-to-God republican was a rarity in Cory's contact book precisely because he'd publicly denounced the likes of Mackers for years. Still, Mackers was a *republican source*, who could be cited anonymously in columns—lending weight to any argument and implying that the author's finger is on the pulse—and was therefore priceless.

Yes, I had kept a secret—miraculously. But I could have owed Cory a "confession," in defiance of a promise to my partner and implicitly to my own government, only because the Pearson case related to the Troubles. Ergo, Cory owned it. I was less obligated to inform him than to beg his permission, as if asking to borrow his car.

Lastly, Cory's charge that I had "endangered his life and the life of his family" made for a painfully predictable clincher. Pure, pitch-perfect Belfast, and leveled at me from other quarters before. In Surrey or Iowa social objections run, "We've had you to dinner three times and you've only had us to drinks once!" In Belfast the default accusation is more flamboyant: "You endangered my life." The hyperbole of a place where murder has joined the ranks of social convention distends the vocabulary even of phone spats.

MY SOIREE HAS NEVER ASSEMBLED AGAIN. CORY, A LOCAL, WAS MORE FOCAL than I, and these days you cannot invite Cory and Lionel to the same dinner. In my social exile, I'm naturally injured, but my friends may have done me a favor. They've made it easier for me to leave.

I will never regret having lived in Belfast, though the town has taught me lessons I'm not sure I wanted to learn. While chums elsewhere may have ferocious arguments, ideological clashes rarely demolish their relationships. Maybe Northern Ireland has taught me the nature of real politics, which are not about what you try on for size but what you are. I do resist the notion that I *am* a unionist, any more than Muriel *is* a nationalist, but I recognize that in a one-issue town, which paints all its residents in a narrow spectrum of green to orange, grossly simplifying and therefore caricaturing all its inhabitants in terms of a single view, I will be caricatured, too. Moreover, if I might justly be accused of having been on a pathetic, decade-long campaign to belong, by securing fierce, personal enmity, I finally fit right in. Denunciation here amounts to a funny kind of acceptance.

I have likewise acquired a begrudging respect for the powers of group allegiance. If there's a moral to Cory's and my falling out, it is to never underestimate the call of tribe. The fight Cory picked seemed so pretextual that in dissecting just what happened and why, I've kept coming back to *Muriel*. I must have downplayed to myself the scale of that couple's discomfort at squaring off in my living room. In fact, I separately emailed both Cory and Muriel after that awful call, if only to solicit an explanation for this terminal tiff that I could buy. I got back gruff reiteration from Cory, but Muriel's perfect silence spoke more loudly than any response. As I flash-sessioned in my study, stale Yuletide waves of resolution washed the flat—the vow those two must have left behind when last at dinner here that their public Border bickering should not recur. In Northern Ireland, to force spouses onto opposite sides of the constitutional question is to raise the specter of divorce.

I, too, am a member of a group: the Visiting Americans, welcome only so long as they raptly attend to every bump and grind of the Troubles like wistful wallflowers, but never overstep themselves to dance. (Recall that Cory could no longer associate with "us." It was my clan that he rejected, though I'd personally nothing to do with the INS.) I've traded on this status, pretending to a fresh perspective from abroad that has become a disingenuous pose. Because I assumed Ulster's passions not by dint of birth into one "community" or the other but of my own free will, I have even less of an excuse than the locals. When I catch myself declaiming that a column of geezers in bowler hats *must* be allowed to troop for nine minutes down a contested Catholic stretch of Garvaghy Road in Portadown, I get intimations that I might be mad. The zeal of the convert has plunged me as blindly into these disputes as my neighbors.

The fact that even I—an American whose technical Protestant parentage is an irrelevance—have been wounded by Northern factionalism helps demonstrate that the conflict is not strictly over religious allegiance. It is cruder than that; it is simply about allegiance. Young and cocky, our little band in my living room imagined that we were above the Troubles, that we could tolerate Catholic (in both senses) viewpoints on the Border, and, our most far-fetched pretension, that we could keep the skirmish in perspective. But in truth until Muriel joined our number we were as politically uniform as any social circle in the city. In the end, Cory's loyalty to his wife dictated a gesture of loyalty to her politics as well: unambiguous disavowal of the trespassing pretend-unionists who were always ganging up on her. At least this much would apply anywhere: friends are more disposable than spouses. That is the only pith I can derive from what seems otherwise a rather small-beer story.

What I will miss about Northern Ireland is also what I need to flee. I will miss my own loamy cynicism, for the North is a playground for misanthropes. There is no one in the cast to admire. Almost to a man, Northern Irish punters and politicians alike act reprehensibly, down to my own friends.

I will miss cheap authority—rattling off the casualties at "Teebane" or "Warrenpoint," as if rote statistics translate to acumen. I will miss cheap status—the reluctant regard I garner when informing strangers in England or America that *I live in Belfast*, and their unwarranted assumptions about my edgy day-to-day. I will miss a neurotically circumscribed and thereby cozily knowable universe. I will miss my superior exasperation with a myopia that I share. I will miss a ready-made cheering section for my opinions and ready-made detractors whose criticisms can be summarily dismissed as partisan mudslinging. I will miss clearly labeled enemies, and I'm sure to founder in normal polities, where heroism and villainy intermingle, often within the same character. Hell, I'll probably even miss hating the bloody place.

I will miss the electricity of impending cataclysm. For years I've been uneasy about leaving Northern Ireland even for a week or two, *just in case something might happen*. On my return from summers in the United States, friends have always taunted me with the ructions that went down in my absence, most notably the infamous "Drumcree" riots of '96; facetiously they assured me, "You were lucky you weren't here." Incitement to jealousy reliably succeeded: a season in *New York City* would appear to have taken me out of the loop. When any bomb goes off back home (for Belfast remains that), when shopwindows are smashed in Portadown and I'm away, I feel excluded.

For anyone infected with the Northern Irish bug, this warped yearning is diagnostic. The diseased can malinger in the North indefinitely, in the hopes that something appalling occurs during our tenure. We're reluctant to schedule the briefest respite from this political closet, lest all hell break loose the moment we step onto the plane and we miss the party. Northern Ireland's mythology that at any given point the place is about to implode into civil war entices Troubles-watchers like myself to remain glued to our seats, like cinemagoers numbed by previews but reluctant to get up for Junior Mints lest the main feature commence. Shamefully, my greatest dread of leaving Belfast for good is that once I've shifted my last sock to London the statelet will go up in flames without me. Witness the ultimate sacrifice trap: after ten years, I have paid the price of admission many times over, and I am owed the show. I sometimes wonder if all Northern Ireland feels the same way, and "civil war" may eventually come to pass from sheer theatrical impatience.

Finally, I will also miss Cory. But since I now miss him even in Belfast, I can do that anywhere.

"No Exit"

HARPER'S MAGAZINE, 2019

[This essay was written during the tumultuous early months of 2019 in Britain, when it was totally up for grabs whether the United Kingdom would stay in the European Union or go, and no prudent punter would have put money on either Leave or Remain at that time. In fact, this issue of Harper's *Magazine went to print on the very day that the UK had long been scheduled to leave the EU—or not. The great achievement of this piece, then, is that despite its having been composed on the political high seas, it still scans. I haven't changed a word.]*

For American liberals, the European Union is a bastion of social justice, secular humanism, and civic virtue. Taxed gratefully into equality, its subjects spend their days recycling kefir containers and protecting the realm from GM foods. Only this wise, collegial institution prevents a recrudescence of World War II. After *Bush v. Gore* and Trump, it's to this land of milk and honey—or crème fraîche and Cointreau—that disgusted Democrats have threatened to decamp, although my compatriots rarely seem to go. That may be fortunate. Fantasies rarely survive close scrutiny.

For it's more the case that the European Union is a bloated bureaucracy packed with pampered timeservers inventing gratuitous regulations to justify their sinecures. A fine idea when first conceived as a free-trade bloc, the profligate, power-hungry body has warped into a centralizing political project without asking the irrelevant little peons it governs whether they *want* a federated Europe. Originally meant to mutually benefit a handful of similarly scaled economies, the now-unwieldy alliance has since absorbed a plethora of far poorer countries and is thus also evolving into a transfer union—to many a German's dismay.

The European Union is antidemocratic by design; as the popularly elected European Parliament cannot originate legislation, its most considerable expenditure must be crate after crate of rubber stamps. Brussels's vaunted "freedom of movement" would be a pleasing arrangement as an exchange of labor—a British engineer moves to Paris; a French carpenter moves to Manchester—but is unworkable when migration gushes all one way. It is NATO that keeps peace in Europe. These days, given the slow-motion car crash of the euro, the jumped-up trade bloc is more a source of discord. Should the departure prompt some soul-searching humility, even a rethink about its ultimate ambition to subjugate and effectively abolish the European nation-state, having one of its largest and oldest members walk out could theoretically do the high-handed cabal a world of good.

Yet American coverage of the surprise victory for Vote Leave in Britain's 2016 referendum was universally aghast. The bigoted barbarians had overrun Buckingham Palace with pitchforks and torches. Curiously, my fellow Americans rarely consider that we'd never have our own country join an autocratic, unaccountable supranational entity whose laws and courts supersede our own. (Well. With Trump? Maybe we would just now.)

A UK resident for over three decades, I doggedly out myself at London dinner parties as a Leave supporter—though I might skate safely on the chummy assumption that of course as a halfway sane person I backed Remain. While most subsequent discussions have been civil, I'm surely pitied and deplored behind my back, for even face-to-face I'm regarded as an exotic if slightly repellant zoo specimen.

Declaring myself in *Harper's* is bound to have the same effect or worse: *Jesus, the woman is a fucking idiot.* Yet perhaps a rare bird of a different color amid the monochrome flock of American columnists writing about Brexit ("economic suicide" according to Thomas

Friedman) will be at least drolly amusing. If nothing else, I can offer up another happy occasion for recreational contempt.

I lived for a dozen years in Belfast, where ongoing disputes about "parity of esteem" were even more mind-numbing than the United Kingdom's argy-bargy over Brexit. Questioning daily why I gave a toss about arcane Troubles politics, I clung to what was really at stake: whether terrorism paid off. In kind, as Brexit has ground on, what has seemed increasingly at stake is whether democracy pays off.

Even if EU membership is indeed to Britain's economic advantage, is a higher GDP growth rate worth the price: the spectacle, conducted on an international stage, of the people's will in a democracy coldly defied? I don't think the answer is obvious.

MOST REMAINERS HAVE NEVER ACCEPTED THE REFERENDUM'S RESULT. LIKE the American press, British Europhiles immediately pilloried Leavers as "racist" for wanting to control their own immigration laws, though the immigrants to whom EU membership was germane were overwhelmingly white. Aggrieved commentators declared that representative democracies should never hold referendums, an argument Remainers never advanced in the days they assumed they would win. Wishing the referendum had never been run became a form of magical thinking, as if marshaling sufficient regret could turn back the clock and unrun the poll. Insults hurled at Leave voters—impugning the capacity of these halfwits and moral misfits to make judgments about complex issues over their heads—echoed historical arguments against women's suffrage and the enfranchisement of the working class.

The effort to subvert the electoral verdict really took off with the ingenious contrivance of the "hard" and "soft" Brexit, when the choice on the ballot was binary. The referendum itself did not present the option "leave sort of but not really." Signally, these textural distinctions never arose during the campaigns, and became common currency only once the incorrect vote was in.

As branding, the "hard" and "soft" polarity is inspired. Softness calls up kindness, compassion, agreeable toilet paper, and bunny rabbits. Hardness evokes obduracy, mercilessness, uncomfortable seating, and extremism—for example, "hard right." At a stroke, anyone advocating *actually leaving the European Union*—hitherto known as a Leave voter—was an intransigent kook from the reactionary fringe. Thus 52 percent of the electorate was neatly exiled to beyond the pale. Advocates of a "soft Brexit"—such continuing entanglement with the European Union as to make the whole fandango of "leaving" utterly pointless—are Remainers in Groucho glasses.

Fatally for Leavers, after David Cameron fell on his sword, Conservatives selected a party leader who'd supported Remain, and who as prime minister would therefore spearhead an extraction that she didn't believe in. Oh, to start, Theresa May talked a good game, eternally perseverating, "Brexit means Brexit!"—a mantra that, tellingly, quite vanished from her speeches by last summer. Like the lobbying group "Leave Means Leave," the tautology suggests insecurity over the government's commitment to honoring the referendum. Otherwise, Brexit would clearly mean Brexit, right? So why repeat the self-evident?

The claim that most British broadcasters, not least the BBC, have consistently displayed a Remain bias isn't even controversial. Eagerly embracing that "hard" and "soft" paradigm, news anchors have constantly referred to the United Kingdom's departure without a deal first as "crashing out," a train-wreck expression that blithely assumes the conclusion.

Journalists and politicians alike have argued for overturning or neutering the referendum result because Leavers didn't have all the facts, had been misled by their politicians, and "didn't know what they were voting for"—allegations that could probably be made about most electorates in the world. Multiple parliamentarians have asserted knowingly that "no one voted to be poorer!"—although when polled in

2017, over 60 percent of Leave voters were willing to accept "significant damage" to the British economy in return for political independence; nearly 40 percent would even accept losing their jobs. Besides, if unintended consequences were grounds for invalidating an election, we'd have to nullify most elections, or we'd simply stop bothering to hold them in the first place.

Meanwhile, British tax authorities have hit major Leave donors with ferocious "gift" inheritance taxes, effective double taxation to which donors to the main political parties (both of which backed Remain) are not being subjected. Leave campaign financing has been vigorously investigated for overspending, while the Cameron government leafleted every British household to promote Remain with £9.3 million of taxpayers' money that didn't count as campaign expenditure. I got that flier. It warned sternly that quitting the European Union would mean leaving the single market, which is one of the things that Leavers supposedly failed to understand.

Despite the tough "Brexit means Brexit!" rhetoric, Theresa May sent an ardent Remainer civil servant to EU negotiations, from which her pro-Leave "Brexit secretary" was excluded; displeased with the direction of travel in Brussels, two such secretaries in a row resigned. At every vital juncture, she has accepted the European Union's terms and often-ludicrous underlying assumptions—most lethally, the premise that extravagant customs arrangements involving perhaps the whole of the United Kingdom were necessary to avoid the terrifying prospect of a "hard border" between Northern Ireland and the Irish Republic.

Out of the gate, Britain said it would not put infrastructure on the border; so did Ireland and the European Union. So where was the insoluble conundrum? This would-be baffling dilemma exemplifies the rubric that, while people can't always resolve difficulties that they're trying to solve, they can always fail to resolve difficulties that they *don't* want to solve. Both highly motivated to stop Brexit in its tracks, the European Union and Ireland have wielded this fake predicament as a shamelessly disingenuous negotiating ploy in the name of "peace."

In any event, Britain is responsible only for its own side of the border, yet Eurocrats improbably persuaded May that she had to sort out their side, too. Presumably even a few cameras are the source of outsize horror because they might present a "target" for ragtag IRA dissidents, whose number is now small enough that they might be downgraded to a mental health problem. Having proved so obligingly useful for tying the Brits in knots, by now those throwbacks should all be on the Brussels payroll.

The resultant withdrawal deal overwhelmingly rejected by Parliament in January entailed a high degree of regulatory alignment, continued subjection to the European Court of Justice, the sacrifice of £39 billion with nothing in return, and potential entrapment in an EU customs union literally forever, with no mechanism of escape beyond "Mother, may I?" No wonder May has also stopped reciting the aphorism from her party's 2017 manifesto, "No deal is better than a bad deal."

The one scalp she waved to the public was an end to EU freedom of movement. Nevertheless, among Leave voters, only 22 percent endorsed her deal, and 58 percent didn't believe it respected their referendum win—belying that Leavers care solely about immigration.

As for still another referendum, it might sound democratic. If some voting is good, then surely more voting is better? The European Union has a history of making electorates go back to the polls until they get their minds right. But early this year, Britons believed by 47 percent to 39 percent that a second referendum was *anti*-democratic. The sole purpose of a so-called people's vote—a tag both bizarre and insulting; I'm sorry, but who voted last time?—is to overturn the 2016 result. (Only one in eight Leavers would countenance a do-over. Even if Leave support were unflagging, the question could be rigged—by splitting the Leave vote, or by taking an authentic departure off the ballot.) It's even argued that because some older Leave voters have died, and younger Remain supporters have come of age, the vote must be run again. But that logic sets one dodgy precedent.

Close elections would be reenacted continually if the votes of dead people don't count.

With 73 percent of Parliament having supported Remain, Brexit has been awkward from the get-go. Parliament delivered a decision to the people. The people gave the wrong answer. Ever since, Parliament has been trying to take the decision back. After all, what happens when you ask powerful people to do something they don't want to? They don't do it. In the political pandemonium following the legislative rejection of May's withdrawal deal in January, all the soft/softer/softest options the body entertained were so close to de facto EU membership as to make the whole exercise a farce.

YET HERE'S A RADICAL PROPOSITION: MAYBE BREXIT, HOWEVER IT ENDS UP, isn't as important as it's made out to be. In Britain's daily media hair-tear, that's a submission you never hear—much as the one true taboo in Northern Ireland is to observe that, for the conduct of day-to-day life, the island's partition or unification doesn't really matter much.

Like many a protracted contest, Brexit long ago became crudely about who wins. Leavers thought they won in 2016, only to find that implementation of that triumph entailed still another fight. But are the consequences of which faction prevails at last really that momentous? While the short term could involve disruption, in the big picture Britain would probably manage well enough outside the bloc; England as an independent nation goes back a thousand years, its union with Scotland three hundred. On the other hand, after participating in the European project for forty-six years, the United Kingdom is still intact, and it would endure bravely, I dare say, through forty-seven. Even a proper UK departure was never going to topple the union.

By embracing the campaign motto "Take Back Control," Leavers were chasing a *feeling*. Yes, they hoped to tap the brakes on mass immigration, but the majority of UK incomers are non-European. Leavers were more broadly motivated to restore British sovereignty, and so to revive national pride and a bolshie islander independence. It was gratifying to defy Britain's elite and refuse to vote as they were told to.

For Remainers, the referendum was also emotional, and also concerned with identity. They were sophisticated Europeans, not "little Englanders." (Do my compatriots ever refer to "little Americans"?) Emulating the very haughtiness that puts their opponents off about their friends in Brussels, Remainers have been driven by a sense of superiority, a certainty that they are right (I've often allowed that on Brexit I might be wrong; I've never heard a Remainer say the same), and a disgust that these ignorant troglodytes could be allowed to victimize the whole population. Remainers have been intoxicated by a messiah complex. Their nation's very survival being at stake more than justifies attempting to overturn the biggest electoral exercise in British history.

Yet as a thought experiment, let's envision each side getting what it wants.

(1.) Britain cuts all institutional ties with the European Union. Street parties in Leave constituencies festoon pedestrianized town centers with bunting. Cakes are iced with Union Jacks. Breweries release commemorative batches of Freedom Ale. Stands flog the tacky gilded coffee mugs of the sort produced for royal weddings.

But most victories are fleeting and anticlimactic. Once the paper flags are swept up, the abundance of these voters' lives aren't faintly improved. If they resented the bureaucracy in Brussels, the British invented bureaucracy. Being clobbered by regulations from Westminster (whose tax code is twelve times the length of the King James Bible) proves little different from being hit over the head by the EU common rulebook. Since tweezing EU diktats from domestic legislation is like picking crabmeat, Parliament keeps most EU laws on the books anyway. Money is still tight. The weather still sucks. Marriages still founder. When anything subsequently goes wrong, whether politically, logistically, or economically, Leavers get the blame, including for anything that would have gone wrong without Brexit. The party sliding to hangover, that stirring sensation of emancipation subsides.

Meanwhile, stewing in antipathy, resentment, and self-pity, Remainers plot to rejoin. Any fallout short of the apocalypse they predicted is annoying.

(2.) Either BRINO (Brexit in Name Only) is locked in, or the referendum is overturned outright. Remainers are smug, not to mention sniffy about submitting to so much turmoil only to sustain the status quo. But arch self-congratulation and palpable relief rapidly evaporate. History doesn't stand still, and EU membership offers no safe harbor. Another, even more overwhelming Mediterranean migration crisis, say, obliges Britain to accept a large share of new arrivals, despite a crippling shortage of housing. Or fiscal collapse in Italy forces Britain to help bail out foreign banks on a ruinous scale.

But here I challenge my own thesis:

For Leavers, failure to honor the 2016 referendum kicks off nationwide consternation. As their country nestles back into the European fold, dissenting commentators warn feverishly that the double-cross is bound to produce a catastrophic breach of public trust in democracy. These threats consistently sound hollow, like the Big Bad Wolf vowing to huff and puff and blow a house in when the little pig's abode is made of brick. That's what Remainers had figured out years earlier: widespread embitterment doesn't matter. Democracy never works all that well; votes are always diluted to the point of absurdity, like the active ingredients in homeopathic cures. The populace is always disillusioned with politicians. So big whoop. A citizenry that doesn't believe in the legitimacy of its own elections affects neither democracy, nor a sham of a democracy.

Now, Brexit-Schmexit does have likely electoral consequences. Should the Tories own the betrayal, incandescent Leavers could put Jeremy Corbyn's Labour Party in power by default. Lo, a Marxist prime minister might pose a far graver threat to Britain's well-being than

Brexit ever did. To accommodate the dizzying scale of capital flight, maybe they finally build that third runway at Heathrow.

Yet on the ground, this isn't France. Disgruntled voters don't burn cars and smash up Oxford Street. Earlier this year, the comment pages of the Tory *Telegraph* predicted that forsaken Brexiteers would: park in the wrong place; burn driver's licenses; buy yellow jackets; carry placards; cancel their BBC television licenses; pay council tax late (but not withhold it altogether), or even pay the tax in person—in pennies. *Ooh-ooh*.

In all probability, they don't even risk a parking ticket. The British are a biddable people, easily cowed by authority. Roundly deceived, defeated Leavers still pay their taxes on time—no pennies.

"Patrios"

HARPER'S MAGAZINE, 2019

"Nationalism" is rapidly overtaking even "populism" as a foremost political bogeyman. Yet progressives will often still embrace "patriotism."
The elevation of the last term is meant to deflect Trump-style accusations that the Left hates the United States and wishes it ill. Liberals
often maintain that true love of country means calling the nation to its
best self and thus subjecting it to criticism.

Hence for progressives, "nationalism" is bad patriotism, associated
with militancy and racism. The word now suggests a blind, ignorant,
belligerent allegiance, whereas "patriotism" is peaceable, noble, and
clear-eyed. Yet in a dictionary sense, the two words substantially over-
lap. Merriam-Webster defines "patriotism" as "love for or devotion to
one's country" and "nationalism" as "loyalty and devotion to a nation"
and notes that the nouns were once interchangeable. But the reference qualifies that "nationalism" especially entails "exalting one nation
above all others and placing primary emphasis on promotion of its culture and interests as opposed to those of other nations or supranational
groups." A blog entry on the dictionary's website observes, "This exclusionary aspect is not shared by *patriotism*."

While accepting the differences of nuance, I challenge this popular but arguably artificial distinction. Liberals' implicit assumption that their fealty to country is rational, healthy, righteous, and altruistic, while conservatives' fealty is unreasoning, tiny-minded, poisonous, and piggy, is, well, a bit too convenient, isn't it? A bit of a stacked deck.

Assuming that you pledge allegiance to the country where you first popped up in the world, any patriotism on your part is arbitrary. What are the statistical chances that out of 195 countries on earth you just happened to have shown up in the one nation that is objectively the most lovable? Whatever you call it, devotion to country is generally dictated by accident of birth and is therefore a matter of chance. For most native-born inhabitants, love of country is a passive affair, a making the best of present circumstances that would be arduous to change. For the majority, patriotism is an expedience.

Apologies to Merriam-Webster, but, like nationalism, patriotism is also exclusionary. If you don't love your own country *more* than other countries—if you love all countries equally well—that affection shouldn't be called patriotism but humanism, if not multiple personality disorder.

Immigrants and naturalized citizens can claim to be patriots by choice. Yet what commonly governs this choice isn't love but self-interest. For that matter, why are so many of you native-born American readers loyal to the United States and not, say, to Denmark? Because you live in the United States, and what happens there affects you. Patriotism is a form of collective self-interest.

Put aside the MAGA caps and simplistic, historically tainted slogans of the Trump administration for a moment. Don't we expect all American presidents to be nationalists, absent the pugnacious jingoism? Surely we want our leaders to put the interests of our country first, if ideally to pursue enlightened self-interest. Were the interests of all the people in the world considered of equal importance, government would be paralyzed. There would be no standard for weighing one course of action against another.

Thus Barack Obama kept us out of a massive military involvement in Syria not for Syrians' sake but for ours. Falling into another bottomless military sinkhole in the Middle East would have been antithetical to America's interest. What's wrong with Trump is that so much of the time he's *not* acting in our country's interest. He hijacks the language of patriotism for self-promotion. He's not a patriot. The country is a mere vehicle. He loves only himself. Actually, I wonder if he loves anything, including himself.

I'M NO NATIONALIST, AND IF THERE REALLY IS A SUBSTANTIAL SEMANTIC difference between the labels, I've long been a lousy patriot, too. In my youth, like many boomer contemporaries, I disparaged my country up a storm while underaware that my very ability to do so without getting arrested was one of the biggest things the United States had going for it. Ditto my freedom to regard expressions of patriotism as elective. Well into my thirties, I still experienced my nationality as something shameful to apologize for. In what passes for my maturity, I've put that embarrassment to rest. I didn't choose to be born in the United States; everyone has to be from somewhere; there are far worse places to hail from. Loyalty to country needn't imply loyalty to a given government, and I don't hold us Americans alive today responsible for our country's numerous historical sins.

Yet to the extent that I am a patriot, I'm a bigamist. Because I have spent the majority of my adult life as an expat, my sense of allegiance to the States has been unavoidably attenuated. (More the result of accident than design, my London residency exhibits much the same arbitrariness of birthplace.) But one can feel loyal to more than one nation, even if my two loyalties coexist in a state of subtle tension. Peculiarly, I've often been asked if I have a clearer view of the United States from abroad, when I have a clue about my own country these days only because I return annually for long, blissful summers.

I do get a warm, fuzzy feeling upon landing at JFK, and that toasty emotion has grown toastier now that I can whiz through immigration via Global Entry. (I prefer patriotism that doesn't cost anything or, better still, that provides perks.) Bureaucratically, it's relaxing to be "home" in the Robert Frostian sense of where they have to take you in, though it's hard to distinguish this gratitude for being back on American soil from the comforts of sheer familiarity. I'm relieved to blend anonymously in, as I can't quite in Britain. Ironically, only in the United States am I not widely perceived as "an American."

My allegiance to my native and adoptive countries is about equally divided. I care about what happens in both places. I want both countries to thrive. The shortcomings and travails of both countries pain me. Yet I haven't applied for British citizenship. I'm currently obliged to declare my worldwide income to two fiendishly complex tax systems, and the prospect of nailing down this odious dual duty in perpetuity, with no option to simplify the paperwork, is disagreeable. But I've wondered whether a deeper reluctance may be at play. I've been referred to as "an American" for so many decades that maybe I've stopped fighting the designation. If anything, I may be more keenly aware of my nationality than most of my compatriots. Trump's election has not only strained my fealty; it's also stirred the tenderness one feels toward the imperiled. (On learning that the shyster won in 2016, this "lousy patriot" surprised herself. I cried.) British citizenship might feel, if not quite like a betrayal, then at least like a muddying of something that is presently clear-cut.

I've never been directly affected by American military adventures, and my patriotism has never been tested. That may be a leading reason why the loyalty feels so feeble, for patriotism becomes truly noble only when it calls you to personal sacrifice. The sole significant sacrifice that my nationality has ever demanded of me is money—and it's not as if I've volunteered these donations.

More interesting than the dubious, often self-serving distinction between nationalism and patriotism is what exactly, when we're loyal to a country, we're loyal *to*. What is a country? I'm not being glib. The answer to that question is not altogether obvious, and the differences between our answers could also hold the key to the modern conventions governing the usages of "nationalism" and "patriotism."

WHAT IS A COUNTRY? AN ACCUMULATED HISTORY. A CULTURE (WHATEVER that means). A legal framework (up to a point, subject to change). A government (very subject to change). Perhaps a set of values, though what those values are may be up for debate. Obviously, a place. Most importantly, a people.

The *National Review* editor Rich Lowry delivered a talk in July titled "Why America Is Not an Idea" in which he criticized this prevailing cliché as an "over-intellectualized understanding of America." Nonetheless, the United States is unusual among nations in believing itself a concept, although we might vary in how we encapsulate what's less a single idea than a set of multiple principles. I'm especially attached to the deeply American proposition that we should all be free to do what we like so long as we're not hurting anyone else. The fact that American laws violate this tenet at every turn doesn't lessen its appeal. Another vital principle is that anyone can become an American; that our nationality is not (or is no longer) dependent on race, ethnicity, or religion. Who all constitute "the American people" is therefore in eternal flux. As we repeat to ourselves endlessly, we're "a nation of immigrants."

Some of the earliest founders of the country, black Americans were "immigrants" against their will who may have a better excuse than anyone for colonizing this continent. The African American proportion of the population has remained roughly steady at around 11 to 13 percent. Chinese immigration in the nineteenth century was culturally important, but by 1910 America's Chinese population was a statistically modest 0.1 percent, perhaps in part because of the 1882 exclusion act. Horrifyingly, the Native American population is still less than 2 percent. Otherwise, the United States has experienced large waves of immigration from Scotland, Germany, Scandinavia, Italy, Ireland, Poland, and so forth—also known as Europe. Take a step back, and despite the commensurate waves of accompanying stigmatization and prejudice, the American people before about 1970 were far more homogeneous than our melting-pot rhetoric would suggest—not so much tutti-frutti as white chocolate with a slender dark swirl. Since 1970, the population's share of foreign-born immigrants has nearly tripled. Non-Hispanic whites have gone from 83.5 percent of the population to about 60 percent today. Post-1970 arrivals have been overwhelmingly from Latin America and Asia.

The point is that we've gone from faux pluralism to the real thing. One of the many reasons for a building backlash against this fifty-year trend is that the country's white majority is constantly bombarded with "nation of immigrants" propaganda that seems to imply that the United States has always been like this—that nothing has changed. In truth, the nature of "the American people" has profoundly transformed, and we now have to live up to our high-minded notion of ourselves as never before. Putting many millions of people from all over the world with different traditions and beliefs in the same place and expecting them to get along is an experiment that's never been tried anywhere, including in the United States. The vote's still out.

Until very recently in modern Europe, a country has been roughly synonymous with a people. These peoples have had an ethnic component as well as a broad cultural coherence. Germans ate schnitzel, ran to fat, and staged polka festivals. Italians whipped up a mean zabaglione, used their hands when they talked, and relied rather heavily on the Renaissance for a sense of achievement. In an era of mass immigration, Europeans are being asked in short order not merely to be welcoming to strangers but to upend their entire concept of country. In the new order, your countrymen do not necessarily speak your language, profess your religion or for that matter your secularism, share your sense of humor, or have any reason to identify with either the long and often tortured history of your nation or its collective cultural accomplishments. The only thing that makes them "German" or "Italian" is their geographical presence on German or Italian soil.

Europeans are thus being asked within a generation to convert from a European to an American concept of nationhood, but without a history of politically servicing this more absorptive, fluid definition. Most European countries haven't fostered an "idea" of the sort that theoretically unifies Americans. British politicians often talk up "British values," but aside from a vague sense of fair play and a devotion to queueing, most Brits would be hard-pressed to identify what these values are. Only France has a similar idea of itself as committed to liberty, equality, and fraternity, which is why the French state refuses to track the nation's racial and ethnic makeup. Otherwise, in European nations whose citizens aren't apt to get sentimental about their legal systems, the concept of a country seems to be shrinking to a patch on a map.

Hence the rise not only of nationalism but also of usage of the word "nationalism" as a synonym for bigotry. ("Ethnonationalism" in most instances is a more accurate word.) The conflict over immigration in Europe is fundamentally an argument over the concept of country. Lest you dismiss all these prejudiced, closed-minded ethnonationalists as backward-looking and disgusting, it's worth asking whether an Italy that no longer has more than a handful of Italians in that zabaglione sense—a country that, for argument's sake, is abundantly populated by Chinese people eating moo shu pork—really remains "Italy," even if the place—the patch on the map—is still there.

WE NATIVE-BORN AMERICANS NOW HAVE TO PUT OUR GENUINE INCLUSIVE-ness where our mouths are. We have been talking the talk for decades. We've long thought of our people as dynamically various, even if until very recently we weren't nearly as various as we imagined. We're conflicted over what to do when Club USA is oversubscribed, but at least the national narrative can accommodate newcomers in quantity. Europeans historically haven't adopted the same story, making mass immigration far more consequential. Intriguingly, I've had multiple conversations with progressive Americans who have no quarrel with high levels of immigration to the United States, but who express quiet queasiness about substantial, largely Muslim immigration to Europe. They're attached to the idea that Germans eat schnitzel and read Heinrich Böll. These otherwise intelligent progressives are embarrassed by that discomfort. By implication, European nations, which many white Americans still regard as their ancestral homelands, have an obligation to stay the same, like natural history museum dioramas, so that we can visit.

Having deliberately committed to another country, as opposed to lazily acquiescing to fate like the native born, many recent immigrants are especially passionate about their new home and less likely to take its benefits for granted. Yet the very etymology of "patriotism"—from the Greek word *patrios*, meaning "of one's father"—is deeply entwined with lineage. In a world on the move that is increasingly severing the concept of country from a recognizable people, Americans can cling to their national idea for coherence, if not always for cohesion. Most Europeans have no such anchor.

Catholic Latino immigrants in the United States should be able to assimilate into a traditionally Christian country with relative grace, while Asian Americans have been getting with the program with such alacrity that they're beating the white majority at its own economic game. Africans and Middle Easterners migrating to Europe cross a greater cultural chasm.

As Europe's dominant cultures grow increasingly dilute, denunciation of all who want to preserve the original character of their countries as "nationalist," meaning "bigoted," has a truth to it, but not the whole truth. (In Turkey, Hungary, and Poland, the greater problem than nationalism is autocracy.) Country-as-patch-on-the-map doesn't in-spire much fervor. Given the demographics of this century, the con-tinuance of an incoming tide from the Continent's south is probably inevitable. That shouldn't preclude forgiving some Europeans for their sense of loss.

GETTING

THE BLOOD

RUNNING

PART IV

"Ode to the Hacker"

PROSPECT, 2011

From running all winter, I have a hamstring injury. Recent efforts to rehabilitate the muscles have been laced with hysteria. Trying to keep my thigh warm, I wear three pairs of cycling shorts under my jeans all day, and I wear all three pairs to bed. This hysteria has nothing to do with yearning to return to my regular running course along the Thames, mind. No, I have a deadline: 15 June, when I fly to New York for virtually the exclusive purpose of PLAYING TENNIS.

The sport may not quite constitute my reason for living, but it comes close. My father taught me to play. He was a restless, ambitious man who squandered little time on family outings. The exception was tennis. About once a week in summer we'd decamp to nearby courts, where my father's type-A personality eased to the far end of the alphabet. No longer tense, irritable, and distracted, he became patient, graceful, and relaxed—almost languid. So from the start I associated tennis with redemption. Within that charmed rectangle lay an alternative universe where the cares and anxieties beyond its perimeter vanished.

In its rudiments, tennis is sublimely simple, and the uninitiated might reasonably be baffled by what is so compelling about repeatedly batting a pressurized sphere across a divide. Yet manipulating a tennis ball is nefariously subtle and addictively difficult. On a summer's first day of play, I never know if the deadly flick of my wrist on the forehand's follow-through will plague me for half an hour or the whole season.

As a physical experience, tennis is uniquely satisfying. I'd never slander scrambling for a dastardly drop shot with the onerous label "exercise," though finishing three hours of rallying wilted from exhaustion is part of the satisfaction. It's fabulous to be able to thwack anything that hard, over and over, and not get arrested. The twang of the ball on the strings delivers the same percussive gratification of plopping a stone into a pool, popping a fresh pea pod, or snapping together the components of a new computer printer without breaking their plastic tabs.

The game may be as mental as it is physical, but playing it well entails making the brain shut up. At my worst, my head is crowded with imperatives—first and foremost, though you'd think this would go without saying, WATCH THE BALL! Then: *Step into the shot! Hit the ball in front of you! Get your racket back!* But these clamoring edicts are an impediment to obeying them. They so clutter my mind that I might as well have strewn a clatter of gardening tools on the court itself.

Why is having hit the ball correctly thousands of times before never any guarantee of hitting it properly this time? That is the central puzzle of tennis, a mystery on parade at Wimbledon as well as in public parks. Even professionals will abruptly futz a shot they've hit dazzlingly since they were five.

Part of the answer is that there is no "this shot." Any impression of having hit a ball before is an illusion. "Baseline forehand" is a crude umbrella under which cluster a constellation of infinitely various circumstances. Geometrical elements make every shot distinctive: angle, velocity, spin, and bounce. More interestingly, emotional variables equally pertain. How confident do you feel today? Did you lose the last point? Did you lose the last *ten* points? Are you still a little pissed off that your partner showed up fifteen minutes late? Are you focused, or merely telling yourself to focus? That is, are you dwelling fully in the moment, or did you just start debating lamb patties versus haddock for dinner?

For tennis tantalizingly offers perfect inhabitation of the present tense, what drummers call playing "in the pocket." During brief, intoxicating periods of hitting at the top of your game, the mental cacophony quiets, and there's no longer any space between "telling yourself" to do something and doing it. This flow state seems like not thinking. In fact, it is perfect thinking.

Alas, then there's the rest of the time—for me, most of the time. The remainder of any given session comprises varying degrees of disappointment in myself, lending tennis a potentially volatile character. To my chagrin, for years I despoiled many a voluptuous summer afternoon with anything from sullen dyspepsia to full-blown rage. I could grow so disgusted with my ineptitude that I'd begin to lose points on purpose—as punishment for losing the one before.

Were tennis a solo pursuit, temper tantrums would constitute mere existential waste. But one of the charms and challenges of the sport is that it's played with someone else. The bond with that ally-cum-adversary across the net is so particular that Abraham Verghese dedicated an excellent memoir to the relationship: *The Tennis Partner.*

The implicit romance of the tennis partnership is consummated in my sixth novel, *Double Fault*, in which two professional players wed. The woman, Willy, is so heartbroken when her initially less accomplished husband first beats her on the court (on their first anniversary, no less) and later beats her in the rankings that she destroys both loves in her life: her marriage, and tennis. Given my self-destructive emotional history on court, it's pretty easy to infer where I got the idea for the book.

Yet the seminal tennis partner in my own life is not my husband.

I've played for thirty-five years with a man I met in graduate school, S., who doubles as my best friend in America. We do other things together, but tennis, and our mutual passion for it, forms the core of our friendship. (Although S. is a whore, and plays with lots of other people, of whom I am prone to grow jealous.) When S. lost a whole season to a dropped metatarsal, I was so bereaved I might have been limping myself. In kind, S. is keeping tabs on my hamstring. His concern is selfish. I take that as a compliment: he's been looking forward to playing with me. Which is astonishing, considering how ill behaved I often grew in the olden days. S. put up with grumbling, curses, equally scalding periods of total silence, balls thrashed furiously at the fence, and even, when my self-hatred spilled over the net, glares of unqualified loathing.

Inexplicably, a few years ago my rages lifted. These days I am cheerful on court, appreciative of my partner's winners, and *almost* forgiving of my shortcomings. After blowing a sitter, I'm less apt to cuss than laugh. The makeover is befuddling. Though as a fiction writer I capitalize on the conceit that people are capable of transformation, I don't really believe we can be born again. In real life, I find character depressingly constant.

Nevertheless, at least on a tennis court, I have profoundly changed. Every afternoon the sky is clear, S. is free, and we meet by the bike racks in Fort Greene Park I regard as a blessing. If I have a pernicious problem with my forehand follow-through, I will continue to work on it, and exult in the occasions on which my follow-through is smooth. Maybe it's finally got through to me that my remaining summers are terrifyingly few. At fifty-four, I no longer take mobility for granted. In future if it's not my hamstring it will be my Achilles, bursitis, or some scrofulous cancer. I'm actively grateful to still be able to swing a racket, to run full tilt for a deep corner backhand and make it about half the time.

I don't credit myself for this reform. I didn't "work on" my temperament. A tranquil, airy demeanor simply descended on me like a gift.

Perhaps, with that quality of redemption I first identified in my father as a child, the ebullient spirit of tennis itself has finally worked its magic. *Look*, it whispers in my ear over Fort Greene Park in a sweltering July. *The sun is high and hot on your shoulders. The leaves of the maples are rustling. The sock of the ball in the sweet spot resonates deep in your diaphragm. Your feet are light. On breaks, the cold tap water in your rinsed-out Campari bottle tastes better than champagne. Your partner is, in his way, a beloved. When you are finished, deliciously tired, you will sit on your usual bench and talk about your day. This is life, this is good life, this is as good as life can be.*

"London's Unofficial Olympic Sport"

THE ATLANTIC, 2012

Impatient with passivity, you've taken a break from the 2012 Olympics to wend along the Embankment on one of London's "Boris Bikes," a public rental fleet colloquially named for Boris Johnson, the boisterous, flop-haired Conservative mayor who introduced them. Be forewarned: the moment you straddle the chunky frame and broad saddle—the bicycle equivalent of a dray horse—you're no longer a spectator. You've joined the games.

In London, urban cycling is an Olympic sport. Without exception, members of the city's farcically dubbed "cycling community" despise one another, starting with visitors on Boris Bikes—whom local cyclists delight in leaving behind in a muddy splatter. Resident pedal pushers resent that City Hall has squandered civic energies on a fleet for tourists, while many of the sporadic "bike lanes" along London's narrow, parked-up roads still extend no longer than ten feet. Whenever a resource is scarce—in this case, space—Darwinism prevails, and only the fittest survive.

When the Tube shut down following the terrorist attacks of 7/7, many Londoners dragged rusted, flat-tired hulks from the cellar to get to work. Discovering that bikes were faster and cheaper than the priciest public transport in Europe, many of these commuters kept biking. The bicycle has also become the ultimate fashion accessory, furnishing a haughty eco-sanctimony that a handbag simply cannot provide. Officially, the number of the city's cyclists has tripled since I moved here in 1999; by my unofficial estimate, that number has burgeoned by more like a factor of ten. Cyclists accumulate in packs, revving edgily at lights in quantities of twenty to twenty-five, toes twitching on pedals like Formula One drivers' feet on the gas at the starting line.

With the Olympics, the capital's derailleur delirium is bound to intensify. Road closures could set London traffic in concrete, inspiring yet more couch crumpets to clue up to the efficiencies of two wheels. As wide-screen images of Saluki-slim cyclists whipping around the new velodrome in East London strobe every pub, loads of potbellied punters are bound to fancy that they, too, can prance the capital pigeon-toed in clip-in bike shoes. Meanwhile, the streets will coagulate with sluggish, wide-eyed tourists on Boris Bikes.

So newbies to this scene better wise up quick to rule number one here: that submitting to another slender tire ahead of you is an indignity on a par with taking it up the backside with a cricket bat. I've biked dozens of American states and all over Western Europe, and nowhere have I encountered a cycling culture so cutthroat, vicious, reckless, hostile, and violently competitive as London's. In comparison, New York City's cyclists are genteel, pinkie-pointing tea sippers who potter the West Side with parasols demurring, "No, after *you*, dear." Bafflingly, Londoners' adrenal outrage at being stuck behind any other bike is universal. Purple-faced octogenarians on clanking three-speeds, schoolkids with handlebars plastered in Thomas the Tank Engine decals, and gray-suited salarymen on tiny-wheeled fold-up Bromptons alike will *all* risk mid-intersection coronaries to overtake any other bicycle with the temerity to be in front. To stir this frenzied sense of insult, you needn't be slow, either. You need simply be *there*.

Mind, nearly all these wheezing challengers are converts, and converts are zealots. They are not merely people who bicycle; they are Cyclists—an identity so embracing that to overtake is to desecrate their deepest sense of self. (Our most inflammatory scenario: any male being passed by a *girl*, who might as well have brandished a scalpel for curbside castration.) So forget any fraternal nods or offers to lend pumps for punctures. Wary, antagonistic, and insecure, these fanatics never meet one another's eyes, much less do they exchange pleasantries when accumulating side by side.

If motorists find cyclists' self-destructive behavior inexplicable, there's often an obvious reason why, say, fifteen cyclists just veered in front of a bus on Waterloo Bridge: they're trying to get ahead of each other. They're not even thinking about the traffic. Operating in their separate, cog-eat-cog world, Londoners on two wheels forget all about the real enemy: the kind that gets about on four.

Consequently, I've grown reluctantly more sympathetic with the city's drivers, who revile cyclists *almost* as much as cyclists revile each other. During rush hours, clouds of gnats in helmets teem at stoplights, in the unusual instance that they don't run the light in a swarm. Cyclists thread perilously through multilane tailbacks, filling crevices in traffic like grout between tiles. Intent only on passing some wally with bulging panniers up ahead, cyclists veer without warning into outer lanes, absent the merest glance over the shoulder. Capitalizing on clout in numbers, dozens of bikes obstruct cars that have the right-of-way while streaking through the hectic roundabout of Hyde Park Corner. London cyclists think nothing of overtaking another bike stealthily *on the inside* without so much as a ding-a-ling—a formula for collision. They cruise alongside a two-ton lorry right in the trucker's blind spot, and then when the lorry turns left and grinds them predictably into biomass everyone is still supposed to feel sorry for them. The London *Times* has used the city's sixteen cycling fatalities last year to galvanize a safety campaign, but the real wonder is that bodies aren't piling up in gutters by the thousands.

Other longtime veterans in cities abruptly churning with fevered nouveau cyclists will share my dismay. I discovered the bicycle in 1965. Having biked for primary transportation ever since, I've nothing to prove, and just want to get where I'm going, preferably with my head attached. Cycling was once my little secret—a sly eccentricity that explained my uncannily punctual arrival at any appointment. While the great unwashed lavished fortunes on train tickets, car repairs, and taxis, I saved a bundle. I got my exercise, while after a prolonged, miserable journey home the proles had to face the prospect of yet another odious trip to a stuffy, jam-packed gym.

My secret is out.

Were I ever genuinely motivated to cycle in order to save the environment, I'd be joyous that so many of my fellow Londoners have followed in my low-carbon tire tracks. Instead I'm resentful. My territory has been invaded. For me, cycling used to be contemplative, solitary, while lately in London I'm apt to get drafted into an impromptu race to the death with multiple members of my "community" at three a.m. These days, I shove off on even the briefest of rides with dread.

And now, to my horror, a "Summer of Cycling" campaign timed to coincide with the Olympic season aims to *double*—again!—the number of bikes on British roads. Oh, NO! NO, NO, NO! Whereas each cyclist is now encouraged to convert one friend, I actively discourage anyone who considers biking in town: "It's *much* too dangerous," I say. "Breathing all that exhaust, too—*terrible* for you." Trashing cycling with a pannier slung over my shoulder, I get some funny looks.

Worst of all, blogs and call-in radio shows teem with irate British motorists clamoring to license cyclists. Our previous mayor, Ken Livingstone, advocated numbered plates for bikes that could be read by CCTV cameras. An *Evening Standard* columnist recently called for cyclists to carry third-party insurance. The chairman of London's leading minicab firm demanded this spring that cyclists pay a "road tax."

Thus popular momentum gathers to subject bikes to the whole grotesque legal apparatus that makes driving such a downer, thereby undermining the very uncomplicated independence that captivated me about my first banged-up hand-me-down mono-speed as a child. It's already fiendishly difficult in London to slip through a red light with no traffic in sight, since with the explosion of cycling the cops are handing out tickets like girlie-show fliers. When we were merely an occasional annoyance, the authorities paid us no mind. Not long ago, my serene, sneaky, below-the-radar form of transport was an option on that ever-greater rarity of modern life: *getting away with something.* As my pastime has been colonized, its popularity threatens the last redoubt of freedom in this world.

"Your Gym Routine Is Worthless"

UNHERD.COM REVIEW-ESSAY ON ALISON BECHDEL'S
THE SECRET TO SUPERHUMAN STRENGTH, 2021

It seems I have a doppelgänger: a self-described "vigorous type" with a lifelong obsession with exercise, although this minor variation on Shriver happens to be gay. Born three years after me, in 1960, Alison Bechdel grew up in roughly the same America as I did—as she notes, "before the dawn of the exercise epoch." Girls weren't expected to bestir themselves beyond fifteen seconds of jogging in place in gym class, while bulging muscles on females were still considered gross. Nevertheless, Bechdel and I both resolved in our scrawny childhoods to become physically strong. We both invented ball games in the yard with rules of our own devising.

As I learned from her new graphic novel *The Secret to Superhuman Strength*, we both eschew team sports, preferring to compete primarily against ourselves. (Bechdel skis, and though I play tennis instead, I prefer rallying for hours on end to matches.) We were both regarded by schoolmates as mediocre athletes; that is, we were both chosen in the middle of the pack for kickball teams. We both took up running as a lark, beginning with short solo distances—in junior high, I did circuits of the football field while the rest of the class scarfed down miniature pizzas; Bechdel started spontaneously running to visit her grandmother. We both steadily increased this distance, and we both pushed our route to ten miles. Over the course of artistic careers, we've both been as dedicated to working up a sweat in a literal sense as we have been to our exertions on the page.

We've both gone through similar phases: weight training, long-distance cycling. Why, I positively seized on the fact that Bechdel spurns swimming—a difference!—and has got into yoga, which (so far) I've resisted. But over the last fifty years, we've both also been subjected to the larger Western world's gathering fixation on fitness, which has overtaken our meager private labors and crashed over our heads like a thirty-foot breaker. Overwhelmingly, then, what Bechdel and I have most in common is that at nearly the same time we both took a step back from what she calls an accelerating "cardio-pulmonary frenzy" and wrote books about it.

A word from our sponsor: my 2020 novel, *The Motion of the Body Through Space*, regards a woman of sixty who's pursued a rigorous, albeit intensely private, fitness regime since childhood. At the very point that regime has almost entirely destroyed her knees—so much for those ten-mile runs—her sedentary husband announces he's going to run a marathon. When he ramps up to the triathlon, for which he engages a sexy younger trainer, the marriage, to put it mildly, is imperiled. The purpose of my project was to examine what in God's name is propelling this latter-day preoccupation with fitness and whether the trend is a force for ill or good. (Answer: both. Now you needn't buy the book.)

Yet the graphic novel may be an even better form than the straight prose kind for exploring this topic. Illustration brings to life various forms of self-torture, and Bechdel's rendering of her multiple exertions throughout the years is dryly self-parodic. The drawings are stylish as well as entertaining. The narrative moves nicely along. Simultaneously detailing her romantic and career travails, Bechdel's accompanying text is lush enough to parse with some profundity our mysterious exaltation of roundly unproductive suffering. The whole package is presented with more than a soupçon of welcome self-derision. I loved it.

Nevertheless, I confess to some ambivalence about discovering that the powers that be created two of me, just in case something unfortunate happened to the spare. One reason people like Bechdel and me avoid competitive sports is that by nature we're *too* competitive, and so might take conclusive defeat fatally to heart. Thus the rivalrous devil on my shoulder jeered over these pages, "Oh, yeah? You've biked a hundred miles in a day? Well, I've cycled so-called centuries cross-country for months!" I know. Pathetic. Indeed, an aim of both my novel and Bechdel's is to question why we've come to invest so much status in fitness. How come many of us now compare ourselves with others in accordance with who does more repetitions of deltoid dips, even more so than with who earns more money or builds the more dazzling career?

When I started running around the football field at lunch and keeping a secret chart of my daily sit-ups, I imagined that these quirky absorptions were entirely my idea. Now I'm not so sure. Recognizing my double in Alison Bechdel (though she's massively taller than I am, damn her) made me suspect uneasily that there might be other copies of me out there—hundreds, thousands, even millions.

Rare must be the parent who looks up "one thousand most popular names for girls" and exclaims, "Look! 'Olivia' is number one! Let's call our baby the same name everyone else is choosing!" Something more enigmatic and subconscious propels "Olivia" to that top slot. "Olivia" is in the air. It burrows into the brains of parents-to-be from the side like an earwig. Meanwhile, all those parents who christened a daughter "Olivia" last year thought the name was fresh, unusual, and *their idea*.

So with fitness. I think both Bechdel and I were suggestible. The nascent cultural obsession with exercise was already in the air. We were early adopters. But we were still earwigged.

I acknowledge this apparent conformity with no pleasure. Like any proper American, I prefer to regard myself as self-created, not as a predictable product of outside forces, like pasta dough forced through the mold for fusilli. But the amount that Bechdel and I have in common cannot be a coincidence. We started out the same loner, high-achiever type and grew up in the same country at the same time.

In one respect the graphic artist and I may part ways. Strewn throughout *Superhuman Strength* are mini-bios of philosophers and poets: Wordsworth, Coleridge, Ralph Waldo Emerson, Jack Kerouac. These inserts are a little tedious. The bolstering of Bechdel's personal story with historical heavy hitters suggests an insecurity about the worthiness of her theme. Writing my own novel about exercise, I shared that insecurity: Is this topic meaty enough to justify a book? For me, what came to seem important about the subject was making it seem less important.

Despite her playful, self-deprecating approach, Bechdel portrays her churn through multifarious routes to exhaustion as a form of spiritual seeking. By contrast, I've come to see this mystical elevation of exercise as a route to enlightenment as part of the problem—and there is a problem. Obviously, a greater focus on fitness comes with undeniable health benefits, but worship of the hard body is a form of idolatry. Taken to excess, fitness fanaticism naturally nurtures narcissism (the endurance-sport-convert husband in my novel becomes unbearable). What we need is not to go back to being slobs, but to restore a sense of proportion.

Keeping the body in working order is a mechanical matter, one best decoupled from status and virtue. I adore tennis. I happily impute to the sport an element of, yes, spiritual satisfaction—because for me tennis engenders joy in its purest form. By contrast, plain exercise—calisthenics, running when I'm not in the mood (almost always)—is drudgery. Exercise constitutes the dullest part of my day. The fact that I keep doggedly at it is one of the least interesting things about me, and I'd rather talk about almost anything but.

The elevation of fitness to the highest of attainments is a sure sign of a culture grown neurotically inward and stunted. It's a sign of diminished aspirations. When "self-improvement" entails not learning German but doing jumping jacks, we're aiming to clear the lowest of bars. We're not producing superheroes, but gym bunnies. In the end, no matter how much agony we undergo to build our biceps, those perishable muscles will still atrophy in old age and then end up on the scrap heap—at which point, what have we got to show? We could stand to demote the push-up back to the floor where it belongs.

The whole purpose of maintaining a functional body is to be able to do something else: write books, invent new software, land a rover on Mars. Theoretically, Michelangelo could have spent all his time on chin-ups and never have got round to the Sistine Chapel. Alison Bechdel won't be remembered for her running time, but for her exuberant drawings, droll captions, and candid self-reflection. The West's obsession with physical strength, perversely, is a weakness.

Against
the Grain

PART V

"I AM NOT A KOOK"

THE NEW YORK TIMES, 2016

Multiple choice: In the primaries, which 2016 presidential candidate should this voter support?

She opposes hate-crime and hate-speech legislation. She dislikes fat taxes; she does like flat taxes. She regards prohibitions of smoking on beaches, or of using electronic cigarettes in public spaces, as evidentially unsupported and merely vengeful. She believes the federal government has bloated all out of proportion to its original purpose. She sees the federal, state, and local governments commanding 38 percent of the economy as a fundamental infringement on our liberty. She perceives American business as over-regulated, and the United States' levying the third-highest corporation tax in the world as economically idiotic. She resists the welfare state and affirmative action.

Easy. This red-state rube can take her pick. But it gets trickier.

She is also pro-choice and endorses same-sex marriage. She opposes school prayer. She is outraged about abuse of police powers, particularly in black communities. She disapproves of farm subsidies and other congressional backhanders to big business. She abhors widespread state surveillance of Americans' emails and phone calls. She would decriminalize assisted suicide, prostitution, and recreational drug use. She believes anyone should be free to publish visual depictions of Mohammed. While a feminist, she wouldn't restrict pornography, however grossly misogynistic. She is skeptical of foreign military interventions, most of which, during her lifetime, don't seem to have resulted in any real net gain for the United States.

If you guessed Rand Paul, that Kentucky senator may minimally approximate this voter's positions, save for the fact that, as of last week, Rand Paul has left the building. No loss, if for our prototype, as for many American women, Mr. Paul's antiabortion stance crosses a red line. Which it does. For no surprise: "she" is I.

The mainstream of neither the Democratic nor the Republican Party (insofar as it has a mainstream anymore) represents my views, which qualify as left-wing or right-wing only on the basis of "eeny meeny miny moe." During the nine months a year I live in London, I'm regarded as an archconservative nut. When I fly home to the United States, I transform, mid-Atlantic, to a leftist radical—with the same opinions. That's because most of my progressive social positions are taken as the norm in Britain by just about everybody.

The socially liberal economic conservative in America has long been disenfranchised. A true foreign-policy conservative is equally at a loss. Democrats and Republicans vary in their eagerness to undertake foreign military adventures by only a narrow degree. Yet whether it's "leftist" or "rightist," my catechism is consistent. The rubric to which those positions hew—we should be free to do whatever doesn't impinge on the rights of others—forms the conceptual backbone of the United States. The Constitution is *libertarian*. To the extent that the unamended Constitution was flawed, it was more rigorous application of libertarian principles that abolished slavery and granted women's suffrage. Libertarians were way ahead of the pack on decriminalizing homosexuality.

We can at least thank Rand Paul for nominally refurbishing libertarianism so that it is halfway respectable. But the real mystery is why American libertarianism was ever marginalized (and why they marginalized themselves). David Boaz encapsulates the essential idea in last year's *The Libertarian Mind*: "You learn the essence of libertarianism in kindergarten: Don't hit other people, don't take their stuff, and keep your promises."

Yet Chris Christie has declared that libertarianism is "dangerous." Its advocates' going on about property rights strikes communitarians as grabby, selfish, and sordid. Libertarians are caricatured as regarding every man as an island. When I announced to my mother in the 1980s that I considered myself libertarian, she recoiled. How did people like me come to seem like kooks?

THIS DISCUSSION ALWAYS ROUNDS ON HARD CASES. DO PARENTS HAVE A right to not vaccinate their children against measles? (No, and Rand Paul got this issue wrong in his own terms. Vaccine refuseniks infringe on the rights of their neighbors' children.) Individual rights can conflict with collective rights. Coercive legislation to secure clean waterways, breathable air, and sustainable fishing practices seems good and necessary, yet unlibertarian. Climate change is unlikely to be sorted out by the free market. Both governments on brief electoral cycles and companies with shareholders hungry for short-term gains struggle to meet long-term goals.

The hardest case is immigration. Libertarians ought to believe that anyone should be free to live anywhere. But in a crowded, mobile world of grossly disparate opportunities, open borders for wealthier countries are impractical. Little wonder that Rand Paul has championed American border security, not international freedom of movement.

In truth, few self-confessed libertarian candidates are purists. Mr. Paul's support for reclassifying possession of "very small amounts" of controlled substances as a misdemeanor is a far cry from calling for the across-the-board decriminalization that a true libertarian would promote (at his or her political peril). Mr. Paul also backed Social Security—anathema! the state saving for retirement *for* you—because the program is so popular. His advocacy for the "rights of the unborn," which run roughshod over the rights of us women who are already here, is glaringly unlibertarian.

I have my own inconsistencies. I have no problem with seat belt and helmet laws. I support a minimum wage—a higher minimum wage—and laws forbidding racial discrimination in employment. There are simply too many crazy people, and I'm keen on gun control out of sheer self-preservation. Having enjoyed a largely positive experience with Britain's National Health Service, I prefer single-payer health care—though in the United States, I'm not holding my breath.

But then, without allowing for qualifications, any standpoint degenerates from pragmatic guideline to inflexible dogma. As with any other broad political perspective, libertarianism can be a useful starting point, but if you apply it in a strict, quasi-religious manner, you'll indeed get consigned to the crackpot's corner. All viable political positions make room for exceptions—leeriness of foreign interventions need not preclude entering World War II—and contend with What Is. So there's little purpose to libertarians holding out for the elimination of the Federal Reserve or a return to the gold standard, especially since neither of those tired tropes flows inexorably from that core rubric that we should be free to do what doesn't hurt others.

I cannot be the only American repeatedly forced to vote Democratic because the Republican social agenda is retrograde, if not lunatic—at the cost of unwillingly endorsing cumbersome high-tax solutions to this country's problems. My comrades and I don't all sit around reading Ayn Rand novels, either. In fact, the abundance of my natural political bedfellows don't call themselves libertarian—though "socially liberal economic conservative" is a mouthful. We aren't bigots, and we're not evangelical. We are live-and-let-live about sexuality, accept human influence on climate change, and believe in evolution. But we're also concerned about the national debt, oppressed by an arcane, punitive tax code, and unenthusiastic about widespread dependency on the state.

Dismayingly, the more acceptable libertarianism has grown, the less often its principles are applied. Defending the rights of people whose views we abhor has ceded to defending our right to take offense. Municipalities are ban-happy—forbidding anything from lighting up on your own balcony to putting a cookie in your kid's bag lunch to placing a saltshaker on the tables of your local restaurant. The total Code of Federal Regulations is now over 175,000 pages in 238 volumes, with compliance costs of $1.75 trillion. Annually, businesses and individuals spend six billion worker hours on tax paperwork. No one has any idea how many federal crimes are on the statute books; there are anywhere from 4,500 to 300,000.

Confirming Milton Friedman's "tyranny of the status quo," government all too readily expands and all too rarely contracts. Not impersonal abstractions but groups of self-interested individuals, federal, state, and local governments will never willingly release their $6 trillion grip on the American economy. It will be a miracle if we merely stop the usurpation from getting worse.

In the last few decades, this country has grown ever more oriented toward control freakery. Rand Paul was an imperfect counterbalance to this trend, if only because neither he nor his father, Ron, before him had the commanding personal presence to win, and lead from, the White House. Yet I hold out hope for a more formidable successor in the years to come. Voters like me—who believe that environmental quality, health and safety, and security needn't be purchased at the cost of our liberty, and who defend the right to make our own mistakes as a crucial aspect of being human—deserve political representation. We're ornery, and we don't like being told what to do, but we're not kooks.

"Ikea's Real Genius"

THE SPECTATOR, 2018

By all accounts, Ikea's founder, Ingvar Kamprad, was my kind of guy, may he rest in peace (on an Askvoll standard double). Like me, he was a skinflint. For a multibillionaire to buy his clothes at flea markets and select his groceries from supermarket quick-sale shelves is charming. About his retail wares, I'm more ambivalent. Look, hats off to Ingvar for making halfway-attractive furniture available to hoi polloi at afford-able prices. Yet every time I've succumbed to the allure of a cheap-and-cheerful Ikea design, I've ended up hating it.

Part of the problem is the look. Cheap and cheerful is not my bag. I'm more into cheap and morose. In a profile a while ago, a journalist characterized my home as freighted with "grandma furniture." Further, that cut-rate Scandi look is now so recognizable that you might as well leave the Ikea price tags dangling off the chairs. I'd rather my house look uniquely crap than exactly like the comely house next door. But the main reason I've come to hate Ikea-anything is that, sooner or later, it falls apart.

Flat-pack furniture is not meant to last. It's taken me too long to understand that flimsiness is much of its appeal. Because when the door of a cabinet starts to sag off plumb and the laminate is curling on its corner, that means you get to buy another one. So long as they can always find another sucker, manufacturers are obviously motivated to sell products that break or degrade. The best thing that ever happened to cookware companies, for example, was the nonstick surface. A solid set of stainless-steel pots and pans will last a lifetime—and, should you inherit "grandma cookware" from an elderly relative, a lifetime after that. Cast iron can last hundreds of years. Such stunning durability is a commercial catastrophe. You sell one complete set of your line to a pair of newlyweds, and even if they adore your products—or especially then—they never buy your wares again. Retailers don't make money on customer satisfaction. They make money on customer dissatisfaction.

Thus nonstick was a godsend. Regardless of how vociferously it is marketed as heavy duty, it wears out, and it wears out fast. Occasional stainless-steel baking pans are making a reappearance (I suggest you buy them up soon). Stainless steel doesn't rust, requires no special utensils, withstands high heat, and stoically submits to any abrasive cleanser or scouring pad with which you care to assault it. But we have now gone through a good fifteen-to-twenty-year period during which this material virtually disappeared from cookery outlets. Stainless steel is too robust and too practical.

If a corruptible cooking surface makes sense from a capitalist perspective, it would seem to make less sense from a consumer one. After realizing that the calories saved are minimal (since nonstick functions properly only with a little oil), that the savings on elbow grease also decline as the coating flecks off, and that this shedding of you-don't-want-to-know is toxic, if not outright carcinogenic, why haven't more customers rebelled?

Because they *like* having to buy another frying pan. Acquisition has become a standard form of entertainment. Perhaps the best definition of the middle class is people who are grateful to run out of shampoo. Needing a consumer good, a far superior experience to merely wanting it, presents the delightful prospect of both purposive activity and one of the few quests in this life that can almost certainly be fulfilled. Indeed, in an era of mass production and inexpensive imports from China, incessant shopping is a form of amusement widely available even to Westerners on low incomes. It stands to reason, then, that durable products are not merely a catastrophe for manufacturing, but for the people who buy them. Sturdy, well-made objects threaten our well-being. Staunchly refusing to break or decay, they ruin our good time. They are the antishopping.

Take towels. Good-quality towels last for decades. Why do so many people persist in purchasing piles of thin discount towels bound to rip and shred? Given that one set of excellent towels will cost less than an endless parade of sad ones, opting for the latter might seem to be a manifestation of self-destructively short-term thinking. It is not. It represents long-term thinking. Whether consciously or instinctively, the purchase of rubbish towels deliberately plants in a consumer's future the happy occasion of having to replace them.

While customers can generally tell at a glance that Ikea furnishings are not destined to be lifetime investments, much less heirlooms to be handed down, their glaringly temporary nature is a large part of their attraction. You are not stuck with this stuff. You can move house and leave it behind. Even before the flat pack is through the checkout, somewhere in the back of the average Ikea customer's mind is the image of that Jokkmokk pine table clattered in the front garden with a broken leg waiting for the council's bulky waste pickup. Both economically and aesthetically, then, even furniture purchase, once a major commitment, amounts to a small decision, and a provisional one.

All this buying and chucking would seem rather harmless fun, except that Sky News was repeating on its usual infinite loop after Kamprad's death that Ikea now uses a full 1 percent of the world's annual wood production. Writ large, the environmental consequences of acquisition-as-entertainment are substantial.

So give me my "grandma furniture" any day. Our walnut dining table is more than two hundred years old. It has therefore been recy-cled in multiple households. It's hand-hewn and funky, and no one else in London has one just like it. I have owned that table for nearly twenty years, and you'd think I'd have tired of it by now. But something happens when you hold on to things: rather than weary of them, you grow more attached. Not unlike some husbands, come to think of it.

"Our Institutions No Longer Understand What They Are For"

THE SPECTATOR, 2018

[To date, there have been three concerted attempts at my effective "cancel-lation," and it's thanks only to the steadfast support of the people who pub-lish my work that these modern-day lynchings have thus far (touch wood) failed. Clearly, the first was the "cultural appropriation" pile-on after my ad-dress in Brisbane. This column kicked off the second.

On the heels of its publication, I got a call from a woman who'd pre-viously begged me to please, please judge her small-circulation maga-zine's short-story contest; huffily, she informed me that my services would no longer be required, and "you know why." I didn't know why, actually, but I was delighted to get out of the chore. I learned that Twitter had exploded only because I kept receiving emails from friends asking, "Are you all right?" Young authors in a Penguin Random House mentoring program published an indignant open letter addressed to me personally. The Guardian com-ment page commissioned an established fellow fiction writer, who is Asian, to write a broadside eviscerating me as a "knuckle-dragging bigot." Taken out of context, the line about the "gay transgender Caribbean who dropped out of school at seven and powers around town on a mobility scooter" is what rammed an electric cattle prod up the wokester bum—if only for being a little droll—though nothing in that composite is derogatory.

In my following Spectator column, which I'm also including here, I at-tempted to explain myself. By the third mugging in 2021, I had learned my lesson and didn't bother.]

I'd been suffering under the misguided illusion that the purpose of mainstream publishers like Penguin Random House (PRH) was to sell and promote fine writing. A colleague's forwarded email has set me straight.

Sent to a literary agent, presumably this letter was also fired off to the agents of the entire PRH stable. The email cites the publisher's "new company-wide goal": for "**both our new hires and the authors we acquire to reflect UK society by 2025**." (Gotta love that shouty boldface.) "This means we want our authors and new colleagues to reflect the UK population taking into account ethnicity, gender, sexuality, social mobility and disability." The email proudly proclaims that the company has removed "the need for a university degree from nearly all our jobs"—which, if my manuscript were being copyedited and proofread by folks whose university-educated predecessors already exhibited horrifyingly weak grammar and punctuation, I would find alarming.

The accompanying questionnaire for PRH authors is by turns fascinating, comical, and depressing. Gender and ethnicity questions provide the coy "prefer not to say" option, ensuring that being female or Japanese can remain your deep, dark secret. As the old chocolate-or-vanilla sexes have multiplied into Baskin-Robbins, responders to "How would you define your gender?" may tick "Prefer to use my own term." In the pull-down menu under "How would you define your sexual orientation?" "Bi" and "Bisexual" are listed as two completely different answers (what do these publishing worthies imagine "bi" means?). Not subsumed by that mere "gender" enquiry, out of only ten questions, "Do you identify as trans?" merits a whole separate query—for 0.1 percent of the population. (Thus with a staff of about two thousand, PRH will need to hire exactly two.) You can self-classify as disabled, and three sequential questions obviously hope to elicit that you've been as badly educated as humanly possible.

And check out the ethnicity pull-down: "Asian or Asian British" may specify "Indian," "Bangladeshi," "Chinese," or "Pakistan"; the correct adjectival form of the latter nationality seems to be mysteriously unprintable. "Black or Black British" may identify as "Caribbean" or "African." "Mixed" allows for the options "White and Black African," "White and Black Caribbean," and "White and Asian," but any other combo is merely "Mixed: Other." As for us crackers, there's "White: British," "White: Irish," and "White: Gypsy or Irish Traveler," but the rest can tick only "White: Other."

Let's unpack that pull-down. If your office is chocka with Italians, Greeks, Spaniards, Germans, Danes, Finns, Bosnians, Hungarians, Czechs, Russians, Americans, Canadians, Australians, Kiwis, Argentines, Brazilians, Guatemalans, Mexicans, Romanians who aren't travelers, and South African Jews—I could go on—together speaking dozens of languages and bringing to their workplace a richly various historical and cultural legacy, the entire workforce is categorized as "White: Other." Your office is not *diverse*.

I see two issues here. First: diversity, both the word and the concept, has crimped. It serves a strict, narrow agenda that has little or nothing to do with the productive dynamism of living, learning, and working alongside people with widely different upbringings and beliefs. Only particular and, if you will, *privileged* backgrounds count. Which is why Apple's African American diversity tsar, Denise Young Smith, got hammered last October after submitting, "There can be twelve white, blue-eyed, blond men in a room and they're going to be diverse too because they're going to bring a different life experience and life perspective to the conversation." She hadn't bowed to the newly shackled definition of the word, which has now been effectively removed from the language as a general-purpose noun.

Second: Dazzled by this very highest of social goods, many of our institutions no longer understand what they are for. Drunk on virtue, Penguin Random House no longer regards the company's raison d'être as the acquisition and dissemination of good books. Rather, the organization aims to mirror the percentages of minorities in the UK population with statistical precision. Thus from now until 2025, literary excellence will be secondary to ticking all those ethnicity, gender, disability, sexual preference, and crap-education boxes. We can safely infer from that email that if an agent submits a manuscript written by a gay transgender Caribbean who dropped out of school at seven and powers around town on a mobility scooter, it will be published, whether or not said manuscript is an insensible pile of mixed-paper recycling. Good luck with that business model. Publishers may eschew standards, but readers will still have some.

In the news last week, we find the ultimate example of this fatal confusion over what is your actual job. Will Norman, London's "walking and cycling commissioner," bemoaned the fact that too many cyclists in the city are white, male, and middle class. "The real challenge for London cycling," he declared, "is diversity." As opposed to building more cycle lanes for *everybody,* or fixing potholes lethal to *everybody*'s wheel rims, Norman regards his principal function as increasing black and minority ethnic ridership. I'll be fascinated how he accomplishes this noble mission. Will he resort to stereotypes—broadcasting gangsta rap from lampposts alongside cycling superhighways, where pop-up snack stands hand out free chapattis? For a cycling commissioner to define his primary remit as "diversity" is no less ludicrous than for Transport for London to turn a blind eye to the chronic tailbacks along the Embankment, just so long as the requisite number of Koreans is stuck in them.

With rare guts, the softball conservative *New York Times* columnist David Brooks recently decried the "misplaced idolization of diversity." Although a laudable penultimate aim, he wrote, "diversity is a midpoint, not an endpoint. . . . An organization has to be diverse so that different perspectives can serve some end. Diversity for its own sake, without a common telos, is infinitely centrifugal, and leads to social fragmentation." Just as Brooks sees diversity as no substitute for "a common national purpose" in the United States, private and public institutions alike need to keep their eyes on the prize: good books. Safe cycling. For everybody.

"Dear WriteNow"

Dear 2016 WriteNow mentees,

Thanks so much for your open letter to me. It seems only good manners for me to write back.

You're rightly proud of having been admitted to a challenging program at Penguin Random House that mentors gifted young minority authors and helps to cultivate their talents. My own publisher, Harper-Collins, runs a similar program, which enjoys my full support. Such proactive outreach is exactly the approach I endorse for helping to vary the voices on our bookshelves. That is why my column of a fortnight ago said not one discouraging word about WriteNow. Indeed, I made no reference to your program whatsoever.

Apologies to *Spectator* readers, any number of whom have contacted me to express their agreement with my real point, and none of whom seemed confused about that point, or ashamed of themselves for concurring with some bigoted screed. To most subscribers, this column will seem a tortured rehashing of what was perfectly clear the first time. But we live in a dour and censorious age. Perhaps in future it will prove necessary to write every column twice, the original with wit, playfulness, and brio. Then I'll draft a pedantic, leadenly prosaic rendition without any jokes.

To recap: I took specific exception to PRH's declared intention to have both its staff and list of authors mirror the UK population by 2025 in regard to race, ethnicity, class, disability, sexuality, and gender. (As for the latter, the company may have to sack a raft of women, who are vastly overrepresented in editorial.) These demographic proportions are statistically ascertainable. So while PRH may claim that the planned reconfiguration of its workforce and catalog over the next seven years is an "aspiration," the aspiration is to pursue numerical quotas. I do not like diversity quotas, in publishing or anywhere else. They can tempt HR departments to value hitting arithmetic targets over hiring competent workers, and editors to value category-bulking authors over the most exceptional writers from any background.

To the degree that PRH genuinely aims to ply its wares among minority communities with historically few readers, brilliant. That is thinking like a publishing company, whose driving purpose should be expanding its market and selling more books. Nevertheless, the manifestation of a narrow, rigid version of diversity, rather than strong book sales and literary excellence, can too easily become an end in itself. With the relinquishment of judgment abundantly on merit, quality could suffer.

Hitherto, the United Kingdom has not extensively employed positive discrimination, which may still seem innocently benevolent in Britain. But as Coleman Hughes explains in the cover article, the United States has rigorously pursued what we call affirmative action, especially in education, for nearly fifty years. The American experience is cautionary. Even the majority of black Americans don't like it.

Combating injustice with more injustice, and racism with more racism, is philosophically contradictory and pragmatically ham-fisted. In the United States, affirmative action has entrenched racial divisions and pitted minorities against one another. These finger-on-the-scale policies have often benefited the economically well off who happen to tick a racial box. Intrinsically paternalistic, affirmative action has stigmatized and demoralized the very populations it was designed to help. (You observed how hard WriteNow was to get into, and what stringent standards you had to meet. You want to have been selected because you're especially talented, right? Not because you improved a PR statistic.) Though brought in to compensate for historical prejudice, this redress has no end point. It is never over. Bring in affirmative action, and you're stuck with it.

Although still defended by most progressives, affirmative action policies have embittered not only America's white citizenry, but also our large East Asian community, many of whose children have been actively discriminated against in college admissions because they work too hard, excel too much, score too highly on standardized tests, and make too many sacrifices of ordinary teenage pleasures in the interest of career advancement. These applicants have not only been roundly punished, but insulted as well—for the only way that colleges have been able to keep admission numbers down among, say, diligent Chinese and Koreans is to give East Asians systematically low marks on "personality." So maybe they're smart, but they're not nice or interesting people. That racist enough for you?

The suit lodged recently against Harvard University by aggrieved Asian applicants is likely to land in the US Supreme Court, and I wish them success. Mind, the last time affirmative action came under the gavel in DC, the decision hinged on whether the University of Texas was employing quotas—exactly what I object to PRH installing, explicitly or implicitly. Across the board, elite American universities have been accepting roughly the same proportions of each racial category for decades, regardless of variations in rates of application. By stealth, these schools are pursuing quotas, which is unconstitutional, and that's why college admissions offices are more secretive than the CIA.

The gist, then, is that I don't want to see the United Kingdom go down this unfair, antimeritocratic, and culturally destructive road, in either education or commerce. But that's not how you interpreted my last column, is it? And your imputations to that piece were mild in comparison to the shriller hysteria I'm told can be found online. The leap is Olympian: Shriver thinks only white people can write. Shriver wants to protect publishing from the barbarians. Shriver thinks diversity necessarily translates into rubbish books. Shriver is a literary white supremacist.

That column wasn't hard to understand, and I can't imagine your reading comprehension scores are quite that low. So we're dealing with what I can only call malicious misinterpretation. No writer can defend against willful misreading. To the contrary, text entails a contract between authors and readers: authors will endeavor to deliver their message as clearly as possible; in exchange, readers will meet writers halfway, and make an effort—for reading is an effort, which is why it's a decreasingly popular medium in an impatient age—to correctly digest this message, even if in the end some of that audience may still disagree with it.

Outrage being the Left's contemporary drug of choice, addiction levels seem to have got so high that it's not enough to grow indignant about what's actually out there; it's now necessary to make enraging stories up. But I have a hard enough time sticking up for what I actually believe, and actually put in print, without defending against all the things I don't believe, and didn't put in print. I'm afraid this is a textbook instance of what's becoming all too common: an internet mob effectively rewrites your views, the better to attack them. But a world in which you have said, not what you said, but what other people *say* you said, is a world in which savvy people stop writing and shut up. After all, this column—it won't make any difference, will it? The verdict is in.

Tell you what. This is what I *don't* hope for you: that you all have long literary careers, weathering many a struggle, setback, and disappointment along the way, and finally establish yourselves as authors to be reckoned with—only to discover that when you write the word "red" your readers picture aquamarine, and when you write "carrot" your readers conjure a tractor. The result is something between cynicism and bewilderment.

As *Spectator* subscribers may recall, one of my earlier columns described the discouraging experience of having your prose so twisted by its audience that you lose faith in the tools of your trade. In a polarized and broadly illiterate digital universe, full of predators gorging on animosity who are determined to read whatever they wish to, words cease to function. All nuance out the window, the language no longer serves to communicate, and what we writers do for a living is worse than pointless. When others can overwrite our work with whatever they feel like, using our text like a blank screen on which to project their personal PowerPoint presentations, at best tearing scraps of our prose out of context to construct their own gaudy collages, writing anything at all, much less putting truly controversial ideas into the public sphere, becomes too perilous to be worth the risk.

At least you mentees and I do share the same ambition: that in due course, after enough open-mindedness, mutual curiosity, and steady incremental progress, occupations like ours are naturally and effortlessly populated by folks from a wide range of backgrounds. We differ only on how we get there. I wouldn't do it with quotas. Because diversity doesn't lower standards. Quotas do.

Wishing you the best of luck in a damnably difficult job,
Lionel Shriver

"He, She, and It"

PROSPECT, 2016

From childhood, I experienced being female as an imposition. Growing up between two brothers, I was the one who had to wear stupid dresses, and worry about—the ultimate humiliation, in my day—letting my panties show on the swings; even the word "panties" was humiliating. My brothers got to take off their shirts during sultry North Carolina summers, while I wasn't allowed to, even during the years my chest looked just like theirs.

Yet the impositions were just beginning. Periods were hideous. Did my brothers get puffy once a month, suffer terrible backaches, and go back to wearing smelly de facto diapers? I was the one, too, who had the fear of God put in her about getting pregnant. In comparison with their ambitions for their sons, my parents clearly had reduced expectations for my career prospects. Ruefully, at eighty-seven, my father finally conceded last year, "You know, we may have underestimated you." He still hasn't quite brought himself to admit why: I was the girl.

But I was historically fortunate. By the time I entered university in 1974, a revolution was well under way. As I understood it, "women's liberation" meant that the frilly cookie-cutter template of femininity had been chucked out. Being female was no longer defined in terms of hemlines, high heels, and homemaking. Men and women were equal. Both sexes were just people. We had entered the postgender world.

Fast-forward to the present: I was wrong.

We have entered instead an oppressively gendered world, in which identity is more bound up in one's sex than ever before. (Note: until very recently, when the terms became politically loaded, standard dictionary definitions regarded "gender" and "sex" as interchangeable, and I will, too.) As Jemima Lewis wrote in the *Daily Telegraph* in March: "You can be agender, bi-gender, cisgender, demigender, graygender, intergender, genderless, genderqueer or third gender—but by God, you will accept a label." The gay and lesbian world having gone so mainstream as to become a big bore, Western media has moved on to an enthrallment with transgenderism bizarrely out of proportion to the statistical rarity of true gender dysphoria—though children and people generally being so suggestible, the condition is growing much more common. Facebook has extended its gender options beyond the seventy-one it reached a year ago (thrillingly, two options in this dizzying smorgasbord of self-definition are "man" and "woman"). Users are now allowed to infinitely customize their profiles. As the Facebook diversity team published, "Now, if you do not identify with the pre-populated list of gender identities, you are able to add your own. As before, you can add up to 10 gender terms."

Presumably, then, where you lie on this infinitely incrementalized spectrum is a key index of your individuality. For one of the biggest transformations in this exhausting conversation about gender is that it's no longer about fucking. (Sexuality makes for an unsatisfying be-all and end-all anyway. In the face of widespread acceptance, gay culture has grown up: homosexuality no more suffices for an identity than heterosexuality ever has.) Gender is not about what you do, but about what you are.

Yet consider: in order to construct this spectrum, it is necessary first firmly to establish what it means to be "man" and "woman" at the poles. Even if you are "genderqueer"—convinced that your gender identity does not conform to the social norms associated with your sex—alienation from social norms depends on the perpetuation of social norms. Thus if you are a gruff, muscular, assertive woman who has adopted the genderqueer label, girlishness must continue to be associated with garrulousness, weakness, and passivity for your identity to scan.

In short, the spectrum depends on stereotypes.

We are told that a trans woman may have been born a man, but "feels like" a woman. I do not mean to be perverse here, but I have no idea what it "feels like" to be a woman—and I am one. My having happened to be born female has always seemed a biological accident, mere luck (or lack thereof) of the genetic draw. Honestly, being female "feels like" it has nothing to do with me. I respect that some people may feel alienated from their bodies (as I age, I'm as alienated as could be; the "real me" does not have arthritic knees), and I realize I am getting myself into trouble here. Nevertheless, the whole trans movement does seem to have awfully to do with clothes. Especially in the male-to-female direction—and I am baffled why anyone would want to be female with any other option available—"feeling like" a woman seems to imply feeling like wearing mascara, stilettoes, hair extensions, and stockings.

Be my guest. I don't care what anyone wears. But I hate to break it to the converts to my sex: women who were born women schlep around most of the time in jeans and trainers. The version of femininity offered up by Caitlyn Jenner is foreign to me: exaggeratedly coiffed, buffed, and corseted. It's a parody of the female wholly composed of surfaces.

In this would-be enlightened age, in which primary schools hold "transgender days" the way they used to sponsor bake sales, we urge children to see their genders as flexible, and to choose to be boys or girls or something in between. But what does it mean to decide you're a boy or a girl? In presenting this choice, we reverse all that progress on gender-neutral toys, inexorably reinforcing the hoariest, most thread-bare versions of male and female. A boy is rough and boisterous and aggressive and plays with trucks. A girl is soft and quiet and sensitive and plays with dolls. Once again, in some dozen faddish television documentaries I have seen about trans children, it often comes down to clothes. A little boy knows he wants to be a girl because he wants to wear a dress.

In which case, being female doesn't mean very much. And I am willing to go there: maybe being male or female doesn't mean very much. Here is not the place to debate the differences in male and female brains; what matters is that those divergences are greatly exceeded by the differences between individuals within sexes. So I am far more interested in heading in the direction of who-cares-what-gender-you-are than in painfully parsing which kind.

This issue is inextricable from the nature of self. In general, identity comprises a set of external facts and the subjective experience of being. Confusingly, self is both something we are born as and something we make.

In the course of things, we may convert to Catholicism or take up waterskiing, but the externals of our birth we don't get to choose: era, nationality, parentage, parental religion, parental economic class, perceived race and sex. We're free to choose our relationship to these externals—to emphasize them, to despair of them, to embrace or to see ourselves in opposition to them, but we cannot change the facts themselves. Over the course of my career, I could have played up my Tar Heel roots, nursing a drawl and latching on to the role of "southern writer" in the United States; instead I've tended to minimize my upbringing. But even living in the United Kingdom for thirty years can't change the fact that I was born in North Carolina. My having been born female is also a fact, one I pretty much stopped fighting long ago—since I'm not convinced that the alternative is that much of an improvement.

Yet advances in plastic surgery have moved whole columns of what used to be immutable facts about ourselves into the realm of the elective. If you're short, you can have your legs stretched (though I don't recommend it). Big breasts can be reduced. Penises can be lengthened (though I don't recommend that, either). Noses can be reshaped, aging disguised. And sex—well, no problem.

Sex is no longer a fact. It is a choice. Which is all very well, except the conceit that "gender reassignment" surgeons operate under is that a self has a sex. The sexed self can be born into the wrong body, so that in transforming the physical signifiers of sex, doctors make body and self match.

But does the self have a sex? Are men and women male and female in their very souls? Or in reconfiguring the body, are we not primarily tinkering with how other people react to us? Isn't plastic surgery predominantly an act of social manipulation?

As externals of identity like the shape of our ears and even our sex become medically malleable, we seem to be entering an era in which everything about ourselves that we don't like is subject to revision. I may have been born in North Carolina, but I feel like someone born in New York. I may have a father who was a seminary president, but I feel like the daughter of a coal miner. Can I expect my fellows to jolly along with this idea of myself, and inquire after my father the New York coal miner? The transgender reversal of pronouns has a disturbing quality of insisting that the outside world conform to subjective experience. Today's widespread compliance on this point has the quality not only of "virtue signaling," but of a creepy pandering, a condescending complicity. For women who transition to being male, having been born female is a fact, even if it's a fact they're not happy with. In actually changing birth certificates to identify babies as the sex this person came to feel like, we rewrite history. This way lies mass hypnosis—an Orwellian sense of truth. Because sex is not merely a social construct. It is a biological construct.

Self, in the contemporary view, is a construct, full stop. It is no longer made of elements we're stuck with but is wholly a made thing. Thus when comparisons were drawn last year between trans people and Rachel Dolezal, the president of a local chapter of the National Association for the Advancement of Colored People who was masquerading as black because she *felt like* an African American, the parallel didn't require much of a leap (even if most black Americans rejected the comparison). We are, apparently, whoever we think we are. And we are within our rights to demand that our peers get with the program. The emperor always has clothes, if sometimes a dress.

Yet having a few givens from the off is a relief. Life's too short to completely make ourselves up—to decide that rather than the son of a Bristol pharmacist born in 1978 we are the daughter of a nobleman born in nineteenth-century France. The particulars of our circumstances may be limiting, but they save us from wandering the hell of the arbitrary. I have resigned myself to being female, because that's what I was born as, and I'd be loath to have all that horror-show surgery only to discover that men have problems, too.

A tomboy as a kid, I scrabbled in the dirt with my brothers playing with model cars and making toy trains crash spectacularly from a height. I shunned Barbies and detested baby dolls. I reviled dresses, spurning lace and flounces for jeans and flannel shirts. At fifteen, I changed my name from Margaret to Lionel. Were I to have grown up fifty, sixty years later, it's entirely possible that my parents would have taken me to see a therapist and put me on hormone therapy.

I'm glad they didn't. Not because being a woman is so swell, but because being either a woman or a man doesn't matter that much to me. I certainly experience myself as female in relation to other people. But when alone in a room, falling asleep, hiking by myself in the woods, writing at my computer, thinking, I do not experience myself first and foremost as a woman. I do not walk around all day contemplating labia and breasts and ovaries, much less determining to get my nails done or to make an appointment for highlights. For me, my very self has no sex. While obviously I can testify exclusively to my own experience of being a person—to my knowledge, I've been only this one—I cannot imagine that I alone enjoy such a self-perception. If selfhood is real and not merely a neurological illusion, it transcends sex.

More apt to regard their sex as a constraint, women are bound to find that proposition more appealing than men will. Men are often underaware of the restrictions their sex places on them, because those restrictions are fewer. Men are still in control, in case you haven't noticed. (Scan any meeting of world leaders if you're in doubt.) Yet for both sexes, deemphasizing the accident of the X versus Y chromosome is surely a more promising direction in which to head than fixating on which exact point we locate ourselves on a spectrum, itself dependent on hackneyed notions of masculinity and femininity that should have grown outmoded.

I am often asked how I manage to write persuasively from a male character's point of view, which I do frequently. The secret? There is no secret. Writing from a male character's point of view is no more difficult than writing from the perspective of another woman. That's because for all of Facebook's seventy-one genders and counting, the experience of self cannot be all that different. Oh, our characters are different. But the crucial constituents of our characters have little to do with sex, unless we insist on labeling clumps of qualities—forcefulness, violence, inability to cry; tenderness, consideration, inability to drive—as exclusively male and female, which they are not.

While I experience my sex as a physical inconvenience, being female has at least had its upsides. I've been relieved to be spared midlife balding and sexual performance anxiety. As I am otherwise circumstantially fortunate—white, prosperous, American—belonging to one class of humanity that suffers from disadvantage has surely benefited my sense of the world, helping me to sympathize with people in other classes who have it even worse. Most of all, the coin toss of my ending up a woman has meant I got to marry my beguiling husband, a heterosexual who might have looked askance at me as a candidate for his affections had I sported his same equipment.

The very fact that this essay will seem incendiary (and save the con-niption fits; I'm not on social media and never read online comments) is testimony to how gender has grown destructively hypersignificant. We're in the process of taking a giant cultural step backward. The women's liberation movement of my adolescence advocated a release from gender roles, and now we are entrenching them—pigeonholing ourselves with picayune precision on a continuum of gender identity, as if arriving at the right relationship to cliché is tantamount to self-knowledge. But I do not want my epitaph to read, "She was a she." I am a writer, a cook, a sculptor, a tennis player. A big mouth, a hothead, a cutup, and a ham. A woman, yes, there's no denying the fact of it. But that detail is incidental—and way down the list.

"A Monumental Matter"

THE SPECTATOR, 2017

Growing up in Raleigh, North Carolina, I took the monuments around the state capitol for granted. Among the first Confederate soldiers killed in the Civil War, Henry Lawson Wyatt has leaned into the wind on those grounds for one hundred years. Atop a pedestal inscribed TO NORTH CAROLINA WOMEN OF THE CONFEDERACY, a mother in billowing skirts reads to her young boy, his hand on his scabbard. Only in adulthood have I done a double take. I was raised in a slightly weird place.

In an era of fungible Walmarts, regional distinction in the United States is hard to come by, and I treasure Raleigh's funk factor. Yet I didn't grow up around folks who wished the South had won the Civil War and wanted to bring back slavery. For much of my lifetime (OK, North Carolina isn't in a salutary political place in Trump World), cities like Raleigh have had better race relations than many northern ones.

Up against the movement to cleanse the American South of Civil War tributes, aesthetic attachment to regional oddity constitutes a weak argument. I'll make it anyway. These sculptures are curious, interesting, specific to one part of the country, and often better crafted than anything that would replace them. Some are defiant; many others have a mournful cast. They are sobering reminders of a dreadful juncture in American history, and you have to remember a war even to regret it. Junking all these memorials off in some cluttered museum would result in an ineffable atmospheric loss for my complicated hometown.

Yet post-Charlottesville, any reflective discussion of the fate of these relics is regarded overnight as over. Mysteriously, after one unfortunate woman was murdered by a single right-wing malefactor with a driver's license, it's a given that every Confederate monument must come down. Dissension, even ambivalence (like mine), means you're a white supremacist.

Columbus cost indigenous peoples dear. Thomas Jefferson owned slaves. As Oxford University was recently reminded, Cecil Rhodes was an imperialist. Prior to 1960 or so, every celebrated man in the Western world would probably qualify in today's hyperbolic terms as a "misogynist."

We now require those we admire for particular achievements to be blameless in every respect, while the very definition of blamelessness, ever stricter, is a moving target. Applying today's demanding standards of rectitude to previous generations—requiring all past notables to have embraced racial equality, feminism, disability rights, anticolonialism, nonsmoking, and gender fluidity—means pulling down virtually every statue standing. Named after the Duke of York, involved in the slave trade, New York could be in for rebranding.

This campaign is potentially limitless, not to mention antihistorical. More, any drive for ideological purity is hair-raising. Can we have a little more "Let he who is without sin cast the first stone"? This rampage against any regard for ancestors who didn't tick every modern political box has a totalitarian texture, and would leave Americans a sterile public environment with only statues of Eleanor Roosevelt and

Harriet Tubman—until, that is, some eager beaver unearths, say, their insensitive remarks about cross-dressers.

Aside from contributing to a general ambience—a sense of something having happened once, of someone having done, you know, *whatever*—most public statuary functions as outdoor furniture. It's decorative. With signal exceptions (DC's Vietnam memorial), most people ignore monuments, never reading the inscriptions—and the older the statuary, the more oblivious the public. They've no idea who's up on that pedestal, and they don't care; at best, little girls fancy the horses. (Don't imagine that I recalled those two bronzes around Raleigh's capitol. I had to look them up.) The only folks I see study big, dated statues are bored foreign tourists. Consequently, the terrible injury these tributes ostensibly cause a range of minorities feels manufactured.

Thus, while I'm happy for statuary to be "recontextualized" with a contemporary slant, the real effect would be negligible. No one to speak of would read the plaques.

In contrast to the spontaneous, celebrative destruction of homages to Stalin or Saddam in the heat of overthrow, this drive to politically decontaminate public memorials is a cool power contest. The social justice brigade is muscle-flexing. Yet their righteous efforts will have little palpable effect on people's lives. Perhaps the most expedient solution is to "recontextualize" what a monument is: a three-dimensional record of what and whom some predecessors wanted to remember at the time it was erected, rather than a lauding in the present of absolutely everything these figures ever said and did.

Symbolism is important, but purely symbolic gains belong low down the list of vital social reforms, when in the United States, blacks' median income is half that of Asians and two-thirds that of whites. Take a jackhammer to Jefferson's visage on Mount Rushmore, and what have you got? Gesture without substance. Do American progressives really want to confront, "Never mind that we let some cops shoot whomever they like and never serve a day in jail, because we chucked that bronze of Robert E. Lee that you'd never even noticed before"?

Bulldozing statuary long part of a local landscape is gratuitously divisive (people do notice memorials when you smash them). We'll have too little to show for these scuffles once the dust settles. Neither Britain nor the United States needs more discord. This short-of-monumental matter is an elective conflict. Let's pick our battles with care.

"Would You Want London to Be Overrun by Americans like Me?"

THE SPECTATOR, 2021

[OK, here's the third cancellation trip wire. I realize that writing about immigration in any but the most enthusiastic terms is incendiary, but I can't help myself. The point of this piece—which does not regard race—was bound to prove unpopular with certain elements. But my central observation is also true.

Standard theater repeated itself. Twitter erupted with accusations that I was promoting the "Great Replacement" narrative of the French right wing and branded me a Nazi. Companies threatened to withdraw their advertising from The Spectator. A long screed in The Observer—the Sunday Guardian—so maliciously misrepresented my views that The Spectator's editor allowed that it was probably "actionable." But life's too short to squander my time in court.]

The Afghans the Home Office is scrambling to resettle in Britain present one of immigration's most sympathetic cases: translators and other support workers for allied troops whose lives are potentially imperiled by the Taliban's revenge against collaborators. Councils are searching for big, multiply bedroomed properties to rent or repurpose, as fleeing Afghan families can have a dozen members. The Home Secretary has offered to resettle twenty thousand Afghans in due course.

Yet if history serves, we'll soon see many more than twenty thousand Afghans land on British shores, all of whom won't necessarily have worked for NATO and few of whom will wait to be invited. Like those of nearly all immigrants, their stories are bound to be heart-breaking. Surely only a monster would deny such decent yet desperate people "a better life." That's the winning moral reasoning that has currently turned America's southern border into no more than a notional scribble on a map.

In Britain, Migration Watch released two reports this summer whose key findings I will try to present as succinctly and neutrally as possible. In the last twenty years, foreign-born residents of the United Kingdom have doubled to nine million, going from 8 percent to 14 percent of the population. In tandem, the white British proportion of the population has fallen from 89 percent to 79 percent, while ethnic minorities have grown from 10 percent to 21 percent. Since 2001, 84 percent of UK population growth has been due to immigrants and their children, rising to 90 percent since 2017—the majority of these immigrants being from non-EU countries.

Over a third of UK births now involve at least one foreign-born parent; in parts of London, 80 percent of births are to foreign-born mothers. Indeed, non-UK nationals are disproportionately concentrated in British cities. The majorities of London, Slough, Leicester, and Luton have an ethnic-minority background. About half the births in London, Birmingham, Manchester, and Cambridge are to foreign mothers. Unsurprisingly, then, a third of British schoolchildren are already from ethnic minorities; in twenty years, ethnic-minority children will constitute over half the students in state schools. As of 2018, 90 percent of immigrants were under forty-five. That means the ethnic transformation of the United Kingdom, whose white population is far older, is destined rapidly to accelerate.

Even delivering those dry statistics feels dangerous. As for their implications, none of you readers is supposed to care. In particular, white Britons who greet those figures with anything short of delight know perfectly well to keep their traps shut. The lineages of white Britons in their homeland commonly go back hundreds of years. Yet for the country's original inhabitants to confront becoming a minority (circa 2060) with any hint of mournfulness, much less consternation, is now racist and beyond the pale. I submit: that proscription is socially and anthropologically unnatural.

We are a political and territorial species. Although Pollyannas push us to regard ourselves as members of one big happy human family, we compulsively clump into groups. These groups claim territory and, under normal circumstances, defend it. For Westerners to passively accept and even abet incursions by foreigners so massive that the native-born are effectively surrendering their territory without a shot fired is historically extraordinary. I'm hardly commending such an approach, but in times past the inflow of newcomers on such a scale would often have been regarded as a military matter.

This is not all about race. Kenyans resent Somali immigrants. Black South Africans resent Zimbabwean immigrants. Colombians resent Venezuelan immigrants. In 1983, Nigeria expelled over two million migrants, the majority Ghanaians, to the cheers of the native populace. Anywhere, when the proportion of the "other," however they may be defined, crosses a critical and perhaps even quantifiable statistical line, people who were born in a place stop getting excited about all the new ethnic restaurants and start getting pissed off.

With no sense of irony, Mexicans resent the droves of American retirees who settle on their coasts, radically transforming the local culture and nattering along the beach exclusively in English. I'm sympathetic, too. This is normal. Call them "xenophobic" if you will, but most people want to live around people like themselves. Most people are capable of hospitality toward foreigners who arrive in modest numbers, but balk when outsiders become so populous that they seem to be taking over. Most people of any race or religion do not like vast numbers of people entering their territory from elsewhere and making themselves permanently at home. This is not some sick, especially Western meanness. This is what human beings are like all over the world. The blithe welcoming of their own dwindling and loss of dominion now demanded of Western majorities is fundamentally inhuman.

After all, try reversing the paradigm. If white Westerners were immigrating by the tens of millions to developing nations—if Liverpudlians were pouring into Lagos—the Left would decry the mass migration as neocolonialism. Such white flight would be denounced as invasion—as it would be. Yet for today's Left, nonwhite cultures must be protected, preserved, and promoted, while evil European cultures deserve to be subsumed. That version of events is neither fair nor salable.

In the perfect world, it's Pakistan that would have to accept still more millions of disaffected Afghans, after harboring the Taliban for twenty years. Yet plenty of Afghans are likely to make a run for Europe. For now, most Britons will feel magnanimous toward anyone who escapes the joyless oppression of rulers who hate music—although a guilty "we broke it, we buy it" obligation to welcome all comers doesn't pertain; Afghanistan was already broken in 2001.

Many of these refugees will be wonderful people, and all thirty-six million arguably persecuted Afghans could probably qualify for asylum. But in the big picture, along with the native populations of other Western countries, white Britons needn't submissively accept the drastic ethnic and religious transformation of their country as an inevitable fate they're morally required to embrace without a peep of protest. Well over half the residents of your capital city weren't even born in your country—a proportion that continues to climb—and a trace of dismay would seem fitting. I'm one of those foreigners myself, and should London have become majority American, you'd have every right to be irked.

"The Criminalization of Making Money"

NEW CRITERION, 2010

[While I'm walking on the wild side with that last one, why not go whole hog? Even more unacceptable than uttering a discouraging word about immigration is making any money and then grumbling about your tax rate. Yet my accountant was so struck by the spot-on nature of this essay's central point that he forwarded the text to all his colleagues at the firm. At least you're unlikely to read such a confession anywhere else. Voicing even a smidgeon of sympathy for the better off is too self-destructive.

This essay has been revised, so any figures are updated to the most recent I could find as of late 2021.]

It's considered unseemly to discuss one's personal finances in public. But I'm not very polite. Furthermore, while we hear a great deal about the overtly sympathetic travails of the poor, the tribulations of the more prosperous go largely unexpressed. If you earn anything to speak of, you're never supposed to complain. You're to feel fortunate, if not sheepish, and keep your mouth shut. But every once in a while, we might allow the people who disproportionately keep state coffers afloat to share their anxieties. Because that's what earning money in the West has become: an anxiety.

Until my late forties, I earned very little. Although I now realize that the taxes I paid in my younger days were trifling, the bills seemed whopping at the time, and being expected to pay any taxes whatsoever struck me as an injustice. I relate this with chagrin. Yet I suspect this attitude is typical for taxpayers in bottom brackets: *All these other peo-ple make way more money than I do, so taxes should be their problem.* I didn't take government handouts, so I fancied that I covered the cost of my communal existence. In retrospect, I doubt that. At best, I may have covered the wear on the roads from riding my bike and the police time required to issue me tickets for running red lights. My tiny taxes wouldn't have begun to educate the next generation or to build the public libraries I frequented, much less would they have financed any wars or bloated bureaucracies.

On the upside, at least my tax returns were gloriously simple. So long as I'd paid my rent for the month, I was free to think about other things besides money.

Then I had a novel take off commercially. Now, authors don't rake in nearly the royalties that most people imagine. Nevertheless, a while back I enjoyed—though I do not believe that is the right word—a sin-gle windfall year. It seemed that every significantly remunerative event in my life occurred within twelve short months.

Given that this sudden embarrassment of riches was the fruit of a lifetime in fiction writing, the experience of that windfall should have engendered a sense of achievement. Instead, I became choked by a rising dread. Every time another payment came in—for a translation, a film option—I groaned. Moreover, when a payment arrived during the latter part of that year, I no longer regarded it as my money. That's because the government didn't regard it as my money, either.

Having to preface this account with assurances about my keen awareness of how lucky I was is a little tiresome. This ought to go with-out saying, but it probably doesn't. Most writers make next to nothing. If you have any sense, you never become a novelist for the purpose of financial gain. Having even one book earn out, much less show a profit, was a stroke of extraordinary good fortune, for which I don't mean to sound ungrateful. In fact, I've had a wonderful life overall, and the expectation that I make some contribution to the general welfare in return is perfectly reasonable. (I would cheerfully pay Estonia's flat tax of 20 percent to the end of my days. Under the aegis of such a sensible, straightforward, evenhanded regime, I hope I'd have matured from a selfish, petulant stripling into a grown-up who gladly recognizes the individual obligation to chip in to defray social running costs. Alas, "sensible," "straightforward," and "evenhanded" are some of the last adjectives we might apply to most Western tax codes.) Obviously as well, the problems of abruptly having too much money cannot compare with the problems of having too little. After living on a ferociously tight budget for years, I should know.

Nonetheless, I believe my *emotional* experience of that windfall year is politically and economically instructive. I don't remember it fondly. I was fearful; I felt stalked. I felt strangely guilty, as if I'd done something wrong—and I don't think that was due to my Presbyterian upbringing. I felt guilty because the experience of entering a top tax bracket is one of being punished.

Being a low earner had been relaxing. I didn't attract attention. The chances of my being audited were low, because even governments have registered that you can't get blood from a stone. But when my income spiked, I felt as if I were in an African game park in the days when they still were full of lions, and I'd done what the wardens always warn you not to: I'd got out of the car. Suddenly worth more than a gristly mouthful for tax authorities, I was fair game.

Doubling my anxiety: I live most of the year in the United Kingdom, where I also pay taxes—although the United States demands that even nonresident Americans declare their worldwide income to the federal government. The United States is the sole country in the world with such a requirement. (The only nation imposing a kindred system is autocratic Eritrea, which levies a 2 percent tax on expats.) Despite the popularity of the term, for law-abiding Americans there's no such thing as a "tax haven." Even if Americans move to another country with lower tax rates, they are required to pay the shortfall to the feds. The only legal manner in which Americans can shelter any income from the IRS is to renounce their citizenship, often pay a whopping "exit tax," and burn their passports—along with their bridges. Thus I felt hot breath panting from both sides of the Atlantic.

I was a good little camper, and that year I delivered to the American and British governments an enormous proportion of my lifetime earnings. (For writers, America's elimination of income averaging has been disastrous. It's not that unusual to labor on a manuscript for a decade. In the improbable instance that the project is a success, you will be taxed as if you earned the proceeds in a single year.) Once I signed over a six-figure check to the US Treasury, I confess that I was furious. I felt robbed. I felt taken advantage of. In having my ship come in only to have the vessel boarded by pirates from the IRS—for entrepreneurs in America, doing well financially is like sailing the coast of West Africa—I felt like a sucker. These are the feelings that no one in the upper tax brackets will talk about in public. Indeed, I went through an abrupt paradigm shift. When I was skint, I naturally sympathized with other people who were struggling. For the first time, I felt just a teensy bit of sympathy for the rich. If I'm to continue to overshare: the very next year, my income plummeted, and thereafter continued to drop. I am much happier. I am much more relaxed. I'd be even more relaxed if I made less money still.

Unfortunately, I marked myself as governmental prey for life. The IRS casts a suspicious eye on anyone who makes less money this year than the year before, especially a lot less. Indeed, in expecting the self-employed to forfeit not 100 percent but 110 percent of their previous year's liability in estimated taxes, the IRS is eternally optimistic on your account. Apparently the one thing about my returns likely to select them for scrutiny is the alarming contrast between subsequent returns and my windfall year's. In terms of pure safety—protection from bureaucratic and legal harassment—I'd be better off never having got out of my car in the game park.

As both the United States and the United Kingdom rack up soaring national debts, earning any money at all in either country marks you as a target. These are very hungry lions, and the only sure protection against them is to be too scrawny to be worth the bother of hunting down.

Worse, well-deserved public outrage over bank bailouts during the Great Recession—welfare for the superwealthy—and scandals like Bernie Madoff's Ponzi scheme or Fred Goodwin's £700,000 annual reward for almost single-handedly imploding the Royal Bank of Scotland have helped stigmatize wealth itself. The default assumption now runs that all gains are ill gotten. The public seems to have forgotten that not everyone with an appreciable income is a shyster financier—that not everyone accumulates wealth by stealing, obscene over-remuneration, or dodgy wheeler-dealering. We no longer seem to believe that there may still be such a thing as someone who works hard and honestly doing something well. Further, (for now; Biden may revise this) both the British and American governments punish hard work as opposed to passive raking-it-in by taxing earned income far more viciously than capital gains—which is morally perverse. To a greater degree than any other form of income, earned money is fined. Experientially, earning money is a crime.

In Estonia, universal contribution to the nation's communal expenses structurally reinforces social cohesion, as well as giving taxpayers a sense of investment in how wisely their money is spent. But one of the most distressing results of the West's more commonplace "progressive" tax policies is the way that they have divided citizenries into two camps: the takers and the taken. Client citizens look to government to solve problems and to give them money; they get irate when their problems are not solved well or when they're not given *enough* money. To the involuntary patrons on whom the state depends for its very existence, government is overwhelmingly a predator. Government creates problems, and takes money. Politically and culturally, this division is poisonous. Folks at the bottom grow docile, and since no set of services or subsidies is ever sufficient, they get resentful. Having difficulty pointing to many real benefits that accrue to them from their prodigious taxes, higher earners get resentful, too. So polarized, neither camp enjoys any real sense of "community," and everyone is ticked off.

Moreover, client citizens—including public employees and contract workers for the state—never seem to exhibit any consciousness that what they get from "government" is confiscated from their neighbors; that, in a fiscal sense, government is merely a shell company, a clearinghouse. For that matter, since it doesn't generate any wealth itself, "government" as a fiscal entity is a myth: it's the dependent class's imaginary friend. Anyone who suggested that recipients of state largesse should be grateful to their real benefactors—those evil rich people—would be savaged. For the notion that lower-income citizens or public employees should be thankful to the better off is anathema. I certainly felt no trace of gratitude toward high earners when I was hard up. After relinquishing a massive whack of my literary jackpot to people I didn't know, I sure didn't receive any thank-you notes, either. Instead I was left with the impression that *I* should have been grateful—that I had anything left.

The top 1 percent of American taxpayers account for over 40 percent of total US income tax receipts. The top 10 percent pay 71 percent of income taxes, and the top 25 percent pay 87 percent, while the bottom 50 percent account for 3 percent. This disproportion has steadily risen since the mid-1980s. From 2010 onward, on average 44 percent of filers in the United States have paid no income tax, including 43 percent of middle-income earners.

In the United Kingdom, even before the generous subsidies of the COVID era, over half of Britons were dependents on the state. In 2019, nearly half, 43 percent, paid no income tax—a ten-point rise over the previous decade. The top 1 percent of Britons pay over a third of income taxes, a proportion that's doubled since 1990. As of 2017, the top 10 percent of individual income tax payers in Britain—6 percent of the adult population—were responsible for 59 percent of these receipts, while the top 50 percent paid 90 percent. The quip that only the poor pay taxes is sorely out of date.

Yet ever since wealth was demonized by a handful of irresponsible financiers in 2008, the rich have become like smokers: one of those groups to whose defense no one dares to rise. The fact that a single packet of cigarettes in New York City now costs $12.85 sets an ominous precedent: well over half that price is taxes, and nothing stops that pack of twenty Marlboros from costing $100 tomorrow. For "sin taxes" are potentially infinite, and wealth is now a sin. The Tories have reduced the "additional rate" bracket to a hardly negligible 45 percent, but when the last Labour government created a new 50 percent top tax bracket, two-thirds of the British public polled as perfectly happy; it didn't apply to them. Were that number ever to rise to pre-Thatcher levels of 90 percent, most of the British would be vengefully delighted.

By contrast, in the back of their minds even many Americans of the lowliest economic station are convinced that someday they, too, will be rich, which keeps some check on confiscatory tax policies in the United States at the upper end. Nevertheless, the Biden administration's proposed tax hikes on the affluent have met minimal popular resistance. New York City's top state-and-local bracket is now nearly 15 percent; given the clatter of add-ons, affluent New Yorkers are in line to lose closing on two-thirds of their income to taxes. Just for a moment, try to overcome an understandable hostility toward the white truffle and Wagyu beef set and imagine how it might *feel* to have that proportion of your earnings confiscated. Are you purely chuffed that you're able to be of such welcome assistance to others? Or are you perhaps resolved to find a cracking good accountant to reduce the bill, if not instead deciding to move to Florida, which at least has no state income tax, like so many New Yorkers since 2020?

The Western state's accelerating reliance on a precariously narrow tax base creates a society that isn't contributory but patrician. Financing the better part of government through a small minority of the well off is inherently unstable. Should that dependency worsen further, it could prove unsustainable. Golden geese can fly the coop. "Soak the rich" is reliably a vote winner, especially in Britain. But "the rich" do not pull in enough to cover an entire nation's bills. Were congressional Democrats' now-defunct 2021 "billionaires' tax" to have commandeered all $4.1 trillion in the hands of its targets, the proceeds wouldn't even have financed the $6 trillion of increased federal spending that Joe Biden proposed at the onset of his presidency. When the answer to every budget shortfall is once more to stick it to the prosperous, governments lull electorates into believing they can reap all the benefits of a welfare state for free.

In the Continental European model, taxes are exorbitant, but at least the entire citizenry benefits from social services like paid maternity and paternity leave, often of six months to a year; after-school childcare; nursing home care for the elderly; and most conspicuously, health care. Yet the American model, which, with the exception of the National Health Service, Britain's closely resembles, tax policy is largely redistributive: pay more, get nothing. Pay-*even*-more-still-get-nothing eventually pushes the sleepiest and most biddable of the well heeled to rebel. The drive to cheat or simply to leave becomes overpowering. Little wonder that Western leaders have mounted a sustained effort to shut down offshore tax havens, to ensure that there is nowhere to go.

It's always assumed that greedy rich people will keep toiling away even if they keep only ten cents on the dollar, because they're so grasping that they'll do anything for so much as a dime. Thus high tax rates do not discourage productivity or entrepreneurship. I think that assumption is open to question, and not only in the top tax bracket.

Take a look at what's been happening in both the United States and the United Kingdom when you get old and infirm. The state will pick up the tab for nursing home care, but only if you've failed to save for your retirement years yourself—that is, only if you're destitute. If you've worked all your life and put together a reasonable pension, bought your own home and paid off your mortgage, *and* paid hefty taxes in the meantime, you're expected to exhaust nearly all your assets, including selling your home and spending down the proceeds. *Then* the state will pay your nursing home fees, and not before. Since full-time private nursing home care can run to over $100,000 per year in both countries, this expense easily depletes a lifetime's savings. So what is the point? Why not spend it all, or earn nothing to begin with, when the results in old age are the same?

Most of all, this "the greedy will keep working for peanuts" theory doesn't take into account the emotional experience of losing half or more of what you earn. In a fiscal environment of state voracity, earning money instills not satisfaction but fear. In a cultural environment in which wealth is suspect and is assumed to have been acquired through shady means, high earners feel criminalized—a sensation bolstered by a punitive tax regime. Nobody likes to be taken. When you put in long hours year after year only to have the proceeds of your labor donated to strangers, you feel like a chump. On top of that, nobody thanks you.

To the contrary, politicians' rhetoric suggests that your earnings are theirs to begin with, and they will let you have some of it back but only if you're very good. We're often told that to repair the national finances the wealthy have to do "their fair share." On the contrary: the wealthy have to do their *unfair* share.

Inured to those "progressive" tax regimes, Western publics routinely overlook the fact that for some able-bodied workers to pay 10 to 20 percent of their income to the state—or nothing at all—and for others to pay 50 percent doesn't, on the face of it, represent any commonsense version of justice. Then again, for a president or prime minister to get on television and announce that it was time for the well off once again to do "their unfair share" wouldn't sound so great on the nightly news.

Even with a moderate income, I am disinclined to accept journalistic assignments unless I'm intent on putting a point across. I won't accept a job for the money alone. Why should I hunch over my computer all day, when nearly half the fee goes to somebody else? In fact, since I have a childish streak, for me, high tax rates inspire spite: no, I won't accept that assignment—I don't feel like it. What I feel like is baking an apple cake. And never mind spite; a disinclination to work hard for little in return is perfectly rational.

With that polite coyness that attends private fiscal matters, we don't hear this very often, but surely earning money should be a pleasure. Why, it's an underrated pleasure, one inherently more gratifying than going on a spending spree. Monetary reward means you've done something that other people value. Yet in a predatory tax environment, we've taken all the fun out of that direct deposit. Is this in the larger social interest?

While governments design ever more top-heavy tax policy to justify yawning deficits, they fortify a giant moral hazard. Low income is rewarded. If you're poor in America, medical care is free, and you'll be taken care of in your old age for nothing. Higher income is penalized, and not only with punitive tax rates but with paperwork: printed out, my US federal tax returns would stack an inch thick. I'm obliged to hire accountants, whose fees amount to more taxes. Indeed, escaping the burden of filing multiple returns, paying two sets of estimated taxes, and conforming to the complex, conflicting tax codes of two different countries with two different tax years—none of that my idea of a good time—may be the prospect that most tempts me to leave the United Kingdom.

For this isn't purely about economics. It's about politics. When a vast proportion of your earnings is appropriated, you're not free. When you live in fear—of the IRS or Vladimir Putin, it doesn't matter— you're not free. When your time is colonized by mind-numbing, mandatory paperwork, you're not free.

Clearly, losing a job or a home to foreclosure is incomparably more anguishing than preyed-upon prosperity. I can't emphasize enough: don't for a moment imagine that I write this out of self-pity. Anyone relatively secure in parlous times is lucky (and all times are parlous, really). Yet the negative emotions I experienced during that one windfall year—from paranoia to suppressed fury—cannot be exclusive to me. Writ large, the feelings I've described demoralize a country's productive citizens and enervate its economy. Resentment, especially the kind you're not allowed to express in public, motivates cheating. It drives the wealthy to lobby politicians for exceptions, which is a leading reason tax codes are such a hash. Earning money out on the veldt— within sniffing distance of the rapacious lions of the state—is joyless. These days, the less I make, the happier I am. The more I make, the more I feel frightened, helpless, humiliated, and stupid.

"Quote-Unquote"

THE WALL STREET JOURNAL, 2008

[This is the full version of what, to my consternation, The Wall Street Journal commissioned and then chopped down to a stump. Lo, another opportunity to right past wrongs. This essay is an "interrogation," as we say now, of the tiniest of flicks on the page, and picayune minutiae call for examinations of picayune thoroughness in return.]

To put it mildly, literature is not very popular. According to the National Endowment for the Arts, nearly half of Americans do not read books at all. Those who do average six a year. Young people aged fifteen to twenty-four—readers of the future—now devote less than 3 percent of their leisure time to reading for pleasure. The review sections on which my own hoity-toity literary fiction depends for exposure are contracting; overnight this summer, the distinguished *Los Angeles Times* book section disappeared.

In comparison with jouncing about the internet or lounging in front of the set, reading seems to demand an onerous degree of concentration. So you'd think that these days literary writers would be bending over backward to ingratiate themselves—to make their work maximally accessible, straightforward, and inviting. But no.

Perhaps no single emblem better epitomizes the perversity of my colleagues than the lowly quotation mark. While the use of quotes to distinguish speech is still standard in English-language fiction, undemarcated dialogue has steadily achieved the status of an established style. In fact, this is one of those stealthy trends that no one confronts directly—much as I noticed suddenly one winter that everyone had started tying scarves by doubling them over and tucking the tails through the loop. Who passed a new law about scarf-tying? In kind, some rogue must have issued a memo, "Psst! Cool writers don't use quotes in dialogue anymore" to authors as disparate as Junot Díaz, James Frey, Evan S. Connell, J. M. Coetzee, Ward Just, Kent Haruf, Nadine Gordimer, José Saramago, Dale Peck, James Salter, Louis Begley, and William T. Vollmann. Although lately enjoying a vogue, the elision of quotes is not exactly new. Cormac McCarthy has nixed quotes since *Suttree* (1979), as did E. L. Doctorow in *Ragtime* back in 1975.

Despite the don't-mention-the-war quality of this practice, when I solicited opinions on the matter from a few dozen agents, editors, critics, and writers on both sides of the Atlantic, a torrent of vociferous, conflicting views poured in. Apparently quoteless dialogue is not only my private pet peeve.

Though typing quotation marks when my characters speak aloud is now a conscious choice, I have always opted to use them. The principal reason is simple: fiction without quotation marks is harder to read.

Petty? Perhaps more small than petty, and indicative of a larger attitude problem among fiction's elite. For by putting the onus on the reader to determine which lines are spoken and which are not, the quoteless fad feeds the widespread conviction that popular fiction is fun while literature is arduous. A reputation for being "difficult" is as off-putting for a book as for a person. Surely what should distinguish literature isn't that it's hard but that it's *good*. Optimally, then, the text should be as easy to process as possible, saving the readers' effort for exercising imagination and keeping track of the plot—assuming that there is one.

As a rule, readers are suspicious of formatting gimmicks, and they quickly tire of special effects (as special effects go, too, ditching quotation marks is pretty lame). They don't fancy window dressing; they want to know what's in the store. Sure, you can write without quotes. And without periods or capital letters. In *JPod* (2006), Douglas Coupland can publish page upon page of prime numbers—but that and a host of other stunts help to explain why I recently threw the book away. W. G. Sebald wrote *Austerlitz* (2001) with no paragraphs, but the result is so daunting that I've never been able to start it. (*Austerlitz* is like a sixteen-ounce steak without a knife.) This summer's rerelease of B. S. Johnson's *The Unfortunates* (1969) is beautifully packaged—a "book in a box" with twenty-seven separately bound chapters that can be read in any order the reader likes—but after a bemused shuffle most consumers are bound to slip it back onto the shelf. The impotent razzmatazz in Jonathan Safran Foer's *Extremely Loud and Incredibly Close* (2005)—single-line pages, photographs of mating turtles, text marked up with hand-written red pen—simply helps illustrate that the sad little graphic tricks available to fiction cannot compete with the pyrotechnic tools of cinema.

What effect is the quoteless format meant to achieve? Ideally, a seamlessness, a smoothness, a minimalism that lends text a subtlety and sophistication. Given that Cormac McCarthy may be most responsible for popularizing the custom, let's examine a passage from *No Country for Old Men* (2005):

> You could head south to the river.
> Yeah. You could.
> Less open ground.
> Less aint none.
> He turned, still holding the handkerchief to his forehead. No cloud cover in sight.

To be generous: The absence of quotation marks may intensify the gruffness of the exchange. Punctuation errors may also imply the lack of formal education typical of his characters. Perhaps the dialogue is all the more swallowed by a vast western expanse, in which human utterances amount to mere tufts of sagebrush. As the novelist Tracy Chevalier observes, McCarthy's technique "blends his characters' thoughts and words with the landscape—which is what his books are about."

Yet take the same passage with quotes added:

> "You could head south to the river."
>
> "Yeah. You could."
>
> "Less open ground."
>
> "Less ain't none."
>
> He turned, still holding the handkerchief to his forehead. "No cloud cover in sight."

Is that landscape any less vast? Honestly, what do we lose when we insert those quotes? To McCarthy's credit, he has at least carved out his own style, which other writers have aped. Yet it is hard to imagine that his often riveting, atmospheric novels would be of any lower literary quality with proper punctuation.

Proponents of quotelessness argue that the practice pays aesthetic dividends. Eschewing quotes herself, the British novelist Julie Myerson fancies "the cleanness of these letters and words without any little black marks flying around above them." The book critic John Freeman believes that no-quote dialogue "lends everyday speech a formal elegance. . . . With McCarthy and [Peter] Carey, the lack of quotation marks gives the story a forward momentum and elemental fury—it's as if their voices are rising out of something so instinctual it can't be put between quotation marks." Having chucked the quotes in his 2008 novel, *Willing*, Scott Spencer declares with the zeal of the convert, "Once you do without them, they look ridiculous. I wonder if I will ever use them in my serious writing again."

Scott is a friend of mine, so I say this in all affection: when it is employed traditionally, the prospect of any punctuation mark looking "ridiculous" is itself ridiculous. One might as well find the comma ridiculous, the semicolon, or page numbers.

Besides, is the style always "elegant"? From Susan Minot's *Evening* (1998):

> But you see I've just been at dinner—he glanced over his shoulder, then
> lurched forward—in Boston with my great old friends—the Beegins—and
> I've only just heard of your mother's—he pressed his chin into his chest—
> misfortune and wanted to pay my respects.

All those dashes simply replace one form of clutter with another. In kind, Roddy Doyle (like James Joyce) employs the French convention of denoting speech with em dashes; the style is at least clear, though seems less superior than merely different. Kate Grenville and Jonathan Safran Foer have sometimes opted for italics. (In *Child 44* [2008], Tom Rob Smith distinguishes dialogue with both dashes and italics, in a disconcerting overkill of alternativeness.) The italics convention lends dialogue *a curiously forceful, emphatic sensation* while still keeping speech pent up, inside, barely audible.

For that is the overwhelming effect of the no-quote style: quietness. The novelist Laura Lippman complains, "I can't help feeling everyone is muttering." Fair enough, when lines are murmured, the emotions expressed seem soft. But lines like these from Susanna Moore's *The Big Girls* (2007) look peculiar:

> Just what is it that you're not getting? he shouted. Your son has been
> molested. [and]
> Is this what you're like with LizAnn? I heard myself scream.

We don't hear any shouting; no one screams. Reading heated dialogue without quotes is like watching chase scenes in *The Bourne Supremacy* with the sound off. It's a tad perplexing why fiction writers would gag their own characters for the sake of typographical cleanliness. The effect is not only quiet but muffled. Speech does not quite happen.

The refusal to make a firm distinction between speech and interior reflection can also evoke a hermetic worldview—sealed up and sealed off. Explaining why she writes without quotes, Ms. Myerson asserts, "In my experience of the world, there are no marks separating out what I think and what I say, or what other people do." (With all due respect, there is indeed a sharp dividing line between thinking and saying something, and whenever I forget that crucial social distinction I get myself into trouble.) Yet when the exterior is put on a par with the interior, *everything becomes interior*. What is conveyed is an insidious solipsism. Characters grow less particular, seeming mere variant extensions of a dominant central consciousness. When thinking, speaking, and describing all blend together, the textual tone levels to a drone. The drama seems to be melting.

Why does this impression matter? The appearance of authorial self-involvement in much modern literary fiction puts off what might otherwise constitute a larger audience. By stifling the action of speech, by burying characters' verbal conflicts within a blurred, all-encompassing übervoice, the author does not seem to believe in action—and many readers are already frustrated with literary fiction's paucity of plot. When dialogue makes no sound, the only character who really gets to talk is the writer.

The new tidiness also produces nuts-and-bolts problems. Stage direction is often put on hold, lest it be confused with chat. To designate conversation, speaker identification can grow incessant. In quotation-marked dialogue, "he said" and "she said" are picked up almost subconsciously, and so rarely grow trying. Absent quotes, one is more apt to read-read the IDs, which therefore become monotonous, as in Ali Smith's *The Accidental* (2005):

What person? her mother says.
In the house, Astrid says.

No idea, her mother says. Is Michael still here?

Uh huh, Astrid says.

Is Magnus up? her mother says.

Don't think so, Astrid says.

Yet it is the issue of clarity on which the enemies of quoteless dialogue universally round. Even no-quote convert Scott Spencer specifically conditions the choice on there being no confusion over what is spoken and who is speaking. Skillful writers like Spencer or Tim Winton can pull off the "look, Mom—no hands!" Others are less adept. From Miranda July's *No One Belongs Here More Than You* (2007):

I was actually just standing there in love. I was not even really standing, if she had walked away suddenly, I would have fallen.

I wouldn't do it, never mind.

You sound disappointed.

On examination, those last two lines are dialogue. On first reading, "I wouldn't do it, never mind" is easily confused with reflection, an assurance that the narrator wouldn't literally fall.

Reading dialogue without quotation marks is like driving without signposts. A tired or impatient reader will easily get lost. For that reason HarperCollins editor Gail Winston assured me that "any 'impossible for the reader to figure out' situation leaves me cold." London's Portobello Books publisher Philip Gwyn Jones is currently making an offer for a demanding novel that he described as doubly laborious to comprehend because the author has eschewed quotation marks. Thus the offer is conditional on their restoration—"It rarely being the case that confusion by grammar is a meaningful or legitimate purpose. It is very rare, in my experience, that their absence improves a book or enhances its literary value."

So a word of warning for aspirant writers. Certainly my queries turned up plenty of open-mindedness on this issue in publishing—from Ecco editor Dan Halpern, for example, or Gary Fisketjon at Random House. Farrar, Straus and Giroux publisher Jonathan Galassi comments liberally, "I have no prejudices about it, but I do notice, and try to make sense of why this is happening. Usually there *is* a reason." But those who give the quoteless author the benefit of the doubt are in the minority.

Two-to-one in my unscientific poll, editors, agents, critics, and established authors bristled at no-quote dialogue as affected, confusing, imitative, and gratuitous. Their most recurrent adjective was "annoying." Bloomsbury editor Helen Garnons-Williams explained, "Dialogue without speech marks crops up an awful lot in novels I turn down at the moment. Young, aspiring writers seem to believe they are making a statement with their choice of punctuation and 'trying to shake things up,' and this can elicit something of a weary sigh." For critic Carlin Romano, "Dropping the quotation marks is the prose equivalent of declaring, 'My car has no windows, but I can drive it anyway.' Yes, dummy, you can, but there's a reason they invented windows."

Signally, not one interviewee asserted anything along the lines of, "When I see quotation marks in a manuscript, I assume the author is a fuddy-duddy, and I immediately pitch it in the bin." Playing with mechanical conventions can appear diversionary and risks seeming insecure—as if the author is worried that written in standard form the dialogue might not scan. At least writers who use quotation marks take responsibility for crafting lines that a given character might plausibly say, and in this sense the conventional, not the experimental, is brave. Besides, quotelessness is no longer experimental. It's old hat. Want your first novel published? It's safer to keep those quotes.

More crucially for the commercial viability of literary fiction, in my casual vox-popping the responses of ordinary readers to the quote-free fashion were, without prompting, fierce, immediate, and hostile. A sampling: "I fluctuate between being irritated and enraged." "It's like hearing someone speak through plexiglass." Half a dozen times I no sooner raised the issue than a friend or neighbor exploded, "Oh, I *hate* that!" By contrast, I've yet to hear any reader despair, "This would have been a great book, if it weren't for all those pesky quotation marks!"

Surely most readers would happily forgo "elegance" for demarcation that makes it easier to figure out who's saying what when their eyelids are drooping during the last few pages before lights-out. Commercial and genre fiction writers almost always use quotes. It's not because they're crass. They want to sell books. Big on action, they would never adopt a convention that promotes the impression that when their characters talk no one is quite saying anything. To the degree that this device contributes to the broader popular perception that "literature" is pretentious, faddish, vague, eventless, effortful, and suffocatingly interior, quotation marks may not be quite as tiny as they appear on the page.

"Lionel Shriver Is Grateful for Pandemic Quarantine (No She Isn't)"

LOS ANGELES TIMES, 2020

[During the first pandemic lockdowns of 2020, newspapers were bloated with filler features in which artists delineated how they were spending their suddenly copious free time. Almost universally, these accounts of reading The Tin Drum *in the original German came across as not only pompous but suspect. So when the Los Angeles Times approached me to submit a lockdown diary, I filed the following, which is not quite what the paper bargained for. In the editor's defense, however, he was delighted.]*

Tuesday, 14 April 2020

Jeff and I arise at dawn, so we can sit out back and watch the sunrise. London is so much more peaceful when no one is doing anything unnecessarily productive in it. The clear sky is undisturbed by planes full of folks who didn't need to go places after all. Now that our neighbors believe that COVID-19 lives on fur, they keep their cats inside. So our garden is full of birds, and I can skip my daily ritual of retrieving all the corpses.

"You know, I'm glad for the lockdown," I say reflectively. "All this opportunity for contemplation and solitude. And the social solidarity is so uplifting."

"Yes," Jeff says. "Social solidarity is a lot easier when you don't see anybody."

I return to *Remembrance of Things Past*, because during this becalming stasis it makes sense to read a book in which nothing happens. Jeff picks thoughtfully at the sitar he ordered on Amazon. I've always wanted to read Proust, Jeff has always wanted to learn the sitar, and thanks to the British government we can fulfill our dreams.

I head to the Tesco Metro covered in "PPE" (gotta dig all our hip new lingo). Thanks to silent, wary social-distance queuing with the fellow Londoners whom I've learned to spurn as leaky vessels of lethal contagion, a fifteen-minute trip now takes two hours. Again I relish the extended meditation and chance for inner wisdom. Lately I really know myself, right? So it hardly matters that I don't know anyone else.

Jeff and I take a lingering online tour of the British Museum, gawking at big chunks of rock that have endured, stoic and implacable, for thousands of years. Their defiant inertia seems to be telling us something. *They're* not going anywhere. So what's our problem?

At dinner I remark beamingly, "I'm pleased we agreed not to drink during this period of enlightenment and cultural enrichment. The mental clarity is so refreshing."

This evening, I read Pushkin aloud in Russian. Jeff doesn't speak Russian, but he gets so caught up in the rolling rhythms of the poems that he is moved to tears. I am so moved that he is moved that I cry, too. Then Jeff is moved that I am moved that he is moved, and the sofa gets terribly wet. We have tender tantric sex, because we've never been this close. Cheers, Boris Johnson.

(I lied. We got up at noon. I read the *Telegraph*, *The New York Times*, and *The Spectator*, then maniacally worked on my new manuscript, the only fiction I can stand to read. We watched the *Channel 4 News*, *Newsnight*, Sky News, *PBS NewsHour*, and one more car-crash presidential press briefing on CNN. We killed a second bottle of wine. We made a fumbling stab at sex, but Jeff was too drunk.)

We stream *Swan Lake* at the Royal Opera House and a host of improving documentaries. We take turns singing karaoke to *Madame Butterfly*. Jeff starts *Moby-Dick*, because the whole human race is also engaged in a noble, death-defying battle with Mother Nature. Disinclined to despoil his enjoyment, I neglect to point out which of these parties usually wins.

"I confess," I ruminate at dinner, "I was peevish at first that my new novel will be released into a black hole, with no bookstores or promotional events. But maybe next month's publication date is another lucky break. Isn't *selling* one's work a little grubby?"

"It's a defilement," Jeff agrees readily, with a sense of excitement.

"An audience for any true work of art," I say with a returning excitement, "is also a defilement. Surely there's a *purity* to a novel that no one reads. Reading is a kind of contamination—or appropriation."

"I feel the same way about jazz," Jeff says vigorously. "When anyone listens to me drum, they interfere with the music. If clubbers pay a cover charge, the relationship is transactional. The music becomes about money—in a way, it *becomes* money. I'm so relieved that, on the other side of this, all the venues will be bankrupt and replaced with pawnshops and off-track betting. That way I can play all by myself, like a real pro."

I pat my husband's thigh with a touch of condescension. "Oh, honey. You're right about how fortunate you are to be shed of a viable occupation. But 'on the other side of this'? Who said anything about another side?"

I take my 2020 appointments diary to bed and put big, joyous black Xs through "Reviewers' Dinner," "Book Launch," "Solo Spectator event at Emmanuel Centre," "Swiss Festival," "Ely Festival," "Bath Festival," "Dublin Festival," and "Hay Festival," and then let Jeff do the honors on his own account. He strikes through "JW tour of Portugal" and "JW tour for 'Bloom' with Carmen Staaf and Michael Formanek" with a zestful flourish.

(OK, the Xs are real. Otherwise, I lied. We got up at two p.m. We watched Knower's video "The Government Knows When You Masturbate" three times. We devoured five episodes each of *Ramsay's Kitchen Nightmares* and *Come Dine with Me*. We streamed *Who Wants to Be a Millionaire?* and then watched *Quiz*, which, being about *Who Wants to Be a Millionaire?*, gave us the cozy Russian-doll feeling of *Gogglebox*: watching people on TV who are watching TV. I can't believe Jeff has already polished off that tequila.)

THURSDAY

Jeff and I divide up the parts of Ibsen's *An Enemy of the People* and perform the script aloud. I decide it's time I learned Greek. I learn Greek. Then I learn to play the violin. It takes a few minutes but within the hour I can get through the Prokofiev Violin Concerto No. 2 at a good pace. Jeff is doing an online course on Indonesian cooking. I take up watercolors. Then I knit bright woolen masks for the National Health Service.

At eight p.m. we lean out our front windows and bang pots with wooden spoons to express our gratitude for NHS staff. We feel a warm glow of conformity. The dented pots are ruined, but that's all right because banging out the window makes so much difference to what happens.

I've been managing emotionally but today I'm anxious. Britain's "three-week" lockdown is closing on four weeks. How will the government keep us safe? Worried, after destroying our cookware, we turn on the news. Dominic Raab announces that the lockdown will last three more weeks.

"Thank God!" I gasp.

"It was super important he didn't even hint when we're going to 'exit,'" Jeff says appreciatively. "The British are a dim and impulsive people, and at even the word 'exit' they'd all rush into the street and start licking each other."

"Back to carving Italian marble?" I propose.

(Not quite. We woke at dusk, which Jeff used as an excuse to crack open the cognac. I carped that he really shouldn't start drinking before we've had our "morning" coffee. Jeff got belligerent and broke the snifter, then tried to blame me for it. We both refused to sweep up the glass. I grabbed the bottle for rewatching Kenneth Clark's *Civilisation*—while we still had one.)

Lionel Shriver's new novel, The Motion of the Body Through Space, *is out in May. Please don't despoil it by ordering a copy.*

End Papers

PART VI

"In Defense of Death"

POPULATION AND DEVELOPMENT REVIEW, 2010

[Although I explored the financially ruinous consequences of the American health care system in my ninth novel, So Much for That, I returned to the interrelated topics of death and money in my most recent novel of 2021, Should We Stay or Should We Go. In the United States, the Affordable Care Act is failing to stem the relentless rise in the proportion of GDP swallowed by medical care—about 18 percent as of 2019. In the United Kingdom, 40 percent of the government's budget goes to the National Health Service, while the proportion of GDP spent on the service since 1950 has doubled. All the issues I raised in this essay remain pressing. If anything, since this piece was published they've grown more so.]

For some years now, when watching exuberant television news packages on some dazzling medical innovation—say, bionic limbs for amputees that can be manipulated by thought alone—I've experienced a queasy double take. I think: "How much does this astonishing technology *cost?*"—a minor detail upbeat newscasters reliably omit. I think: "Doesn't this technology's per capita price tag limit its beneficiaries to a tiny handful of the well insured in the developed world?"

Most Americans would consider such nay-saying churlish. High-tech medical advances are an unquestioned virtue, a sacrosanct moral good. We may prevaricate about being short of cash, but we don't slam the door on a volunteer collecting donations for cancer research because we don't *want* more money poured into cancer cures—although next time, after reading Daniel Callahan's brass-tacks analysis of what ails American health care, I might slam the door at that.

A distinguished biomedical ethicist and president emeritus of the Hastings Center, Callahan completed *Taming the Beloved Beast* just as health care reform was coming to a boil in Congress, but before a finalized bill narrowly passed this spring. Fortunately for the author, his book does indeed address itself to the nature of the pale, incremental measures in "Obamacare." Unfortunately for the American people, his warnings about the real inflationary drivers of unsustainably escalating medical bills are as germane as ever.

One of the only elements of the Affordable Care Act designed to control costs relies on the knee-jerk American default, commercial competition—hence the creation of state "exchanges" designed to pit health insurance companies against each other in offering fair value for money. Callahan assembles conflicting data to conclude that for health care competition will not keep down costs, though he might have saved himself the trouble by visiting his local supermarket.

Commerce is not only competitive but collusive. Last year, the standard size of a can of tuna fish shrank to five from six ounces (not long ago, that was seven) for the same price. This shrinkage occurred across all national brands—StarKist, Chicken of the Sea, Bumble Bee, you name it—and all at once. Not a single mainstream manufacturer skipped the retooling costs and undercut its rivals by maintaining the larger size. (Cannily, so to speak, the smaller product is no longer quite large enough for one decent sandwich, which now requires opening two.) In kind, the universally inflated cost of American breakfast cereals has risen in suspiciously perfect unison, bearing no relation to the price of comparable products abroad; Weetabix in the United Kingdom costs half the price of American Shredded Wheat (aptly, the same goes for the cost of British health care). Helping to explain why plane tickets from multiple airlines to the same destination are often identical to the penny, informal, unactionable price fixing defies standard capitalist theory. Rather than competing to offer the best deal, whole industries act in mutually beneficial concert: you raise your price, we'll raise ours, and everybody (aside from the consumer) wins. Having colluded for years in exactly this fashion, health insurance companies are currently raising premiums with all the fine-tuned coordination of an orchestral performance of Mahler's Ninth. Little wonder that competition has historically failed to rein in medical bills.

Yet even the wicked health insurance industry is victimized by what Callahan identifies as the prime single driver of rising medical costs: those very dazzling medical inventions that we have enshrined in the United States as a sacrosanct moral good. Nearly half the cost escalation of medical care is due to spending on technology.

Overuse of expensive imaging equipment, for example, is economically irresistible. Excessive testing helps protect physicians from malpractice suits. More crucially, the fee-for-service model ensures that more tests make everyone more money: hospitals and doctors, sometimes keen to make a gizmo earn back its stiff sticker price, as well as the medical device manufacturers that often buy doctors' lunches. Health insurance fee structures and Medicare reimbursement schedules guarantee that MRIs are vastly more remunerative than consultations.

High-tech specialists in surgery or oncology can earn many times more than hands-on general practitioners, who provide the unglamorous primary and preventive care in desperately short supply in the United States. Indeed, Callahan makes the case that by converting medicine from a calling into an industry, we have signed our economic death warrant. It is in the interest of doctors, hospitals, medical researchers, medical appliance manufacturers, and pharmaceutical companies for health care to be as expensive as possible, and more and more expensive it duly is. Worse, the industry as a whole has no interest in making Americans healthier, but rather an interest in convincing increasing numbers of well Americans that they are sick. Though the United States spent only 7 percent of its GDP on health care in 1970, it lavished 17 percent on same in 2009. With simply keeping the population alive and biologically functional on course to consuming a *third* of GDP by 2040, it's surely not far-fetched to suggest that health care costs have the capacity to single-handedly bury the American economy. They are well on their way to becoming the American economy.

Yet all this expenditure is not even buying us a sense of physical well-being. Dr. Arthur Barsky's study *Worried Sick: Our Troubled Quest for Wellness* documents that people now feel worse about their health than forty years ago, although by objective criteria their health is better. The lesson seems to run that you can't be healthy enough, and that the quest for perfect medical reassurance boomerangs into anxiety.

Callahan's finest observations aren't economic and systemic, but cultural, even existential. Since our increasingly secular people are losing faith in pearly gates, we will pay any price to delay oblivion. The virtue of extending life expectancy goes as unquestioned as the virtue of the technologies that facilitate it.

The developed world's oft-cited "aging population" is the result of two factors, one of which, high postwar fertility suddenly dropping below replacement rate, has lately been the sporadic target of (usually ineffective) pronatalist government policy. Hence the hefty payments to new parents in countries like South Korea and Australia. But the second contributing factor, ever-extending life expectancy, is blithely accepted as the inevitable, inexorable, and altogether marvelous march of progress. We don't see legislation offering to pay people to die sooner. Politicians never campaign to rescind National Institutes of Health grants for research on lethal diseases of the elderly. To the contrary, we're meant to greet the revelation that up to half of today's American babies will make it to age one hundred as unalloyed good news.

As Callahan observes, death is no longer regarded as a natural constituent of the life cycle; it is an enemy, and enemies must be defeated. I would go further and submit that in contemporary America dying has become an outrage. Death is a technological failure whose solution isn't mature spiritual resignation but know-how. ("Some 34 percent of Americans believe that medicine can cure any illness if they have access to the most advanced technology and treatment," notes Callahan, a conviction he describes as "preposterous.") What *Beloved Beast* dubs the "infinity model" of health care entices us with the notion that mortality can be indefinitely forestalled and that life expectancy can be indefinitely extended, a prospect that subscribers to *Population and Development Review* have every reason to view with horror.

Alas, for many patients we don't extend life but drag out death, as wrenchingly illustrated in this June's number one most emailed essay by Katy Butler in *The New York Times Magazine*, "What Broke My Father's Heart"—about an accomplished father whose pacemaker, installed when he was eighty, kept the poor man technically alive through a long, burdensome, and humiliating dementia and bedridden incontinence. Be careful what you wish for. Indeed, many of the real-life results of "life-extending technologies" have all the ghastly, perverse consequences of the seemingly innocent wishes granted in W. W. Jacobs's macabre short story "The Monkey's Paw."

Callahan offers a range of solutions. Given the author's advanced years, some qualify admirably as admission against interest: Stop spending so much money on old people; weight the health care dollar toward primary and preventive medicine for the young and middle aged. ("A health care system should help young people to become old, but not to help the old to become even older.") Focus research on emerging threats like childhood obesity, in preference to squandering vast resources on frail elderly patients with multiple diseases who have already enjoyed what the author terms "a full life." Introduce cost considerations to Medicare, along with Medicaid currently on track to consume a stunning 21 percent of US GDP by 2050. Conceive a regulatory body along the lines of the United Kingdom's much-maligned National Institute for Health and Clinical Excellence (incongruously abbreviated NICE), which could disallow entitlement funding for treatments not determined cost effective. Reject fee-for-service and put physicians on salary. Return to a medical model that treats injury and disease, not dissatisfaction—thus relegating redress of infertility, erectile dysfunction, and gender reassignment, for example, to elective procedures that the disgruntled are obliged to finance on their own dime. On a popular level: resign ourselves that some physical discomfort comes with the territory for us animals; recognize that medicine cannot ameliorate our every ache and pain. Accept that with aging comes deterioration, which mountain-biking baby boomers will have especial difficulty accommodating.

"Curing disease," Callahan observes bluntly, "does not cure death." But curing disease and delaying death is expensive, since when you cure one illness another will come along to take its place. A major driver of the 10 percent annual increase in medical spending for the last forty years is progress with cancer, whose survivors either fall prey to a costly recurrence or yet another ailment. (The best explanation I've ever heard for the rise of cancer in Western populations is that "you have to die of something." We've cured enough of its competitors that cancer is one of the few fatal illnesses left.) Meanwhile, we reap diminishing returns, "achieving ever higher costs for ever smaller health gains."

The political likelihood of these prescriptions being filled is minute. To bring about most of those structural reforms, the United States would require the very national health care system that Congress signally refused to consider from the get-go in 2009. Moreover, it's one thing to make broad cultural recommendations like "We die; get used to it," quite another to manifest them. Culture by its nature is deep and intractable, going to the very heart of what people most profoundly think and feel. Americans believe in technology with the ferocity of religious faith. Access to high-tech medicine is a right, and the more the better. Moreover, technology is expected constantly to improve; hence the resistance to any policy that would seem to hamper the hallowed medical "innovation."

Yet I have made my own tiny contribution to incrementally shifting American culture in these respects. Fiction writing may be a feeble vehicle through which to influence my country; nevertheless, *Taming the Beloved Beast*, while full of wisdom, is also dry, repetitive, and woe-

fully lacking in flesh-and-blood cases that might have brought medical
dilemmas to life. My ninth novel is not as statistically trenchant, but
it's much more fun.

So Much for That is about people on the receiving end of "the beloved beast," whose hot breath is pretty rank up close. My protagonist,
Shep Knacker, has saved all his life for a retreat to a more tranquil,
simpler existence in the developing world, where his dollars would
stretch much further than in New York. Yet Shep is obliged to relinquish his idyllic so-called Afterlife when his wife announces she
has just been diagnosed with mesothelioma. Going back to work as
a peon in the company he founded, if only to keep his health insurance, my friend Shep watches his substantial savings steadily eroded
by all the extras and "out of network" care that his insurance doesn't
cover. Alternate chapters begin with his latest investment account
statement, whose diminution of funds is intentionally sickening.
(Eventually dwindling to less than a month's rent, that Merrill Lynch
account is one of the book's main characters.) Yet from the start we're
aware that Shep's wife is expected to live little more than a year, a
grim prognosis that exorbitant surgery and chemotherapy never manage to budge.

What a drag! This is entertainment? Yet as with many of my
novels, I conceived the ending first, and wrote toward this one with
gleeful enthusiasm. Out of exasperation and a newly discovered self-
empowerment, Shep finally defies his culture's edicts about What People Do and the medical establishment's bullying takeover of the most
intimate event in life, second only to birth: death. I'm loath to spoil
my own story, of course, but the climax entails a multiple kidnapping
from the clutches of modern medicine, and I've been pleased to gather
from readers that the up-yours ending is convincingly triumphant. In a
gesture of sweeping authorial benevolence, I give each character what
he or she needs, which in more than one instance is a gentle, meaningful departure from this earth, without being hog-tied with tubes or
drugged into a vacant stupor. Surely it's a formal achievement for any

novelist to kill off that many sympathetic characters and still pull off a happy ending.

My motivations for designing such a plot were cheerfully political. On the road to publicize the novel this spring, I made it my mission to hawk not merely literary fiction but an even less salable product: mortality. Covering one of my book festival events, the *Sydney Morning Herald* characterized me harshly in its headline as "Pro-Death Author Lionel Shriver" and I was not offended; I was pleased. Besides, I've not been promoting just any old death, but the *good death*, in an era when Western culture has ceased to believe there's such a thing.

One version of a "good death," of course, is a quick one, so folks who get run over by buses are fortunate in their way. Yet many other deaths would be mercifully rapid if we weren't so insistent on our horribly imperfect, horribly expensive, and horribly temporary cures. Hooked to IVs and ventilators and chemotherapy bags, whose very presence seems to promise reprieve (why else would doctors deploy them?), moribund patients are cheated—emotionally and personally cheated, denied the full inhabitation of their last and potentially most profound experience. Unlike many novelists, I know, just a bit, what I'm talking about.

So Much for That grew out of losing one of my closest and dearest friends, Terri Gelenian-Wood, who was diagnosed with peritoneal mesothelioma in 2005 when she was only fifty. Doubtless caused by exposure to asbestos in materials with which she worked in her early years as a metalsmith, the cancer must have been gestating for up to thirty years; mesothelioma is hopelessly advanced by the time it's detected. She lived a year and three months thereafter, most of that time in pain or at least, that beloved medical euphemism, in "discomfort." Little of that suffering was due to the disease itself; rather, to recuperation from major surgery and the host of awful side effects from chemotherapy. She died anyway. Her treatments cost $2 million.

But the cheat in this case was not simply Terri's failing to get her money's worth. A woman with a ferocious will, she bought into the "battle against cancer" lingo wholesale, perceiving death as capitulation, failure, and personal defeat. Until the last few moments of her life, when in her husband's arms she finally asked him haltingly to "help her die," Terri was determined throughout her illness that she was going to pull through. Though she was a rational, well-educated person, she still fell implicitly into that third of the American population that believes the "preposterous" notion that there is nothing medicine can't cure with a can-do attitude and good enough insurance.

It's worth noting that in the United Kingdom Terri would have been given palliative care alone—which might have shortened her life by three months or so, months dreadful enough that I wonder if she'd have missed them. NICE is not as hesitant as NewYork-Presbyterian to label an illness "incurable," which peritoneal mesothelioma most certainly is, and the Brits figure that, if you can't cure it, you don't try. I wonder if Terri would have been better off, spiritually and psychologically, in London. For all those treatments and their empty promise of remission serviced her denial. As a consequence, she and I never spoke to one another frankly about what we'd meant to each other; worse, our latter exchanges were contaminated by a big lie. She and her husband never enjoyed those exchanges, either—never discussed what his life would be like without her, never addressed any remaining conflicts between them while there was still time. But the person most cheated by this deceit that she was getting better was Terri herself. She never plunged into the deep, reflective internal reckoning that I imagine is the primary advantage of a terminal illness over getting run over by that bus.

Somewhere, Daniel Callahan's abstract, holistic analysis and my friend Terri's small personal story meet. I'm no Pollyanna regarding the power of individuals to solve big, systemic problems. But this neurotic health care overspend, whose escalation shows no sign of slackening, is so threatening to American life—to the sustainability of our entitlement programs and the solvency of our government; to the ability of companies to hire American workers, whose costly health insurance drives employment overseas; to the economies writ small of families across the nation, with a policy for a family of four now averaging nearly $15,000 [as of November 2021, an employer-provided family health insurance plan cost the worker and employer more than $22,000 per year], with all manner of co-pays and deductibles on top—that surely we need to work on this dysfunction at both the political and individual ends.

My biggest concern about the passage of Congress's limp Band-Aid fix of the Affordable Care Act is that we may not return to this headache for decades. Americans cannot assume that just because that one bill passed we have now addressed the health care crisis in this country. That bill does little to contain costs. Costs are the nugget.

I'm not holding my breath for this, but politicians sooner or later will have to start telling Americans things they don't want to hear. It may be "ageist" to deny certain treatments to people just because they're eighty-five, but Daniel Callahan is right: octogenarians have had their day. Having yet another day, and not a very fun day at that, comes expressly at the price of rudimentary medical care for younger people. Financed with taxes from those very younger people, Medicare will have to start weighing costs as a factor in the provision of treatments, which the program is currently forbidden from considering. We have to publicly repudiate the sentimental notion that "you can't put a dollar value on human life," since no expenditure can be infinite in a finite fiscal world. We have to accept that some form of health care rationing is not just what those evil, Godless Europeans get up to, but a sensible, practical apportioning of a limited pie. And that pie has to be kept to a reasonable size. We don't want to get to the point in this country where the only thing we produce is ourselves. (Throughout the Great Recession's economic doldrums, where have American jobs still been abundantly available? At medical device manufacturers and pharmaceutical companies. The very morning I'm putting the finishing touches on this essay, the front page of *The New York Times* profiles a man who succeeded in getting a small business loan from Sam's Club in order to buy a second truck. What is his trade? Delivering emergency equipment to hospitals whose MRI and CT scan machines have broken. He plans to add a third and fourth truck. Business is booming.)

Still, if the problem is as much culture as politics, cultures comprise individuals, so individuals can make a collective difference. Living wills are a start. For his own part, Callahan vows, "I believe I have an obligation at our moment in history, and at my stage of life (age 79), to make use of as little expensive technology as possible, using only that technology that will do me significant good and not just add a few more months of life. I therefore resist heavy diagnostic screening to turn up asymptomatic problems, and no less resist follow-up treatment of the low-probability, 'better safe than sorry' variety."

Me, I have sturdy genes, and I keep reasonably disciplined health habits. I avail myself of very little health care—an eye exam; stitches for an embarrassingly middle-class injury from ineptly removing an avocado stone—and so belong to the half of the American population that consumes a mere 3 percent of the costs. (Five percent of the population consumes 50 percent of the costs; the top 1 percent consumes 22 percent of the costs.) [All these figures have remained constant as of late 2021.] My resolve on these matters has not been tested. Nevertheless, I feel no great desire to live to one hundred. Not from political conviction, but because, having been spoiled by good health my whole life, I'm a big baby. Were I unable to play tennis, cycle, or even think straight, I don't see the point. Granted, one grows readier to accept less when the alternative is nothing, so as I age I hope to hew to the same modest commitment that Daniel Callahan has made: to go gracefully, and cheaply, once I have lived the "full life" that, in truth, I have lived already. Let's hope that when the time comes I've the courage and humility to put your money where my mouth is.

Calamities arrive, of course, well before one hundred. As it happens, I also trained in metalsmithing during the same period that my friend Terri did, and I worked with many of the same asbestos-laced products. The fact that those deadly fibers could have lodged in my own abdomen is not a possibility that I take very seriously; I don't want to. Be that as it may, and you can call this a vanity, but in my mind's eye, delivered a diagnosis of peritoneal mesothelioma? I buy two or three cases of extravagant cabernet, host a big party, and book for Switzerland. Keep the two mil, buy yourselves a little something, but don't spend it all in one place.

"I Was Poor, but I Was Happy"

THE GUARDIAN, 2014

In the United States, we're sufficiently consumed by the concept of happiness that the right to its pursuit is enshrined in the Declaration of Independence. But what is happiness? I fear that for too many people the word conjures "a condition of ceaseless ecstasy and perfect self-actualization (whatever that is) experienced by nearly everyone but me."

When we conceive of happiness as a static state, effectively a place toward which we are aimed but at which most of us will never feel we've quite arrived, then the vision becomes exclusionary. Before us lies Alice's tantalizing garden, and we're too gangling to fit through the door. Happiness-as-mythic-Valhalla cultivates envy and disgruntlement. The suspicion grows that everyone else is in on some secret that eludes us, that everyone else is sipping cocktails at a party to which we're not invited, that everyone else is having a fabulous time while our life sucks.

But maybe the solution to this sense of being shut out is to shift the paradigm—to reconceive what happiness means. What if contentment isn't a state, a place, an emotional location that so many of us will never feel we've reached? What if instead this process of trying to get there, this trudging toward the distant light, this often frustrated battling from Point A to Point B, only to find that Point B is fraught with just as much travail and turmoil and sorrow as A, so we have to keep slogging toward Point C . . . What if that whole ceaseless cycle of exertion and exasperation, of failure, of try-try-and-try-again, *is* happiness?

I spent twelve years in the literary wilderness as a nobody, with a horribly high likelihood of getting nobodier. But a manuscript under way always gave me something to do. I had a sense of purpose. I knew what I wanted, which may have been more important than getting it.

Furthermore, I belonged to a tennis club back then, and tennis acts as an example in miniature here, as it meets all the requirements for bliss: it's hard. I am mediocre. Thus on court I always have a sense of purpose, and I am never confused about what I want: to get better. I will never *arrive* and possess a perfected game like a trophy. A higher level eternally beckons, just as I will eternally remain a hack. Brilliant.

Add the magic ingredient: during those struggling years, I fell properly in love at last. A raft of asymmetric romances with disastrous boyfriends beforehand didn't count, because you experience real love only when the feeling is roughly reciprocal. Stepping back, I might prefer career catastrophe with a hand to hold to a lonely success.

In sum, I was engaged with my work. I had a complex relationship to my environs (I adored Belfast; the town also drove me crazy). My emotional life may have been turbulent, but at least I *had* an emotional life. If I got mostly bad news, I did get news—which dangled the possibility of felicitous news in due course. I was making an effort, which must be a more considerable aspect of the kind of happiness I'm talking about than whether the effort pays off. The fact that my fortunes on the fiction front have now improved does not, I hope, excessively color my retrospective assessment that all those setbacks took place over some of the happiest years of my life.

The inert vision of happiness—as a location, a veritably geographic end point, a private promised land that you attain, maintain, and defend—is the real enemy here. We tend to generate a hazy impression of contentment as an island resort where we wiggle our toes in the pool and sip piña coladas. But what is there to do, amid such suffocating repose?

I associate happiness with energy, with direction, with being interested—whether that's interest in figuring out what happens next in chapter 11, in reading an article about conflicting research on the economic effects of immigration, or in deciding how much to increase the allspice in a Yotam Ottolenghi recipe.

I associate happiness with having a plan. The Plan, mind, doesn't have to be grand, like "Write one thousand pages in three weeks" or "Save the world." It can be, "Find out if Lidl is still selling shelled pistachios" or "Please get around to replacing the water filter in the cellar this afternoon, you idiot." Happiness isn't a position. It's a trajectory.

Surely happiness needn't imply singing, laughing, and leaping the livelong day. In the big picture, I've been most gratified by taking on difficult projects that often involved unpleasantness. In my twenties, I took several long-distance cycling trips, during which I got rained on, I got cold, I got hot, I got worn out, and I couldn't always find shelter overnight. During five months on the road in western Europe, I enjoyed a tailwind for all of two days. Yet these journeys were satisfying for the very reason that they were arduous. Climbing Alpine slopes in first gear wasn't always fun, but broadly speaking it made me happy.

Taking on challenging projects is not only a prescription for writers or sports enthusiasts. Difficult undertakings that can "often involve unpleasantness" include raising children, staying married, holding down a job, supporting friends having hard luck, and caring for elderly parents. None of these commitments is a location, a point. Each is a trajectory, a purpose. The rewards of pursuing such purposes determinedly and well are what most people must summon for comfort on their deathbeds.

A passive, static version of happiness—one that puts the statement "I am happy" on a par with "I am in France"—implicitly casts the contented as smug, placid, and self-congratulatory. They don't do anything or go anywhere, since they're already where everyone else wants to be. So if happiness is a place, a little club that admits a select few, then its members are unbearable, with spreading bald spots from patting themselves on the head.

Granted, single highlights in my life have triggered flashes of that classic outsize joy, which shoots through your veins like a narcotic: winning an award, say. But the euphoria fostered by glad tidings is staggeringly brief. You're usually treated to those few short minutes of exhilaration only because the peak experience represents a larger achievement that may have required years of work. Single injections of great news can raise your tolerance, too; it will take a higher dosage of good fortune to get off next time. You'll never string together enough of these lotto wins to make a life. Dependence on infusions of pure elation turns you into an emotional crackhead.

More a continuous affair, happiness isn't getting something, but wanting something. It's having appetite, being filled with desire. It's being pointed in a direction. It's caring about something, which means the condition always comes with the threat of disappointment, injury, or loss. As giving a toss about anything or anyone makes you a sitting duck, happiness is intrinsically precarious; it entails putting yourself at risk. It has nothing to do with feeling pompously, fatuously puffed up over your wonderful self and your wonderful life. It's being too driven, too busy, too focused on what's on the docket for today to remember to even ask yourself if you're happy. If you're really happy, you're probably thinking about something else.

"FRIENDSHIP AGONISTES"

PROSPECT, 2011

[For the record, thanks to the invention of electronic cigarettes, my husband kicked a nearly lifelong smoking habit later this same year. My prospective widowhood may have grown a few years shorter.]

Owing to my husband's seven-year seniority, smoking, and lower male life expectancy, actuarily I should live two decades as a widow. So vivid is this dismal future in my mind's eye that I already maintain a shadowy parallel universe, in which I rarely shop because I've no one to cook for and I can't marshal the resolve for daily exercise with no one to lie to me about how well-preserved I look. Assuming a credible romantic exhaustion, what would keep me going?

My friends. Since in our ever-longer-lived species some people will still live longer than others, droves of my boomer cohort are destined to lose spouses early and will need to rely on whatever network of companions we've built in tandem with our marriages. How well or badly we manage those potentially desolate years will depend in large part on how good a job we've done at friendship. Now that "friend" is a transitive verb, the social networker should bear in mind that 350 "friends" on Facebook aren't going to be much use the morning a spouse has collapsed from an aneurysm onto the kitchen floor.

As Josie Barnard notes in *The Book of Friendship*, Aristotle divided amity into three camps: friendships of "utility," of "pleasure," and of "excellence." Similarly, the twelfth-century abbot Aelred of Rievaulx distinguished between "carnal" friendships based on "hope of gain" or "mutual harmony in vice," as opposed to "true" friendships. But my friendships slop merrily into all these classes. We gladly use each other, for practical help or counsel. We have a good time. And we engage in the heart-to-hearts and political dustups of which Aristotle and the good abbot would approve.

What use are these categories? Something about the character of friendship eludes capture. For friendship is elastic, readily morphing from one purpose and one nature to another. It can be frivolous; it can be life-and-death. Unlike blood ties, it is elective. Unlike conventional marriage, it is cheerfully promiscuous. Of all human relationships, it is perhaps the most naturally forgiving. In contrast to the climactic or apocalyptic structure of romance, adult friendship has a quality of *ongoingness*, which may be one reason that as an abstract topic in Barnard's overview ("Friendship is confusing"; "Friendship is strange") it tends to fall flat. This distinctive *ongoingness* is the reason that friends, like the eponymous program, are so perfectly suited to the TV series: despite frequent spats, there will always be another episode next week.

Of course, many a friendship does die. But beyond the tearful betrayals of adolescence, most grown-up friendships end on an ellipsis. You lose touch, you move house, the emails and phone calls grow gently further apart. Sometimes one party is more disenchanted than the other, but a disparity of affections is likely to take the passive form of a dinner invitation that is not returned. By and large the demise of adult friendships is slow, unspoken, soft—less like murder than prolonged bedridden illness.

I THINK THAT'S WHY THE ABRUPT, EMOTIONALLY VIOLENT CONCLUSIONS OF two close friendships in my young adulthood have preyed on me so.

I could understand a friend gradually losing interest, moving on. I could not understand brutal denunciation, a hot-headed tearing up of contract that I associated with implosions between lovers. While I've long since recovered from old romantic injuries, the sheared friendship has left a raw edge, which I've tended to seek out obsessively, as one's tongue compulsively traces a broken tooth.

I first met N. in graduate school, where we were both earning MFAs in fiction writing. Again, this rule of thumb is more apt to apply to lovers: that what first brought you together will tear you apart.

Post-graduation, N. wrote a new novel every six months. Because these manuscripts did not see print, I admired her resilience even more than her industry. Enough rejections, no tears; she simply started a new book. Me, I deep-sixed my first novel (wisely) and at twenty-eight had only just finished my second, by which point N. had already dashed off a baker's dozen. Meantime, N. and I may have shopped, dined, and swam together, but what most bound us was mutual ambition. We wanted agents. We wanted publishers. We argued about whether Ann Beattie's tiny sentences were genius or a gimmick. It was an anxious, insecure era, for neither of us was guaranteed ever to see our name on a hardback. Yet in your twenties, a friend who shares the same vision is fortifying—right up until your fates threaten to get out of sync.

A little older and already married, N. dished out a great deal more advice than she took. She was an attractive, angular woman with whirlwind energy and a distinctive slam-bam quality that extended beyond her whoosh-whoosh production of manuscripts; slash-slash, chop-chop, she could mix a tuna salad in ninety seconds flat. Like so many New Yorkers, she saw a therapist, routinely expressing an eye-rolling knowingness about the deep, dark motivations that drove everyone she knew. Her most common charge about other friends was that they were hopelessly "competitive."

Given her prolificacy, perhaps justice would dictate that N. would get an agent first and publish first. No doubt that's how she saw it. But

I wasn't especially involved in this fairness issue, since matters suddenly started to go so swimmingly for me.

An editor at HarperCollins had tried to buy my novel, which was encouraging, even if she failed to get the company on board. Three literary agents were bidding to represent me. For an aspirant nonentity, this was heady stuff. After consulting a former teacher in the MFA program, an editor at the *New Yorker*, about which agents had good reputations, I naturally rang N. But when I noted that an agent who'd shown interest in N.'s work was on the *New Yorker*'s B-list, N. got frosty. The reasoning was a little skewed, but somehow by relating someone else's dissing of an agent who had liked N.'s work, I had dissed N.'s work.

"Frosty" was just the beginning. I sought N. out in person to sort us out, and she screamed at me for an hour while I cried. Then the letters started. (God forbid how much more frenzied this epistolary onslaught could have become in the age of email.) Long ones—going on for pages about what a terrible person I was, while sharpening every confidence I'd ever shared into a machete. N.'s *husband* sent letters, equally insulting, and we barely knew each other. I'm sure those letters are still in a box somewhere, which is where they can stay.

Fifteen years later, I was picking the dried sour cherries from the fruit plate at a literary party in Manhattan when I looked up and my heart rate doubled. I felt a bit sick. A few feet away, nattering ebulliently, was N.

While I was debating whether to make a quick exit, she saw me— acting delighted to meet again. The only reference she made to the barrage of hate mail was, "Oh, that all seems a long time ago." It seemed like yesterday to me, which is why I instantly felt small, cringing, and inarticulate. When I said in all sincerity, "Wow, physically you've hardly changed!" (she did look terrific), she batted the compliment away. "You just think that because we've aged *together*."

But we hadn't aged together. N. had made sure of that.

We exchanged email addresses, I imagined purely for form's sake, so I was surprised that N. soon availed herself of mine. She wanted to meet for lunch. I allowed that I was game, but my openness never extended to an exact date. I kept remembering my metabolic reaction to setting eyes on her. N. still frightened me witless. Though she was persistent, I continued to be mysteriously unavailable—I might have been giving her lessons in this-is-how-grown-ups-retreat-from-friendships—and finally, to my relief, she gave up.

YET THE SECOND SAVAGE SPLIT WAS STILL MORE WOUNDING. P. AND I WERE running buddies in high school. *Everyone* loved P. in those days, so why should I be an exception? Cute, with bright bow-tie lips, full cheeks, and a spatter of freckles, she'd an unconstrained hoot of a laugh and a punny sense of humor that only P. could get away with. Warm, gregarious, smart, and hilarious, she drew a retinue the size of half our sophomore class. I admit it: I adored her. Far too serious in adolescence myself, I was dazzled by her uninhibited effervescence and riotous sense of fun. But P. could be serious as well, her depth of feeling derived in part from having been fat as a child. She'd walked on the other side. She hadn't always been this popular.

I kept up with P. with determination. She went to university in Wisconsin, where I visited her from New York. Once she moved to Napa Valley, I traveled to California to catch up about once a year. One of those visits in my midthirties tripped a detonator.

I was leaving the next day, and we'd just driven up in her van to her funky clapboard with its fruiting fig tree. Making no move to get out, P. looked to her hands as it all disgorged in a gush: I was always saying how much she and I had in common, P. said, but honestly she couldn't see it. She found me "arrogant," "self-absorbed," "judgmental," and—the ultimate clincher, from P.—"humorless." I was stunned. What made matters worse: there was a grain of truth in each of these invectives. Her disgust with my screwed-up relations with men was entirely justified.

As a package, the message was stark. One of my oldest friends didn't like me. And probably never had. Mixed with the sting of her renunciation was humiliation. Clearly, I had misread the signals from day one, starting in my sophomore year of high school. I had tagged after her like a pest. My visits, to Wisconsin, to Napa, had been unwelcome—so unwelcome that P. had finally lost it. Anything to get these awful impositions to stop.

Well, they stopped. Although P. recanted her lambaste in a phone call two months later, I wasn't about to risk another trip to Napa Valley. Surely there was still a high likelihood that the antipathy spewed in that front seat was the truth. We dropped from each other's lives.

Seventeen years later, in 2007, on an author's tour for my eighth novel, I had a gig in a bookstore on the outskirts of San Francisco. Before my event, the manager handed me a card. It was from P. She apologized that she couldn't come to my reading, but asked if I had time to have dinner, including her email address and a cell number.

I'd been here before, right? I could fob her off with "maybe next time," just as I had with N. I'd plenty of other friends, none of whom had strafed my whole character. These are the "frenemies" whom therapists advise one to purge.

But I wasn't in therapy. I rang the number.

We had a wonderful dinner and killed a bottle of wine. We talked out what had happened in 1990. As I'd known at the time, during my final visit to Napa her beloved older brother had been dying of melanoma, subjecting her to an anguish I wasn't then equipped to handle. I probably wasn't much help, and she'd taken her grief out on me. Even now I suspect her exasperations with me were genuine, but, hey—I *can* be arrogant, self-absorbed, judgmental, and humorless. Yet despite my shortcomings, she loved me. I loved her as well, and still do. We've reconnected since, and P. visited for a week in New York this last summer—after which I asked my husband if he liked her. He responded with indignation, "Well, who *wouldn't*?"

Many years after each rupture, why did I gladly patch things up

with P., while with N. I passed? P. had indulged a single outburst;
N. had engaged in a sustained hate campaign—and even the law distinguishes between crimes of passion and premeditation. P. deliberately reached out to me and risked rejection herself; N. merely ran into me by accident at a party. P. apologized profusely and addressed our rift; neither in person nor in emails did N. ever acknowledge having done me any harm. And I have some modest influence in the world of letters. Having then just published a first novel at last, N. may have been shopping for Aristotle's friendship of "utility," her let's-have-lunch emails driven by abbot Aelred's "hope of gain." Whereas P., an accomplished chef, wouldn't reap anything from our restored friendship besides the odd free hardback, which she would more than repay with great recipes and little presents of fennel pollen and powdered portobello.

BY THE TIME OF HIS DEATH AT NINETY-SIX, MY PATERNAL GRANDFATHER WAS bereft. Oh, he still had family—my father, my aunt, and seven grandchildren. But they didn't understand him completely, nor he them. He missed his friends. When his last friend died, he was ready to go. So for my own old age, I hope to store up plenty of companions in advance, as if stacking a bomb shelter with tinned beef stew.

Yet this ambition to stock up is thwarted by the befuddling difficulty of making new friends later in life. Extending that first come-hither somehow seems more drastic than when I was younger, and even when we get past the first dinner date one or the other party will often drop the ball. Usually not out of uninterest, either, but from simply not having enough time and emotional energy to keep up with the friends we already have. Making and keeping new comrades requires a doggedness, because it's so easy to fall back on your traditional stable and let the new friends—who are slightly harder work—slip out the gate. The two or three solid, permanent additions to my little network in the last few years have therefore filled me with not only joy, but triumph.

Friendship may readily foster forgiveness, a quality of which I take full advantage by disappearing with impunity on even close friends for months at a time. But as N. illustrates, that forgiveness isn't limitless, and I shouldn't expect to rock up after fifteen years of total silence and announce, "My husband is dead now. Can we pick up where we left off?" Be that as it may, my reunion with P. suggests that friendships are remarkably *mendable*, and my really old ones are lumpy with darns.

What strikes me most about both traumatic breakups is the shock of their intensity. Romantic love gets more than its share of focus, in art and real life; in most plots, friends don't play leads. But deep friendship is a romance as well—capable of inflicting the same pain and inflaming the same passion.

"'I'll Never Put Up with Life in a Care Home,' and Other Lies We Tell Ourselves"

THE OBSERVER, 2021

[Miraculously, after lymphoma had spread to every major organ of his body, my father was put on an experimental, off-label chemo drug in 2013 and survived. In fact, he fully recuperated. Did that sermon in part 1 work magic with some higher power I don't even believe in?

I regret to report that two months after the following essay was published my father died. Bereft, my mother followed him four months later. But both my parents had lived exactly the rich lives they'd wanted to, and it had to happen sometime.]

For those of us with elderly parents, countless news broadcasts of bewildered residents cruelly exiled in care homes during the pandemic have been especially raw. Even so, I can't be the only one who's thought reflexively, *That will never be me.*

My friend Jolanta in Brooklyn has made that vow official. Put through quite the medical ringer herself, she tended a difficult mother through a drawn-out decline. Not long ago, she declared to me fiercely that she'd no interest in living beyond the age of eighty. Dead smart and not given to whimsy, Jolanta was already about sixty, the very point at which old age starts to seem like something that might actually happen. I couldn't help but wonder, should she indeed turn eighty, will she take matters into her own hands—or not?

That, in a nutshell, is the genesis of my new novel, *Should We Stay or Should We Go.* A nurse and GP in the NHS, Kay and Cyril Wilkinson have treated numerous patients eroded by aging's remorseless decay. After Kay's father finally dies in a state of ruinous dementia, the couple is determined to avoid the same grim fate. Having concluded, like Jolanta, that beyond the knell of about eight decades life is all downhill, they make a pact: once they've both crossed that threshold on Kay's eightieth birthday, they'll commit joint suicide. They're still in their early fifties, and this prospect seems a long way off.

Whoosh, whoosh, we fast-forward their story, just as our time on this earth seems to race by before we know it in real life. It's Kay's eightieth birthday. What does the couple do?

Despite the book's morbid premise, I'm hoping a playful parallel universe structure makes *Should We Stay* improbably fun. The novel spins out a dozen alternative scenarios: one spouse goes through with it, the other doesn't; they enter a Club Med care home, or their children section them into a *Cuckoo's Nest* care home. Some chapters veer into speculative fiction—cryogenics, a cure for aging. The point is to parse their dilemma. If they cut their lives artificially short, what delights might they miss out on, and what horrors might they escape? The novel considers what we all do, fleetingly, as the years advance: Under what terms will we concede to keep living? Beyond what line does sticking around entail such suffering, diminishment, or humiliation that we'd rather call it quits?

Whether or not we feel like thinking about it now, many of us will turn to this matter in time. Globally, the elderly have the highest suicide rate of any demographic. Derek Humphry's 1991 self-published how-to, *Final Exit: The Practicalities of Self-Deliverance and Assisted Suicide for the Dying* became an unlikely *New York Times* bestseller for fourteen weeks.

This is a personal matter for me, and not only because I'm sixty-four myself. Both my parents are still alive—although in my mother's case that may be stretching the meaning of the word. My father is ninety-three; my mother turns ninety in July. Watching their old age progress has been mystifying, painful, and sometimes heartening.

Class valedictorian in high school and college, my Iowan mother was a sharp cookie. She worked full time as a researcher first for the Presbyterian Church, then for the National Council of Churches. She played the cello and published two volumes of poetry. And it may mean too much to me, but my mother was a beautiful woman. A petite, brown-eyed brunette with a killer smile, she showed up with my forgotten lunchbox when I was in second grade, and the boy in the next desk gasped, "Your mom looks like a movie star!" She did. She looked like a movie star.

Whoosh, whoosh. After a massive stroke in 2015, my mother can't walk. She can't use her right hand. She's incontinent. Her body has grown plump and soft. She can still talk—sort of. That is, she can form words, but rarely has much to say. Much of her scant discourse comprises polite vacuities. Asked how she is, she'll say, "As well as can be expected." Our sparse, formal phone conversations are full of silences.

When diagnosed with low-tension glaucoma in the 1990s, she was warned that, if she lived long enough, she'd go blind. She's lived long enough. As of last year, this formerly voracious reader can't discern a carryout menu, nor can she lay eyes on her beloved husband. A television is a radio with lots of dead airtime. Mostly, she sits in her wheelchair, chin on chest. I've no idea what goes on in her head.

Her demeanor is pleasant. She's undemanding and benevolent. She's perfectly nice. But my real mother was not nice! Our relationship was often prickly. Real Mother was prone to sudden, unexpected bursts of resentment. Real Mother was a touchy, complicated woman who banged about the kitchen in unexplained white rages while giving us all the "silent treatment." I'd trade all that niceness for one more night of crashing silverware in a heartbeat.

If Real Mother could see herself now, would she wish her elderly self were dead? Even Fraudulent Mother often asserts that she's ready to die. This may be the most content-rich statement I've heard from her since 2015: "I don't want to die, but I *need* to die." In most meaningful senses, my mother is no longer here, but I've been cheated even of my bereavement.

A Virginian with a long, distinguished theological career, my father was a handsome, ambitious, vigorous man in his day, one possessed of a towering ego. On retirement, he declared vehemently that he did not want his savings frittered on end-of-life care.

Whoosh, whoosh. Steadily, his savings are frittered on end-of-life care. Since my mother's stroke, my parents have hired full-time live-in help. Like so many elderly pandemic shut-ins, they've barely left the apartment in over a year. My father is still—pretty much—cogent, but with odd lapses; someone seems to have put a cigarette out on the part of his brain that stores numbers. He announced three times not long ago that this summer he'll have been married to my mother "for two hundred and sixty-eight years!" But we continue to conduct engaging conversations, and in the last month he's finally stopped railing against Donald Trump.

His body, however, is failing. He can no longer bear his own weight. A recent infection mandated the amputation of one of his toes. His digestive system keeps packing in, and subsequent avoidance of food has made him gaunt. It's disconcerting to see such a powerhouse contained in a vessel so weak.

I noted that some aspects of this parental passion play have been "heartening." At ninety-three, my father is still fundamentally himself. He has accommodated the steady shrinking of his life—no more New York Philharmonic or Metropolitan Opera—with resigned grace. Prepandemic, he resisted a mobility scooter at first, but rapidly reconciled to the perceived demotion, zooming the Upper West Side with gusto. These days, he accedes to his faithful carer's necessary involvement in his intimate bodily functions without a fuss, for he's not hung up on younger people's strangely bathroomy version of what constitutes "dignity." My father still has dignity, or the kind that counts. He remains in the grip of an astonishing life force. He's proud of his accomplishments and won't let anyone forget them. Despite the imposed compromises of advanced age—compromises that, in my naivete, I imagine would be unacceptable to me—my father clings ferociously to survival. Glimpsing this future, his younger incarnation would be sobered, but lifelong self-regard would preclude his ever vowing that he'd rather be dead.

We enter into an implicit contract with ourselves regarding what we're willing to put up with in order to stay in the game, and when we're younger the conditions under which we'll submit to continued existence can be strict. Maybe it sounds ludicrous, but for much of my life I'd have told you that a future in which I could no longer play tennis was out of the question. I'm an intensely physical person, and the notion of sitting indefinitely in my mother's wheelchair strikes me as intolerable. Faced with some mildly disagreeable prospect, I'm given to tossing off carelessly, "I'd rather kill myself!"

Yet only during one short period did I made that declaration in earnest. For this implicit contract with ourselves must be at its most sincere in respect to physical pain. For five days last summer, I experienced a degree of agony that, had it endured as a condition of my existence, I'd have headed for the ultimate exit to make it stop. (There's nothing worse than *nerve pain*. Fellow sufferers know what I mean.) Dial up the pain high enough, and five seconds passes like a week. Above a certain subjective threshold of torment—the limit must be particular to the person—life is not worth living. It fails a primitive cost-benefit analysis. Being is purchased at too high a price, and pain is so despoiling that existence compensates with little, if any, reward.

That's why the cause of legal assisted dying is usually taken up by people who are physically suffering, often from a condition that will only worsen. Although physician-assisted death is now permitted in half a dozen countries and several American states, it's still illegal in the United Kingdom, where a doctor who helps someone to die can get up to fourteen years in prison. Yet the MP Andrew Mitchell, cochair of the all-party parliamentary group for choice at the end of life, believes British laws on assisted dying could soon be liberalized. Already underprosecution is rife, and in plenty of gray-area instances fading patients are quietly allowed to die or given extra pain meds that speed the process.

Katie Engelhart's compelling 2021 book *The Inevitable* is about people determined to exercise control over their own deaths. While some of the author's interviewees are aiming for Dignitas in Switzerland (where locals allude drily to the "suicide tourism industry"), to which 475 Britons have traveled to end their lives this century, the majority are taking death into their own hands, regardless of the law—purchasing veterinary drugs from Mexico or researching online how to autoasphyxiate with nitrogen. Yet most people who ask to die, Englehart reports, are "not in terrible pain, or even afraid of future pain." Instead, they want to die at a time of their choosing for "existential reasons." They fear "losing autonomy," "loss of dignity," and "losing control of bodily functions." Indeed, the latter two anxieties are often synonymous: "A lot of people I interviewed equated dignity precisely with sphincter control." (In one hospital survey, more than two-thirds of patients over sixty considered double incontinence "as bad as or worse than death.") Strikingly for me, one entirely healthy subject announces, "I'll be eighty in four years' time and eighty is the time to die"—just like my fictional Wilkinsons. Four years later, the woman overdoses peacefully on barbiturates, right according to plan.

Most of all, Englehart's subjects dread losing their identity to dementia. Yet nipping dementia in the bud requires acting before the disease has advanced—thereby sacrificing a period of unknowable duration when you might have been nearly yourself. That is, only giving up some good life guarantees being spared bad life. I've another friend in the United States, the author Amy Bloom, whose droll, beguiling husband was diagnosed with Alzheimer's last year at only sixty-seven. (He'd played a lot of American football.) With his wife's sorrowful blessing, while still of broadly sound mind, the talented architect

---

ended his life at Dignitas a few months later. That took stupendous commitment and courage. Most of us couldn't do it.

In the 2014 film *Still Alice*, Julianne Moore plays a linguistics professor diagnosed with early-onset Alzheimer's at fifty. She leaves a list of simple questions for her future self, along with the location of the sleeping tablets if she draws a blank. But when Alice fails her own competency test and finds the tablets, she gets distracted and forgets what she was about to do. She's missed her chance to exercise control. In dementia circles, this is known as the "five-minutes-to-twelve syndrome." The temptation is to hang on until it's too late, and the opportunity to exercise agency over the end of your life has passed.

It's difficult to kill yourself painlessly—one reason most suicides fail. We produce drugs to put down suffering animals, but we don't design drugs to kill people. Thus a slogan of the right-to-die movement runs, "I would rather die like a dog." Lethal drugs are hard to come by and can be confiscated by customs or the police. In *Should We Stay*, Cyril readily acquires "an effective medical solution," stored in an upper corner of the couple's refrigerator for decades, only because he has prescribing privileges as a GP. The rest of us who live in places where assisted dying remains illegal are obliged to order underground books like *The Peaceful Pill Handbook* and commence furtive subterfuges to secure a stash.

Where the practice is permitted, qualifications for assisted dying vary, often involving a terminal diagnosis and a prognosis of death within six months. But more interesting to me is our private stipulations. In what circumstances do we personally regard life as unbearable?

While still on the cusp of this negotiation, I imagine that the journey from our often-hale sixties to the life of the "old-old"—my parents—entails getting stuck on the "bargaining" phase of the five classic stages of grief:

All right, maybe insisting that if I can't play tennis I'll dive off Blackfriars Bridge is unreasonable. Obviously, the number of press-ups I can do will gradually drop. No press-ups at all, you say? Fine. Bit of a relief, actually: no press-ups, good riddance. At least I can still cycle. No? You're kidding me. I've cycled everywhere since I was eight! It's part of who I am! OK, OK. They say walking is the best exercise anyway. . . . Oh. Too painful? I can barely make it to the shops? Well, that's what they make online delivery services for. Gosh, I just went through three solid days unable to remember the name of my best friend in primary school. Happens at any age; one of those "blocked neural pathways." Came to me in due course. But it's harder to explain why I just found a pair of socks chilling in my vegetable drawer.

I always thought I couldn't live without my husband, but apparently I can, though some days I suffer under a cloud of desolation, like a low-pressure weather system that won't budge. It's at least a comfort to remain in the home we shared. What do you mean my relatives have expressed "concern"? What's to be so bleeding concerned about? I do, too, wash! Well. After a fashion. See, I hate having to sit on that plastic chair in the shower. Nevertheless, I promised myself that I'll never submit to a care home. I won't, I won't! Reluctantly, I concede my niece's point: I forgot about the chicken. Without her impromptu visit, that grease fire could have proved my funeral pyre. Besides, I'm not as special as I imagined. I guess people always think they'll never submit to a care home—and then they do, and so do I. At least the staff are kind. The other residents aren't all my cup of tea, but it's a relief to talk to anyone. Bland institutional meals still punctuate the day. I used to love cooking—but only when fixing dinner for two. Nappies? You get over the embarrassment, and the carers are brisk and professional. No one here knows who I am, what I was, all the books I wrote. But that Lionel Shriver is one more thing I've learned to forgo.

We make these compromises by degrees. Legalize assisted suicide in Britain and only a tiny minority will avail themselves of it, because most of us will put up with anything rather than die. My father is apt to put up with anything. He's not checking out of Hotel Terra Firma unless he's actively ejected by the management.

I fancy Katie Engelhart's characterization of a chosen death as "an authorial act," and I've never cared for stories that end on ellipses. Thus I desperately don't want to end up like my mother, who on my brother's latest visit no longer recognized him. She's grown, he said, "unreachable." My mother's dazzling, articulate younger iteration would recoil from a version of herself that is unseeing, inert, and unresponsive. Yet she long ago signed a living will, as I have. Had she kept an "effective medical solution" at the back of her fridge, after that Blitzkrieg of a stroke she'd have lacked the self-possession to take the tablets. Genetically, I will have inherited many of her medical vulnerabilities. So how will I *not* end up like my mother?

I have no idea.

"Just Because We've Been OK Doesn't Mean We'll Stay That Way"

Ramsay Centre Virtual Address, 2020

[This speech was delivered online for a foundation in Australia, a country nearly impossible to visit or leave during the COVID pandemic. Although Western economies have so far bounced back from lockdowns more readily than I expected in September 2020, if anything my warnings about soaring sovereign debt and excessive money production in the second section of this address are already proving all too prescient. Vast subsidies for furloughed employees and businesses have only increased appetite for social welfare spending in both the United States and United Kingdom. Across a mere eighteen months—December 2019 to August 2021—the US Federal Reserve increased the dollars in circulation by 35.7 percent. It's estimated that by the end of 2024, the money supply will grow nearly that much again.

Eighteen months after I delivered this address, Vladimir Putin's invasion of Ukraine further underscored the West's previous complacency and "the fragility of order."]

Well. This has been a weird year—and having lived largely in the UK for over three decades, I'm demonstrating my acquired gift of British understatement.

• 2020 began with the withdrawal of the United Kingdom from the European Union, with astonishingly little ceremony, which would have seemed unimaginable only five years ago.

• In response to a novel pathogen, world leaders cupped suffocating tumblers over their own economies for months on end, like an interminable episode of *Under the Dome*. Bizarrely, Western politicians copied this heavy-handed and hitherto unheard-of protocol for the suppression of a fairly low-fatality infectious disease from, of all places, authoritarian China.

• In June, a single instance of abuse of power by a single policeman in Minneapolis, Minnesota, fired up a worldwide protest movement that was affecting at first, but that rapidly grew violent and fanatical. Supporters of Black Lives Matter have demanded the defunding or even dismantling of police departments. They've inflamed racial grievance and accelerated the campaign for socially divisive and impractical racial reparations. They've frightened institutions and corporations across the Western world into proclaiming fealty to, and even donating large sums to, an organization dedicated to the fall of capitalism.

• Now in the United States, we have active anxiety that a sitting president will not necessarily hand over the keys to the Oval Office if he loses a national election.

Regarding the first and last of these juddering turns of the wheel, I'm relatively at ease. I freely confess to having supported Brexit. From the start, Brexit struck me as the scale of disruptive "revolution" that Europe and the world could afford. When the referendum results came in, I was surprised that more than half the almost uniformly small-C conservative British people were willing to gamble on such radical change. Barely two months after the UK's exit from the EU, that change abruptly appeared insignificant. Few Brits talk about Brexit anymore. As for the US, I'm anxious about dysfunctional postal voting and any protracted period of post-election uncertainty about who won. By contrast—and maybe this makes me naive, but if so I will cling to my naivete for six more weeks—I still have faith in the structural workings of American government to overcome the ungraciousness of one sore loser.

The widespread COVID-19 lockdowns and the increasingly venomous Black Lives Matter movement strike me otherwise. Both destabilizing phenomena have been instigated by people suffering from a perilous complacency. A surfeit of Western security, with no major wars and nearly uninterrupted prosperity for seventy-five years, has created an ahistorical underappreciation for the fragility—and not only the white kind—of order.

PERHAPS THE HYPER-RACIALIZING OF THE WEST IN THE SECOND HALF OF this year will prove a temporary mania, at the end of which we'll have fairer, more sensitive societies. But somehow I doubt it.

We don't commonly characterize folks who want to altogether overturn the way a country works "systemically" as *complacent*. But I would argue that most of this year's abundantly white, middle-class protesters embody the epitome of complacency. These are not people who expect to make any personal sacrifice to make the world a better place. To the contrary, by positioning themselves as "allies" on "the right side of history," they expect to reap rewards, and to jettison older, purportedly prejudiced generations even more rapidly than younger generations do as a matter of course. BLM bandwagoners assume that they can change everything while everything they fancy stays the same.

Weekend revolutionaries imagine that they can bring an end to capitalism and still keep all the fruits of capitalism that they take for granted. They think they can install a neo-Marxist equality of outcome, boot out all the wicked old white guys like Tim Cook, and keep their iPhones, replete with regular OS updates. They imagine that they can pack faculties and student bodies with minorities regardless of qualification and "decolonize" the curriculum to rid it of "white knowledge" and still have prospective employers regard their degrees from Harvard as meaningful commendations. They want to undermine the means by which their parents earn a living, yet still expect to crash back home when they're low on cash, where they can always raid the refrigerator when feeling peckish. Woke white activists want to demonize "whiteness" as the sole source of all evil, while mysteriously believing that this does not entail demonizing themselves. Apparently the joyful embrace of one's own "fragility" grants the right to hector others while triggering a racial opt-out clause.

The same brand of white activist helped draft this last summer's ubiquitous "open letters" to Princeton and Stanford, the Poetry Foundation, and a beleaguered liberal bookstore in Denver, to name a few. The signatories reliably demanded aggressive, instantaneous affirmative action, often well in excess of regional or national demographic proportions. Yet it never occurs to our worthy white young folk that if these institutions comply, they themselves won't be admitted to universities that are drastically privileging nonwhite applicants with lower scores. If employers across a range of industries are scrambling to cover their moral backsides by filling all available posts with nonwhite hires, it never occurs to our white "allies" that they themselves will be out of a job.

If governments, schools, and businesses embrace "antiracism" as their sole prime directive, as opposed to producing a salable product or performing a valuable service, competency is bound to decay at what was once these entities' driving purpose: to provide for the common defense, to educate students for viable careers, to manufacture products that consumers want to buy. Demonstrably ineffective, even counterproductive "unconscious-bias training"—which leaves many resentful subjects of compulsory antiwhite brainwashing more bigoted than they were to begin with—not only wastes resources, but pits employees destructively against one another. Should most Western institutions and corporations devote their principal energies to "antiracism," China will clean up. As a result, "equity" zealots will only level the playing field by making everybody poor. Forgive me for stating the self-evident, but advocates of wealth redistribution need wealth to redistribute.

Rioters are dependent on a functional society, or they have nothing to disrupt. Hoodlums still assume that if they get shot or thumped with a truncheon, an advanced, well-funded, and skillfully staffed hospital will patch them up. Looters rely on a generous supply of operational businesses whose premises can be ransacked, and which are chock full of the fruits of capitalism, like high-end trainers and headphones. Eager to acquire more free stuff, looters blithely expect these businesses to replace their windows and restock, the better to get ransacked again. (In many cases, fat chance. If I were Satya Nadella, after June's free-for-all by baseball-bat-wielding bargain hunters in Manhattan, I'd close the ravaged Microsoft store on Fifth Avenue for keeps.) Hey, even criminals rely on the fruits of capitalism. Gang members place their trust in weapons produced by companies that manufacture to a high standard. Drug runners need airplanes and SUVs to deliver their product to customers. If nothing else, criminals need solvent, hardworking, taxpaying suckers who own something worth stealing.

As with cake, this summer's activists wanted to have their police and defund them, too. We can take it as a given that none of these often well-off white protesters have any desire to live in truly lawless cities—where their phones are snatched on the street and their homes are repeatedly burgled. Where women are raped with impunity and petty grudges are settled with violent assault. Where cars are routinely T-boned by tearaways running traffic lights—who will keep driving like hellions because they face no consequences. Where everyone lives in fear of arbitrary injury or even death, because this is a city without legal recourse. By the time this summer's failed utopian project nicknamed CHOP in Seattle had lived with no police presence for three weeks, four shootings had occurred within the zone's mere six blocks, one of them fatal. With chastened, demoralized police forces embracing passivity as a means of self-protection, murders in Chicago, Minneapolis, and New York City have been soaring. Yet according to a core tenet of the BLM-inspired American medical students in "White Coats for Black Lives," "Policing is incompatible with health." You've got to be kidding me. Nothing is less "healthy" than being dead.

For all their demands for "systemic" transformation, 2020's protesters don't really want that much to change. They want to keep curating their playlists on Spotify and ordering oat milk from Amazon Fresh. They want Netflix to keep churning out new entertainment, through whatever nefarious corporate machinations, because they've already binged the fifth season of *Ozark*. Thanks to horrible racist capitalism and centuries of oppression, their computers can communicate instantaneously with Minsk. They have not only enough to eat, but a range of dim sum in their local supermarket's freezer, from shrimp to pork to vegan pumpkin. This last spring, you can be sure that these same young people got as consternated as everyone else when those supermarkets ran short of paper towels (and I recently read a fascinating *Wall Street Journal* article on paper-towel manufacturing; the process is far more intricate and sophisticated than you'd think). Thanks to the police they detest, these protesters still enjoy "safe spaces" in many smaller cities—in the sense that "safety" used to mean: protection from physical harm.

Up to a point, dedication to racial equality—in countries that have never been less prejudiced—is laudable. But in a society that provides shelter, clean water, and sustenance to the vast majority of its inhabitants, even in densely populated cities where otherwise we'd be slaughtering each other in packs, the opportunity to obsess fetishistically about "microaggressions" and "unconscious bias" is one more luxury borne of the system these activists abhor. Even the right to demand curtailment of free speech requires the right to free speech.

In the United States, I'm loath to histrionically predict a second civil war. Nevertheless, in Minneapolis, Portland, Seattle, DC, San Francisco, New York, and Kenosha, arsonists are both literally and figuratively playing with fire. This summer has seen the most tumultuous civil unrest since the 1960s. Opposing sides in the culture war no longer seem to feel like citizens of the same country. Few in the white majority feel any responsibility for slavery, and many white Americans are themselves struggling to pay bills or unemployed; should the reparations movement be victorious, white resentment could be incendiary. And if a deadly confluence of logistical disarray and mutual distrust means there's no clear winner after November's presidential election, I foresee mayhem. (For that matter, if Trump wins clearly fair and square, I especially foresee mayhem.) Left-wing rioters, looters, and vandals already have form. Self-nominated defenders of the republic already have guns.

Centuries in the making, contemporary Western civilization is so complex that it shouldn't really work at all—but somehow, after a fashion, it does. In fact, on the whole we've never lived more comfortably, more peaceably, or more justly. Yet shrill voices on the hard left preach that countries like the US, the UK, and Australia are a disgrace and should inspire only shame. Subjecting the fruits of one's forebears' toil to contempt signals not only complacency, but ingratitude.

NEVERTHELESS, I RESERVE MY OWN CONTEMPT NOT PRIMARILY FOR CALLOW protesters, with no appreciation for how utterly dependent they are on social order to afford to dabble in disorder. Young people have always erred on the side of poorly thought-through idealism and sanctimonious hotheadedness. In my own teens and twenties, I wasn't any different. Far more do I deplore the grown-ups: global leaders in 2020 who should know better.

With rare sane exceptions like Sweden's, Western governments have installed unprecedented nationwide lockdowns of their whole societies for month upon month, and continue to threaten the reimposition of economically catastrophic, near police-state conditions on their ostensibly "free" populations. These governments are also guilty of an obscene complacency. Having done no cost-benefit analysis before pressing a giant pillow over the territories entrusted to their guidance, politicians have credulously assumed that civil liberties can always be magically restored (and that's assuming these officials don't come to rather fancy wielding unlimited power). There will always be more tax-payers. Treasuries can always "borrow"—meaning print—more money, and the currency will still retain its value. Is that so? Politicians' obliv-ious, tunnel-vision focus on a single pathogen only moderately more lethal than the flu is not only wreaking short-term fiscal havoc, but is pumping up the Ponzi scheme of escalating sovereign debt, which no one really imagines will ever be paid back.

The authorities' wholesale capitulation to COVID hysteria—which set the emotional table for racial hysteria—has inflicted a scale of de-struction that might, had leaders looked before they leapt, have been anticipated. Indeed, a 2006 paper by Dr. Thomas Inglesby, the director of the Johns Hopkins Center for Health Security at the Bloomberg School of Public Health, predicted nearly every disastrous consequence of a theoretical lockdown that we can now verify in practice. This ex-pert on epidemics wrote, "The negative consequences of large-scale quarantine are so extreme . . . that this mitigation measure should be eliminated from serious consideration." Yet even poor countries have aped this clumsy protocol, which may kill millions from starvation.

Once lockdowns are finally eased, successfully terrified work-forces refuse to venture out their front doors—especially in the UK, where two-thirds of employees are still working, or neglecting to work, from home. For some processes are far easier to set in train than to reverse. It's not that difficult to frighten people. Unfrightening them is a bastard.

Small business has been ravaged by bankruptcy. Public transpor-tation with minimal ridership is running unsustainable deficits, and many systems could enter a death spiral of reduced services and higher fares followed by even smaller riderships. The financial and commer-cial centers of great cities like New York and London are hollowed out. Midtown Manhattan, Wall Street, the City of London, and Canary

Wharf are currently all ghost towns, as if commandeered by film crews for movies about the end of the world. The West's collective GDP look like an apple that a Saint Bernard took a bite of. The performing arts, precious in and of themselves but also vital engines of tourist revenue, have been incinerated. Airlines are on their knees. Unemployment is high, and job losses are often as irreversible as fear. Swaths of restaurants, bars, hotels, and nightclubs have closed for good. Tax bases have effectively been plunged into vats of acid—at the same time as demand on the public purse has skyrocketed. Focused myopically on COVID, many health systems are failing to treat more lethal ailments like cancer.

Look. A short, sharp shock, such as a fortnight's cessation of business-as-usual in March, however also extraordinary, might have been safe or even prudent: life briefly on hold, as health care systems prepared for the unknown. But instead some lockdowns have already lasted six months. They've been only timorously lifted, always with the threat of reintroduction with no warning. The grotesque consequences were entirely foreseeable. What were politicians thinking? They weren't thinking. They were reacting. They were "doing something" to disguise the fact that they had no idea what to do. In preference to making measured, informed trade-offs, Western leaders mindlessly copied both the worst possible model for governance, Communist China, and each other. They implicitly relied on the excuse many a parent has found wanting: "Well, everyone else is doing it!" To whatever degree our leaders have exercised any independent judgment whatsoever, they've trusted naively that an effective vaccine will put everything back to the way it was.

The same complacency extends to us, the citizens of once liberal democracies. At least in comparative terms, we assure ourselves, we're rich. We're used to being rich, just as in terms of worldwide military havoc we're used to relative peace. So of course we're going to *stay* relatively rich and *stay* relatively peaceful. No matter the scale of the upheaval, in the long run we'll be fine, because we've been more or less fine for seventy-five years. As peoples, we have ludicrous faith in the state to take care of us—underaware that at least financially we *are* the state. We watch disaster movies all the time, yet no longer believe in the possibility of proper disaster on the near side of the screen. We're lazy. We have flabby imaginations.

But as a novelist, I'm paid to have an athletic imagination.

Set in a near-future America, my 2016 novel *The Mandibles* describes a dystopia of an expressly economic sort. The book begins on the centenary of last century's stock market crash, October 2029. Because China and Russia are mistrustful about America's towering national debt, the "almighty dollar" is replaced by a new international currency that's actually worth something and backed by real assets. Thus the dollar loses its status as the world's reserve currency. In retaliation, the president renounces the national debt—some of which is held by foreign parties, but the bulk of which is owned by domestic investors and pensioners, whose bonds convert overnight to poorly absorbent toilet roll. As a faithless debtor unable to borrow on world markets, the US government frenetically prints its way out of a fiscal hole. Surprise: inflation soars. First food is scarce; then food is available but insanely expensive. Social order unravels. My middle- and upper-middle-class characters go from impatiently awaiting the trickle-down of a sizable inheritance to growing their own vegetables (which are all stolen), mugging schoolchildren for groceries, and panic-buying paper clips, in the wan hope that at least stationery, unlike their currency, will retain some value. At length—spoiler alert—the Mandibles are forced from the family house at gunpoint.

It was supposed to be fiction. I would like it to stay fiction. Writing that novel gave me an appreciation for the frailty of civilization—more appreciation, honestly, than I want. As we only half-learned in 2008, when we came closer to worldwide fiscal collapse than anyone cares to recall, the financial systems on which we now rely are impenetrably complicated and precariously interrelated. Complexity theory foretells that complex systems collapse catastrophically. Even violent anticapitalists, much less presidents and prime ministers, take for granted that there will always be affordable food in supermarkets. That when you flip a switch, the lights will come on. That the taps will always flow with potable water. That in the main, come what may, citizens can walk down the street without being murdered for a pound of hamburger.

Widespread, simultaneous, long-lasting, and often repeated international lockdowns may be unprecedented, but COVID-19 is not. The 1957 Asian flu killed between one and two million worldwide. The 1968 Hong Kong flu killed between one and four million. During both pandemics, world leaders didn't close so much as a newsagent. The disproportionate response to one more disagreeable albeit sometimes lethal virus boggles the mind. Thus far, real-world data demonstrate *no* correlation between the stringency of government restrictions and COVID infections, hospitalizations, or deaths. There's growing acknowledgment that lockdowns will cost many more lives than they saved—and that's assuming they saved any lives, rather than simply dragging out inevitable fatalities over a longer period of time.

But my biggest worry isn't the immediately devastating economic losses and personal suffering that this copycat, knee-jerk overreaction has wrought on the ground. I'm worried about implosion on a more historic scale. COVID lockdowns have massively sped up the rate at which national debts are burgeoning. How tall can a house of cards rise before it topples?

According to "magic money tree" thinking, a.k.a. modern monetary theory, a government that controls its own currency can print money to cover its expenses *without limit*. We can see why this theory is so popular: everything for nothing. For a sneak peak at my latest novel, *Should We Stay or Should We Go*, here's a passage from a chapter set in a fairy-tale near future:

> After the scare of what, in historical retrospect, proved a relatively
> brief economic downturn following the global lockdowns to suppress

COVID-19, an obliging monetary theory was demonstrated to be faultless. Lo, it was more than possible for the government to print an infinite amount of money and then give the money to its citizenry to buy things. If the citizenry ever wanted to buy more things, then the government could print still more money so that the citizenry could buy more things. Everyone marveled at why retrograde economists had ever installed the unnecessarily convoluted business of employment and taxation. The technique caught on all over Europe, and effectively established an indefinite lockdown, except in this one you could leave the house.

What's wrong with this picture? It's deeply counterintuitive, and never underestimate common sense. I can't cite a single product that can be manufactured in infinite quantity and still retain its value. Flood the market with corn, and the price of corn plunges to below the cost of production. Our gut intelligence dictates that the logic of oversupply also pertains to money: the more you conjure from thin air, the less it will buy. As an ominous early warning, the US Federal Reserve announced last month that it will *not* be raising interest rates, even if inflation rises to above the Fed's target. Stay tuned for more such cheerful news from the Bank of England and the European Central Bank.

The international monetary system is held together with rubber bands, bits of string, and appeals to divinity. Because it's in everyone's interest to have confidence in this fragile kludgeocracy, we all determinedly have confidence in it. But frankly, ever since all money became fiat money—backed by nothing and therefore generated ad infinitum at no apparent cost—countries have competed with one another over whose currency could be more worthless. The race to the bottom is well under way. Me, I'm astonished that any currency in the world right now is worth anything at all. I'm positively impressed that the pound and the dollar continue to be accepted in exchange for genuinely valuable tangibles like wheat and oil. But we have succumbed to complacency. The insouciant assumption runs that because we've been getting away with murder for all this time, and because so much rides on our continuing to get away with murder, we will therefore be able to get away with murder forever more. We can thus pile up national debts of over 100 percent of GDP, even 200 percent, so why not 300 or 400 percent? A thousand? Isn't the sky the limit? Yet *all* Ponzi schemes collapse. The only uncertainty is when.

I yearn to be wrong. I would love for modern monetary theory to prove astonishingly sound, so that the two governments under which I live in the UK and the US can continue to provide services like health care and national parks, and fund the military, and pave the roads, while my taxes never rise, all the people I care about thrive, and peace and goodwill toward men descend upon all the earth.

I'm not being entirely facetious. I feel an enormous personal investment in the economic stability of the next couple of decades. I'm already into my midsixties, which puts me on the cusp of both physical decline and an inevitable drift toward the professional sidelines. But I worry that no matter how much I save for my retirement, national or even international economic implosion could wipe me out (and in any financial apocalypse, I'd have a horrifying amount of company), thus leaving me destitute in my old age, when I'm at my most dependent and most disposable. As a character observes in my new novel, "The only thing worse than being old is being old and broke."

I ALSO DREAD EVER HAVING TO WATCH THE CIVILIZATION THAT HAS NURTURED me, and that has provided me such an exhilarating cultural inheritance, fall apart. I could not bear a real-life dystopia in which the Statue of Liberty is toppled and Parliament burns to the ground. In which libraries and online search results are strictly policed in order to serve a single, narrow, fanatical dogma (a process that Facebook and YouTube have already begun). Today's hard leftists are eager to bulldoze their "systemically racist" societies into landfill, but have no constructive replacement for what they would gleefully destroy. Their blind rampages go hand in hand with our idiotic COVID lockdowns. Both the Marxist Trojan horse of BLM zealotry and these suicidal, shortsighted "public health" policies eat away at everything in Western life that I treasure, from reading artful, ideologically unorthodox books to being able to buy a chicken. Yet in protesters and politicians alike, I detect that deadly complacency, as if you can rock a boat as wildly as you want—all because it's stayed afloat so far.

Sure, I may be an alarmist crank. In a few years' time, this address may seem hilarious. I hope so. Bring on the ridicule. I'd welcome being laughed at, so long as I'm spared any real-life manifestations of the visions that haunt me.

The relatively safe, prosperous, tranquil existence I've unthinkingly inhabited my whole life was many centuries in the making, the fruit of endless trial and error by our forebears. It could be destroyed in a weekend. Trying to exorcise anxieties about my own life as I enter its last tranche, I set *The Mandibles*, you'll recall, in 2029. I'm not known for being an optimist. But as of 2020, I now worry that my fictional choice of year zero was on the late side.

"Catastrophizing Is My
Idea of a Good Time"

THE SPECTATOR, 2018

When, on a test of general knowledge, the highly educated score far worse than chimpanzees, university degrees may be overrated (definitely). But something more interesting may also be going on.

According to the newly released *Factfulness* by Hans Rosling, we would-be smart people would improve our results on multiple-choice questions about the current state of the world (16 percent) if we picked the answers at random (33 percent). We all seem to think that humanity is in the toilet and swirling more deeply into the sewer by the day. We're willfully blind to social progress. The more cheerful a host of indices look, the more belligerently we cling to the conviction that everything is getting worse.

Strictly speaking, I might score more highly than the average chimp on Rosling's twelve-question quiz, because I'm technically aware that human history has become steadily less violent, extreme poverty has plummeted during my lifetime, education of girls is on the increase, and immunization against the likes of polio has been so successful that until very recently the WHO was on the cusp of eliminating the disease from the planet. But temperamentally, I flunk.

I am a self-confessed catastrophizer. As a novelist, I'm a professional catastrophizer. According to *The New York Times Book Review*, Shriver is "the Cassandra of American letters"—which sounds like quite a claim to fame, except that according to *Factfulness* that makes me an ignoramus.

When global literacy has soared and wars are dramatically on the decrease, it's baffling why people like me continue to lavish a staggering proportion of our mental, conversational, and literary energies on how bloody terrible everything is, and on how terribly much terribler it's all bound to get.

Part of the trouble is presentism. Myopically, we don't see modernity in context. Take two steps back, and barely yesterday we were hunched round a fire roasting voles on sticks.

On the other hand, subjectively, life is getting worse. That is, for individuals, every day that passes makes the time remaining twenty-four hours shorter. The very structure of biological existence is apocalyptic, which may incline us to look for mirrors of our own horrifying mortality in the outside world. For all us pre-dead people, catastrophizing is a form of projection. On a subconscious level, too, some of us bitter oldsters may relish the prospect of taking everyone else with us when we go. The notion of all these blithe, carefree younger folks having a wonderful time without us is irritating.

My business is story, and story entails something crap happening. If everything is eternally sweet and good and nice—if life for everyone on earth just keeps getting better and better—I'm out of a job. (Try selling this plot to HarperCollins: "Mary gets her vaccinations, eats well, graduates from primary school, lives in a democracy, has access to clean water and electricity, and buys a mobile phone.") More, given the persistence of an audience for fiction—and for nonfiction, which these days is even doomier than the made-up stuff—novelists are clearly not the only ones who crave stories with crap happening. Crap happening is, if you will, a human need.

The news cycle is equally dependent on crap happening, so that news junkies like me are continually having our bleakness bolstered. Amid the smorgasbord of awfulness to choose from, we focus on stories that arouse the most emotion. I'm not apt to zero in on a more effective treatment for hives, but rather on the "trash vortex" of plastic in the Pacific that's three times the size of France—an image that sends me into an almost hallucinogenic high of self-immiseration.

Most of us, too, have pet catastrophes—to which we grow attached, and which we're always looking to feed, like puppies we hope to nourish into full-grown rottweilers. Suffering from an avocational confirmation bias, some of us keep a lookout for verification that Syria is insoluble and getting worse as a hobby. Others have a professional investment in the problem with which their own field grapples being far more dreadful than any other field's darling difficulty. Researching my fourth novel, *Game Control*, during the African AIDS crisis, I discovered that epidemiologists were convinced HIV would destroy the population of the continent. By contrast, demographers dismissed AIDS mortality as a drop in the kicked bucket and believed that Africans would overpopulate themselves into oblivion instead. The scientists in both fields were in love with their adopted problem.

My pet problem is human population. I think those demographers were right. Because I'm so fiercely attached to my own version of the world—even more so than to the future prosperity of humanity, apparently—you should distrust anything I say about population. In kind, left-wing Westerners are mightily attached to a gaping gulf between developed and developing countries that doesn't exactly exist anymore, the better for progressives to feel as guilty as possible, because, gloriously, it's all their fault. Tell them that poverty is on the wane, most of the world lives in a medium-income bracket, and the gap between rich and poor has narrowed, and they will get annoyed. They also won't believe you.

The idea that the end of the world is nigh is invigorating. A dark horizon makes the foreground more vivid, and life seems more precious when it's imperiled. Contented recognition of how delightfully matters are puttering along feels passive and soporific. For those of us addicted to shooting up gloom and collapsing in an ecstasy of inexorable Armageddon, optimism appears pallid, nay, repulsive—not an opiate, but a disgusting mug of warm milk.

However: Catastrophizing is an armchair pastime. It's fun. It's surprisingly comfortable; it goes well with wine and cheese. It's an active pleasure—the veritable antithesis of being broadsided by catastrophe itself. Hair-tearing and hanky-twisting about imminent disaster is an entertainment. The only danger of catastrophizing, as opposed to catastrophe, is that we lull ourselves into the mistaken impression that we're prepared for the real thing.

"The Nobody at Cannes"

STANDPOINT, 2011

You'd think swanning to France for the premiere of a film adapted from your own novel would give anybody a fat head. To the contrary, my visit to Cannes to see *We Need to Talk About Kevin* screen in competition was humbling, and I've felt put in my place ever since.

That place is somewhere between the second assistant cameraman and the catering staff. Even the invitation to bring the author over for a night was a last-minute afterthought, so I was thankful that my husband, Jeff, and I were included at all. After driving around for an hour and a half, the driver sent to pick us up from Nice airport admitted that he'd been given the wrong address for our hotel, and if I'd not thought to scribble down the address from the Web we'd still be teeming back and forth along the Med.

Getting ready for the prescreening dinner, I learned once more that a lifelong tomboy isn't cut out for this stuff. I tried putting up my hair seven or eight times—after which, strands flailing, I looked less like a woman on her way to a gala evening than one en route to a police station to report a brutal assault. I've never understood makeup, which I wear rarely, and once I'd daubed ineptly in the dim wardrobe mirror (while Jeff hogged the loo) my face resembled a preschool finger painting. While I was feverishly trying to adjust the bow tie from Jeff's rental tuxedo, I smeared beige foundation on the bright white collar of my Alexander McQueen dress, a thing of beauty with which a charity-shop slob should never have been entrusted.

By seven p.m., it was obvious that our six thirty p.m. festival car was not showing up. No one had provided me any contact details, so we hailed a taxi. Fortunately, I'd jotted down the name of the villa where we were dining, or Jeff and I would have eaten minibar maca-damias in front of CNN. When we arrived, a production staff member took one look at me and blanched. Too grateful to feel embarrassed, I gladly took her up on the offer of on-site hair and makeup.

At least meeting the cast was a kick. Tilda Swinton is unexpectedly warm, though she's scary; in heels, I come up to her waist. Ezra Miller is a wiseass, sharp and wickedly charming, while John C. Reilly is solid, salt of the earth. The director and her husband, Lynne Ramsay and Rory Kinnear, were unfailingly gracious, and I was touched by how profoundly pleased they seemed that I think their film is great.

Nevertheless, once our car drove us up to the famed red carpet, I took my husband's arm and strode up the stairs, and . . . With some two hundred photographers on both sides, not a single flashbulb went off. I might have been the popcorn vendor.

Breakfast was on me. Hungover, Jeff barely touched his stone-cold eggs; I had half of a miniature jelly donut. Total: €56. And the coffee sucked.

Writers in Film World are extras. Moreover, wandering around the dazzling marquees and snaking queues of fans the next day, I real-ized that literature enjoys no equivalent hoopla. In comparison with Cannes, the London Book Fair is a church social. Feature-release film may be under strain lately, but it still involves money that dwarfs publishing's outlay to chump change. Writers sometimes inspire mov-ies, but the movie is cultural king. A hardback makes a respectable showing when it sells ten thousand copies, while a film counts its audience in the millions.

Yet I returned from France with a renewed sense of calling. I have the job I want. Explaining the difficulties of filming one (very funny) scene in *Kevin*, in which the mother is so desperate for relief from her screaming infant that she seeks out the merciful obliteration of a jackhammer, Lynne Ramsay despaired that it took them days to rent the equipment and get health and safety go-ahead—all for thirty seconds of film. In my occupation, I write, "Eva stood by the jackhammer," and voilà: Eva is standing by a jackhammer. Even in the United Kingdom, health and safety inspectors don't immediately rap on my door.

I needn't raise millions to start a novel; I press command-N on my keyboard and part with a few pence for tea. Writer World may be a cultural ugly duckling, but within the manuscript itself I enjoy godlike omnipotence, dishing out birth and death, success and failure, on my whim. I can conjure a jackhammer with ten letters, the end of the world with a few more. And I don't have to get along with hundreds of difficult creative people; I email my publisher from time to time, chat with one agent, and save my social energies for dustups with tin-eared copy editors. Exiling the Alexander McQueen to the dry cleaners, I shamble joyfully to work in filthy jeans.

[PS: I returned to London that May with the worst cold I've ever contracted in my life. Instilling an appreciation for the dangers of foreign viruses well in advance of 2020, the six-week marathon so devastated my nasal microbiome that I proceeded to catch cold after cold once a month for the following year. Moreover, when my local dry cleaner removed that makeup stain, he permanently stretched the fabric of a crisp check-shaped white collar into a drooping, floppy mess. I've never worn that dress again. At £700, it was by far and away the most expensive piece of clothing I've ever purchased. That'll teach me. I believe we can pronounce conclusively that the humiliation was complete.]

"Semantic Drift"

HARPER'S MAGAZINE, 2019

Regarding the purported rules of English syntax, we tend to divide into mutually hostile camps. Hip, open-minded types relish the never-ending transformations of the way we speak and write. They care about the integrity of our language only insofar as to ensure that we can still roughly understand one another. In the opposite corner glower the curmudgeons. These joyless, uptight authoritarians are forever muttering about clunky concepts such as "the unreal conditional" that nobody's ever heard of.

I've thrown in my lot with the pedants. Yeah, yeah, language is a living tree, eternally sprouting new shoots as other branches wither . . . blah, blah, blah. But a poorly cultivated plant can readily gnarl from lush foliage to unsightly sticks. The internet has turbocharged lexical fads (such as "turbocharge") and grammatical decay. Rather than infuse English with a new vitality, this degeneration spreads the blight of sheer ignorance. Hence I propose to address a set of developments in the prevailing conventions of the English language whose only commonality is that they drive me crazy.

I long ago developed the habit of mentally correcting other people's grammatical errors, and sometimes these chiding reproofs escape my lips ("You mean, 'Ask *us* Democrats'"). Marking up casual conversation with a red pencil doesn't make me popular, and I should learn to control myself. Yet fellow philological conservatives will recognize the impulse to immediately regroove one's neural pathways, the better to preserve one's fragile ear for proper English. That ear is constantly under assault by widespread misusage that threatens by repetition to be—another on-trend verb—"normalized."

For even we rigid, grumpy anachronisms are vulnerable (a blobby political catchall adjective I now encounter dozens of times a day). I recently received what I pleasantly mistook for a fan letter, only to unfold the very sort of mortifying reprimand that I myself hurl at grammatical slackers. My most recent column in Britain's *Spectator* had employed "laid" as the past tense of "lie." The stern correspondent was disappointed in me, as he should have been. Granted, I don't envy second-language speakers obliged to memorize the perverse tense pairings "lie/lay" and "lay/laid," but for me those conjugations were once second nature. My instincts have been contaminated. Proofreading that column, I'd sailed right past the mistake. Those prissy mental corrections my only protection from descent to barbarism, I resolved forthwith to be more of an asshole, if only in my head.

I had the good fortune to be raised by articulate parents who spoke in complete sentences. They didn't talk down to their children; we imbibed vocabulary like "echelon" along with our strained peas. I had no idea at the time what a favor they were doing me. I owe my parents for that ear.

Consequently, when my seventh-grade English teacher spent the whole year on grammar, punctuation, and sentence diagrams, I was contemptuous. I wanted to write stories. I didn't need to learn the rules. I could hear when a usage was incorrect without resort to *Fowler's*. Yet I later felt I owed that teacher an apology.

When I taught freshman composition as a university adjunct in my twenties, knowing the rules facilitated passing them on to my charges. I hammered it home to hundreds of eighteen-year-olds that, aside from rare instances of extremely short sentences that effectively function as a list ("I came, I saw, I conquered"), you absolutely must not join complete sentences with a comma, which may constitute the only true altruism of my otherwise selfish life. Put it on my tombstone: SHE BATTLED COMMA SPLICE.

As far as I can tell, most schools today downplay grammar and punctuation if they teach these subjects at all. (Last year in Iowa, authorities banished S. Keyron McDermott as a high school substitute teacher for criticizing "second-grade" grammatical errors in students' prose.) The neglect shows. I resist teaching creative writing if only because, on the few occasions when I've done so, the students have proved all too creative. Young aspirant writers are working on novels but can't produce comprehensible, error-free sentences. Whether they know it or not, today's MFA candidates are crying out for primitive instruction on the accusative case, mastery of which would readily clear up any confusion about "who" versus "whom" (a perfectly civilized distinction that the animals are now clamoring to revoke). Though what they want is tips on character development, what they need (and in my classes got) is a five-minute lowdown on the semicolon.

Absent such instruction, this endangered punctuation mark has slid willy-nilly to the em dash, a crude demarcation that cannot imply relatedness or contrast, much less clearly separate list elements that contain commas. Capable of being inserted whimsically just about anywhere, the em dash effectively has no rules, and is therefore horribly suited to an era of semantic anarchy.

Education's having turned its back on teaching the technical aspects of composition is partially responsible for deteriorating standards in prose and speech. When lacking any familiarity with the structure of their language, people find linguistic rubrics arbitrary and unreasonable. Utter grammatical dereliction in English departments conveys that knowing the rudiments of one's language is unimportant, in which case "correct" English is unimportant, too. This pedological short-shrifting also feeds the lazy, convenient, and therefore wildly popular view that there is no such thing as correct English.

Hence we witness the precipitous demise of the adverb, now that the very word "adverb" is lost on most people; even mainstream newspapers now use "quicker" rather than "more quickly" to modify a verb. Many a subeditor suffers under the misguided impression that when the subject of a sentence comprises a fair number of words, it is not only acceptable but mandatory to put a single comma between the subject and the verb. (For example, "The Jack and Jill who went up the hill to fetch a pail of water, fell down." Anathema!) Comparative and superlative forms are no longer prescribed but a matter of mood; one of my favorite movies might be titled today *Dumb and More Dumb.* "Literally" now means "really," or, worse, "figuratively." (Anyone claiming that "my head literally exploded" would not have lived to tell the tale.) "Notorious" is employed with such abandon as a synonym for "famous" that when using it correctly one can never be certain that one's pejorative intensions have been understood. The differentiation between quantity and number having been deep-sixed, "less" and "fewer" are now interchangeable. Thus on the rare occasions these adjectives are actually deployed accurately on TV, my husband and I will interject mischievously, "He means *fewer* water," or, "She means *less* bottles."

Just try explaining that "as" is used with clauses while "like" takes a direct object when your audience hasn't the haziest idea what a clause or a direct object is, and don't expect your average American to infer that a direct object will therefore take the accusative case. In the absence of any structural grasp, even examples ("as I do" versus "like me") won't make a lasting impression, and meantime you've merely identified yourself as a pain in the butt. So forget the even more tortu-ous (as opposed to "torturous," though perhaps that, too) explanation of the restrictive and nonrestrictive uses of "that" and "which," even though this distinction can have huge implications for the meaning of a sentence. (Fun fact: the British are universally oblivious to this nicety. They use "which" as a conjunction higgledy-piggledy in all circumstances. "The Queen's English" my foot.)

When writing dialogue in fiction, I often feel guilty. I'm supposed to make my characters speak as (not "like") they would in real life. Yet rhetorical verisimilitude propagates the very errors that (not "which") I revile. Now that the predicate nominative is dead and buried, I can't have a character announce, "It is I!" without also conveying that this person is unbearable, perhaps outright insane, or imported from a previous century through time travel.

Therefore I, too, contribute to semantic drift. In our digital age, online dictionaries are revised almost continually, whereas the issuance of a new print edition of *Webster's* or the *Oxford English Dictionary* is the expensive labor of many years. In the analog world, then, official changes to meaning and usage were subject to considerable scrutiny, discouraging the institutionalization of commonplace mistakes. These days, what were once authoritative and inherently conservative reference sources easily acquiesce to mob rule. Misconceptions transform lickety-split into new conventions. We consolidate ignorance.

Although well spoken, my parents nevertheless embraced two errors of usage, both of which my brother and I have struggled to rectify in our own speech, because misunderstandings instilled in childhood are tough to override. Hence when the copy editor on my first novel claimed that there was no such word as "jerry-rig," I was incensed. Determined to prove her wrong, I went to my trusty, dusty-blue *Webster's Seventh* (based on the august *Webster's Third*), only to find that she was right: "jerry-rig" wasn't listed. Apparently, I'd grown up with a garbled portmanteau of "gerrymander," "jerry-built," and the word I really wanted: "jury-rig." The scales fell from my eyes.

A convert, I explained to my mother her lifelong mistake, but she was having none of it. "Oh, no," she said gravely. "'Jury-rig' refers to rigging a jury, which is very serious." Explaining the allusion to a "jury mast," a makeshift sail, with no etymological relationship to a judicial "jury," got me nowhere. It's fascinating how ferociously people will cling to their abiding linguistic assumptions, however wrongheaded.

Although this is an argument I should have won in 1986, I'd lose it today. Dictionary.com informs us, "Jerry-rigged is a relatively new word. Many people consider it to be an incorrect version of jury-rigged, but it's widely used in everyday speech." With no such embarrassment, Merriam-Webster's online dictionary now proudly lists "jerry-rigged" as meaning "organized or constructed in a crude or improvised manner." The mob—and my mother—have won. So much for my precious filial condescension.

Or take "nonplussed," which I was taught meant "blasé." When another copy editor forced me to look this one up, it turned out to mean almost the opposite: "at a loss as to what to say, think, or do." What I thought meant "unruffled" pretty much meant "ruffled." But after laboriously internalizing the correct meaning of "nonplussed," I find I needn't have bothered. Enough other people have made my parents' mistake that at the top of a Google search "nonplussed" is defined as both "surprised and confused so much that they are unsure how to react" and "Informal, North American: not disconcerted; unperturbed." Great.

I ask you: What good is a word that now means both "perturbed" and "unperturbed"? This democratic inclusiveness of delusion effectively knocks "nonplussed" out of the language's functional vocabulary. If it means two opposite things, it ceases to communicate. If I say I'm "nonplussed," what do you know? I'm either dumbfounded or indifferent. I might as well have said nothing.

So, given the pervasive misunderstanding of "enervated," any day now online dictionaries are bound to start listing an accepted meaning of the word as "excited and keyed up," and that will be the end of "enervated." If the adjective ever formally means either "energized" or "without energy," we'll have to chuck it on the trash heap.

We also find semantic drift in pronunciation, one instance of which has ruined a favorite party trick. I used to love submitting that "flaccid" is actually pronounced "flak-sid," challenging my incredulous audience to look it up and sitting back to watch the consternation. (That un-onomatopoeic hard "c" in a word for "floppy" is counterinstinctual.) Traditionally, my defiant company would always vow to keep mispronouncing the word anyway. But mass cluelessness has at last prevailed. According to *Business Insider,* "The standard pronunciation is 'flak-sed,' not 'flas-sid.' . . . Until recently, most dictionaries listed only the first pronunciation." That "until recently" pours cold water on all my fun. The accepted pronunciation "flas-sid" has even slithered into the modern *OED.*

Within the past few years, one misappropriation has spread like knotweed. In linguistics, "performative" has an interesting and specific definition. It describes a verb whose usage enacts its action, as in "I promise," "I curse you," "I apologize," and "bless you": these are performative verbs. "I now pronounce you husband and wife" is a classic "performative utterance." In my old print dictionaries, the word meaning "relating to performance" is "performatory"—an adjective that has failed to catch on—and the linguistic meaning of the now-fetishized word has been lost. For "performative" in the sense of "posturing and insincere" is everywhere, now that "virtue signaling" appears to have exhausted itself. As we went through "virtue signaling" like single-ply toilet paper—the term took off only after a *Spectator* piece in 2015—there must be a brisk market for descriptions of left-wingers vaunting their ethical credentials with self-serving theatricality. (When I search for "performative," Google suggests "performative wokeness.") Given such a hunger for words to capture it, fraudulent moral flamboyance is clearly a mark of the age.

The steady decay of English syntax is a first-world problem par excellence, and tsk-tsking over sloppy grammar amounts to a haughty and rather geriatric form of entertainment. Besides, my own generation probably instigated this decline in the first place. For my erudite father, "decimate" can mean only "destroy a tenth of"; hypocritically, some semantic drift strikes me as sensible, and I happily employ the verb's broader sense. My father decried Captain Kirk's "to boldly go where no man has gone before!" though split infinitives leave me, if you will, nonplussed.

We let-it-all-hang-out boomers may have celebrated lingual creativity, but the dangling dependent clauses and modifiers that have grown rife, even in books, hardly qualify as inventive. Neither can "between you and I" pass for a form of self-expression. Honestly, English requires so little declension in comparison with most languages that expecting the declension of pronouns in compound objects isn't asking for the moon.

However picayune and pitifully old-fashioned the bereavement may seem to most people, for me the erosion of style, clarity, and precision in everyday speech and prose is a loss. Call it a quality-of-life issue. A century ago, in diaries or letters to the editor, ordinary people wrote with astonishing elegance and correctness. Elegance is related to correctness.

In the fiction biz, of course, syntax is a matter of craft. Early in my career, I still had a blind, unjustified confidence in my semantic inner ear, often railing against the edicts of officious, nit-picking copy editors. I was always wrong. If nowadays I also wrangle with copy editors, that's because the more recent crop's acquaintance with English syntax is abysmal. Their poor grasp of the discretionary and nondiscretionary comma is not their fault. Never having been taught the rules in seventh grade, they don't even have the vocabulary to cogently discuss our differences, because they don't know a predicate nominative from a hole in the ground. But I *want* to be saved from myself, because I suffer from the same misconceptions as anyone else. (I'm still shaky on "may" versus "might.") I want an expert, a stickler, a real whip-wielding dominatrix. Yet all the terrifying taskmasters bashing me over the head with Strunk and White appear to have died off.

It's always dangerous to display hubris about one's proper English, since pedants like nothing more than to catch out other pedants. Fellow curmudgeons will also recognize all of my bugbears as losing battles. Ultimately, the evolution of language is a story of mob rule. But surely there's a tattered nobility to valiantly fighting wars that we know we can't win.

ACKNOWLEDGMENTS

I get few opportunities to thank the people with whom I work in non-fiction; journalism is often a hasty business with little time for such courtesies. But I've never heard anyone carp about being subjected to too much gratitude, so:

Apropos of my dedication, first and foremost I thank Fraser Nelson, editor of *The Spectator*, who took me on as a new columnist in 2017 with the heartening assurance that I was the one candidate for the position on whom the whole staff could agree. Ever since, I've found a political home in a magazine that I genuinely like to read, and it means the world to me that I can finally file text that, aside from a few tweaks for adherence to house style, is never mangled, neutered, boring-ified, or censored. Although my frank pieces on incendiary topics like race and immigration have sometimes put the magazine in jeopardy, Fraser has stood by me and stoically withstood the flak. If more people in positions of authority did the same, there would be no such thing as "cancel culture." I'm also glad for fellow columnists such as Douglas Murray, Rod Liddle, and Toby Young, whose daring and often droll journalism provides a context in which my own pieces look a little less barking.

I'd also thank Rick MacArthur, publisher of *Harper's Magazine*, for coming to me to fill the "Easy Chair" slot for a year; apologies the stint wasn't longer, but I found holding down two columns while working full-time as a novelist was a bit much. Nevertheless, the essays I wrote for *Harper's* I regard as some of my most mature nonfiction, and I was honored to appear in such a storied magazine.

On the publishing side, thanks to William Callahan at InkWell Management, who helped cull the appallingly extensive longlist of possible inclusions down to manageable size and made an initial stab at organization; a second opinion was invaluable. Thanks to my agent, Kim Witherspoon (as ever), and my editor, Gail Winston (as ever); your advice has been astute, your enthusiasm for this project reassuring. Thanks also to Suzie Doore, my UK editor, who disagrees, I suspect violently, with more than one of these essays, yet who hasn't sought to veto any selections and still cheerfully expresses seemingly sincere support for this collection, perhaps over her own dead body.

Lastly, thanks to Brian Murray, HarperCollins CEO, who first mentioned that he'd like to publish a book of nonfiction by that Shriver woman. I needed the nudge. Had he never expressed such interest from on high, I doubt *Abominations* would have come to fruition. I'm glad it did.

About the Author

LIONEL SHRIVER's fiction includes *Should We Stay or Should We Go*; *The Motion of the Body Through Space*; *The Mandibles*; *Property*; the National Book Award finalist *So Much for That*; the *New York Times* bestsellers *The Post-Birthday World* and *We Need to Talk About Kevin*, an international bestseller adapted for a 2010 film starring Tilda Swinton. Her journalism has appeared in *The Guardian*, *The New York Times*, *The Wall Street Journal*, *Harper's Magazine*, and many other publications. She's a regular columnist for *The Spectator* in Britain. She lives in London and Brooklyn, New York.